Why Quality Is Important and How It Applies in Diverse Business and Social Environments, Volume I

Why Quality Is Important and How It Applies in Diverse Business and Social Environments, Volume I

Paul Hayes

BEP

BUSINESS EXPERT PRESS

Leader in applied, concise business books

First published in 2021 by
Business Expert Press, LLC
222 East 46th Street, New York, NY 10017
www.businessexpertpress.com

ISBN-13: 978-1-94709-853-4 (paperback)
ISBN-13: 978-1-94709-854-1 (e-book)

Business Expert Press Supply and Operations Management Collection

Collection ISSN: 2156-8189 (print)
Collection ISSN: 2156-8200 (electronic)

Cover design by Charlene Kronstedt
Interior design by S4Carlisle Publishing Services Private Ltd., Chennai, India

First edition: 2021

10 9 8 7 6 5 4 3 2 1

Printed in the United States of America.

Description

These two volumes are about understanding—why—and application—how—with the aim of providing guidance and introduction to both. Quality is the consistent achievement of the user's expectations of a product or service. The achievement needs to be "The right thing, right first time, every time, in time." Beginning with manufacturing and services, it also includes professional, personal, and spiritual dimensions.

Variation does not sit happily with consistency and skill in handling risk and opportunity requires competence in the use of statistics, probability, and uncertainty; and needs to complement the critically essential soft dimensions of quality and the overarching and underpinning primacy of personal relationships.

There are no clear boundaries to the applicability of quality and the related processes and procedures expressed in management systems, and this is why it matters so much to show "how it applies in diverse business and social environments." Increasingly, the acceptability of boundaries that are drawn depends on their effect on the user and the achievement of quality, and the latest standards on quality management are explicit on this key point.

Quality is everyone's business, and there is no single professional discipline that can properly express this. Insights, knowledge, experience, best practice, tools, and techniques need to be shared across all kinds of organizational and professional boundaries, and there is no departmental boundary that can stand apart from the organization-wide commitment to quality achievement.

Keywords

quality; management; systems; uncertainty; statistics; probability; humility; arrogance; love; attunement; mastery; ascendancy; holiness

Contents

Acknowledgments

The opportunity for this book came from an invitation to write something for Business Expert Press. The, somewhat pretentious, title I offered was changed to this wider scope and gave me the opportunity to share the experience and understandings from a varied career.

After starting in Aluminium Chemicals research, I moved into technical paper-making with Wiggins Teape, which was then owned by BAT (formerly British American Tobacco) and is now Arjo Wiggins Appleton. I started at Glory Mill near High Wycombe in Buckinghamshire and the graduate intake scheme I was fortunate to join introduced me to their very mature leading-edge approach to quality management. Experience at Stoneywood Mill in Aberdeen and then the paper-converting operation at Dyce as a quality manager provided a base in the best practice in quality assurance and quality control well before there were international standards to support it. My mentor throughout those years and for a number afterward was Peter Daisley, and I would like to acknowledge that deep debt of gratitude for all his support and particularly the direction to the statistical disciplines that are such an important part of quality.

Dental Chemicals, with the very wide range of materials science involved, and testing laboratory supervision introduced me to Pharmaceuticals and the Orange Guide as some of the chemicals claimed therapeutic benefits.

This was followed by quality management in a medical devices company making single-use sterile and reusable Class II anesthetic and sterile single-use class III blood circulation devices and device sets. This also involved regulatory responsibilities setting up registration and all the device forms with the U.S. FDA and hosting one of the early Good Manufacturing Practice inspections in the UK. The quality management systems developed used local access to computer bureaux for the documentation. The work also involved national and some international standards experience.

In both experiences I was deeply indebted to the very able and experienced team members and have many happy memories of the individuals.

The next steps involved training in use of the emerging business microcomputers and software to develop quality management system, and this interest has been a constant theme beginning with the help of Roger Chambers in Aberdeen, who worked in the NHS on the IT side and is now a long-term family friend and fellow believer.

Quality management in computer and software manufacturing brought invaluable experience in this area followed by the first exposure to quality consultancy using the new, at the time, UK government grant scheme for development of basic quality management systems (QMS) but also included development of QMS software for gauge control and hospital ward management.

Contacts made in the time with Wiggins Teape resulted in a move into pre-clinical trial testing of chemicals and pharmaceutical testing with responsibilities in training and quality improvement. The experience of developing trainers and resources, and then delivering the programs, was a rich development time and contact with the four key original directors of the organization and the key QA and human resources staff a great joy. I am deeply indebted to Geoff Cox of New Directions for all the vital input to our quality and management training in the pre-clinical chemicals and pharmaceuticals organization and particularly for the pointer to the work of Roger Harrison that forms such a key foundation of the later chapters of this work.

Experience of independent auditing for the UK Competent body for medical devices just prior to the passing of the first EU Medical Devices legislation was accompanied by a large team project work on the establishment of an early ISO 9000 QMS preparatory to the floatation of a major Scottish government building management organization and also experience in delivery of auditor training for the major UK standards and quality training and consultancy body.

Working in ISO 9000 and then TQM Quality Consultancy for the Renault Institute of Quality Management was founded on very well-developed training materials, which were a joy to deliver. This work also included IT support network creation and support for the team of consultants in the days when ISDN was the preferred, and the only really feasible, option for Wide Area Networks for staff teams.

Recent years have seen specialization in test laboratory and calibration systems in the Marine Energy Renewables sector, long-term indwelling sterile Class III Medical Device specification and prequalification with major international agencies, authorized representative role with the same medical device, inspection body, and Innovative Environment Technology Verification (ETV) assessment, and work as an EU expert arising from this, quite apart from keeping the professional competence up to date in ISO 9001 certification.

The support from John Griffiths and the whole team at EMEC, including Lesley Bews, Chris White, and Neil Kermode, and those that I have worked there over the years has been key over the past decade and more, along with the EU ETV colleagues arising from this association.

The very rewarding long-term association with EMEC sprang from a membership of the UK Chartered Quality Institute (CQI), which was then the Institute for Quality Assurance (IQA). The consultants register for this body led to long-term associations with Ian Dalling, John Jeffery, and Roger Horne and others, and many opportunities for enjoyably widening, deepening, and maintaining quality management competences.

The understanding, support, and learning from Dr Bill Potter of Stapleford Scientific Services, and John Hurll of Hurll Technical Services have been rich friendships and have been invaluable in many important connections and particularly the statistical and scientific dimensions and connections.

Andy Taylor worked with me on eLearning and with his authoring of training material and with the science and quality background, his encouragement on reading the first draft was crucial. The help from my daughter Fenella Hayes throughout and in preparing the document for copy editing was greatly appreciated.

But without the long-term support of my wife Maureen and family, of which two of my three children have worked with me in my business for differing times before moving into their own careers, none of this would have happened. And we are both so grateful for the overarching care and leading that we both depend on in life.

CHAPTER 1

Introduction

This is about understanding—why and application—how.
The aim is to provide guidance and introduction to both.
The book is in two volumes, with the first ending with
Chapter 12, Quality Management.

What Is Quality and What Does It Entail?

Consistency and Variation

Quality is the consistent achievement of the user's expectations of a product or service. The achievement needs to be "The right thing, right first time, every time, in time."[1] We begin by looking at manufacturing and service industry and we wrap up by looking at the professions.

Immediately we can see that variation is not going to sit happily with consistency and that we must consider risk, and its converse—opportunity, likelihood, and probability and understand and use statistics. There are common and special causes of variability and with each we need to apply the related statistical techniques.

Products, even if produced by robotic machines, still involve human agency individually and in teams at key points throughout production and then in the use and service phases even more so. We need to be confident that we can deliver to the standards required and this needs to be established by a whole range of means.

---

[1] Phil Crosby "Do it right first time, every time" amended according to R.G. Boznak. July 1994."When Doing It Right First Time Is Not Enough," *Quality Progress*, pp. 74-78.

Processes, Procedures, Best Practice, and Their Expression

The creation and delivery of products and services depends on processes, and more detailed procedures when necessary, within and across organizations of all kinds. Processes are assembled, established, and maintained in management systems inside and across organizational boundaries. We are going to need to describe these processes and communicate them within and across organizational boundaries.

Best practice that is known to enable and assure consistent achievement of user's expectations must be captured and shared and leads to standards, specifications, and many related documents, which increasingly are created and shared, sometimes exclusively, within virtual information technology environments. There is a natural flow from statements of objectives, with their associated measures of achievements, through policies on how they will be achieved in different areas, to the enabling processes and procedures for the use of those individuals responsible for their operation.

A record of how processes and procedures are operated, and the outcomes are documented also needs to be captured, stored, and shared.

Scope and Boundaries

There is no clear boundary to the applicability of quality and the related processes and procedures expressed in management systems, and this is the main reason for this work and its stated aim to show "how it applies in diverse business and social environments." Increasingly the acceptability of boundaries that are drawn depends on their effect on the user and the achievement of quality, and the latest standard on quality management is explicit on this key point.[2]

Quality is everyone's business and there is no one professional discipline that can properly express this. Insights, knowledge, experience, best practice, tools, and techniques need to be shared across all kinds of organizational and professional boundaries, and there is no departmental

---

[2] See ISO 9001:2015, "Quality Management Systems—Requirements."

boundary that can stand apart from the organization wide commitment to quality achievement.

Foundations of Society

In early society, weights and measures were the basis of trade and international collaboration, and the ethics of honest accurate traceable measures is reflected in their reference in the law codes and spiritual reference works of the day.

Modern science is based on the higher and higher discriminations and the lower and lower uncertainty in measurements that permit testing of the most revealing, and often counterintuitive and disturbing hypotheses and current findings of modern science.[3]

Health and Safety

Quality failures have consequences, and these can be extreme, so this topic has traction well outside the immediately obvious scope.

Improvement and PDCA

Quality is a journey and continual improvement is a driver and motivation, goal, objective, aim, and expression and will be central to everything we say about achievement of quality. Not only is this a truism we used heavily in the 1970s and 1980s, but it reflects the widely accepted belief that achievement and maintenance of quality is central to business and organizational success.

Continual or Continuous Improvement is a process with four very well-established steps PLAN, DO, CHECK or STUDY, and ACT (PDC[S]A), that have clear links to the scientific method (Figure 1.1) which it probably even predates.[4]

---

[3]See Nova, "Einstein's Quantum Riddle", https://www.pbs.org/wgbh/nova/video/einsteins-quantum-riddle/ and https://www.youtube.com/watch?v=Mn4AwineA5o
[4]See R. Moen and C. Norman. "Evolution of the PDCA Cycle." http://www.idemployee.id.tue.nl/g.w.m.rauterberg/lecturenotes/DG000%20DRP-R/references/Moen-Norman-2009.pdf.

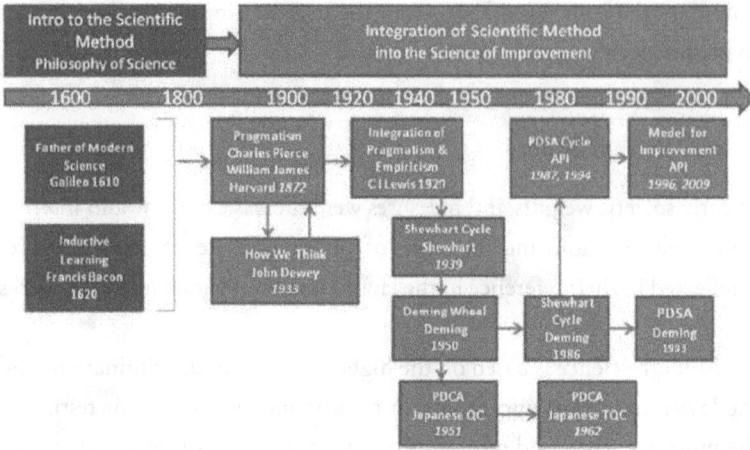

Figure 1.1 Evolution of the scientific method[5]

The very largely accepted standard for management systems—ISO 9001 (now version 2015)—has this statement "The PDCA cycle enables an organization to ensure that its processes are adequately resourced and managed, and that opportunities for improvement are determined and acted on." The open source Management System Standard[6] describes it as "Plan–Do–Check–Act" (PDCA) is a cycle that individual people naturally follow to varying degrees of competence. PLAN is the preparation for doing something. DO is the execution of the PLAN. CHECK is monitoring to confirm the PLAN is being properly followed during DO and that nothing unexpected occurs. Finally during ACT, a review of PLAN, DO, and CHECK processes is conducted to see if the approach used can be improved the next time around plus agreeing actions to make it happen.

PDCA is therefore a natural potentially universal cycle of continual learning and continual improvement applicable to organization strategy, tactics, and operations. The fourth element ACT can also be conducted proactively to ensure that the organization remains aligned with future stakeholder needs and expectations by trying to anticipate future likely innovation and change."[7]

---

[5]Ibid.

[6]See "Management System Specification and Guidance MSS 1000:2014," *CQI Integrated Management SIG.* https://www.integratedmanagement.info/mss-1000.

[7]"Management System Specification and Guidance MSS 1000:2014," *CQI Integrated Management SIG.* https://www.integratedmanagement.info/mss-1000.

"Check" is sometimes replaced with "Study" for non-native English speakers if "Check" has negative connotations of "holding back." It is also conceived as applying more explicitly to improvement.[8] This gives rise to the equivalent PDSA cycle.

Excellence, the Destination

The journey has a goal, and this is explored in several ways. Excellence is a common aim. It is expressed in many ways as follows:

- Customer delight—see "Going the extra mile and the importance of family"
- Total Quality Management—see "Total Quality Management, Company Wide Quality Control"
- Personal Mastery[9]—See "Personal Quality and Mastery"

Touching Lives

Quality is all about relationships and the motivation and values expressed. It is concerned with building values and community and expressing the highest ideals—see Quality, Life, and Service and the concluding Chapter 24—Quality, Faith, and Transcendent Values.

Who Is the Publication Aimed at and How Could It Be Used?

This is an introduction to quality to assist those responsible for the product or service they provide in many diverse situations and organizations to help them see the common issues they face and find the support, references, and links to take their exploration and understanding forward.

To handle the many issues we all face, and which we touch on in Volume 2, it is important to at least review and be confident in the basics we cover in Volume 1.

---

[8]An Introduction to the PDCA Cycle Webcast, Part 1. http://asq.org/2011/07/continuous-improvement/intro-to-pdca-1.html.

[9]See D. Kachoui. April 2018. "Personal Improvement—Becoming A Master—Do you have what it takes to achieve mastery?" *Quality Progress*, pp. 38-43. http://asq.org/quality-progress/2018/04/career-development/becoming-a-master.pdf.

CHAPTER 2

Quality and Manufacturing Industries

The Role of the Specification

The customer expectations of a manufactured product are expressed in specifications. Users come across them at a summary level in product and service marketing literature in brochures, catalogues, and increasingly online in web pages.

Manufacturing to specifications is underpinned by processes, procedures, and systems that enable and assure delivery, use and disposal of the product according to the specification.

System Approaches to Conformance to Specifications

The aim on all sides is "Do the right thing, right first time, every time, on time."[1] No one wants anything less than perfect conformance to their expectations as defined in the specification and perceived and stored in their expectations.

The management discipline of obtaining and maintaining conformance to the specification is "quality assurance." This developed from the more "hands-on" disciplines of quality control when the verification and inspection processes of the day in World War II were found to be inadequate to the level of assurance needed for high integrity life critical product (see Chapter 22, Quality in History and Time of War below— Second World War).

---

[1]Phil Crosby "Do it right first time, every time" amended according to "When doing it right first time is not enough" *Quality Progress*, July 94, p. 74.

Total quality implies something beyond quality assurance and implies an all-encompassing approach based on measurement and aiming for excellence and involving the whole product and service delivery life cycle.

Scope and Boundaries of Quality

Some perspectives on quality, quality assurance, and total quality set limits and draw boundaries for sometimes archaic and restrictive reasons. Quality, in some situations for instance, is perceived to only be related to the measurement and control of product and service characteristics and the processes that directly and indirectly support these. The latest management system standards now require these boundaries to be clearly and transparently stated and exclusions can only be made where it can be shown that they do not negatively impact product or service quality. Finance and the flow of revenue and expenditure has been a common exception.

Because quality is perceived only to be realized in the repeatability of delivery then there is also a belief that "one-off" projects are not susceptible to, or helped by, the disciplines associated with quality management in its different expressions. We may call the quality discipline by a different name such as project management, but the quality needs to be right first time, every time, in time even if it is only a single time.

Conversely a great deal of what is central to quality in all the sectors and dimensions of life we shall list and explore is addressed by many, many disciplines that resource and support improvement and change. Principal among these is information technology which has revolutionized so many areas of life worldwide and the ubiquitous smart cell phone has done amazing things toward linking the whole of humanity. An example of this is provided in a valuable reference work on business analysis,[2] which is about "The successful implementation of valuable business change" and presents the tool set that would also figure in many works that have "quality" in the title. Similar relationships and perspectives apply to management consultancy, training and education and many other disciplines that seek to make things better.

---

[2]See D. Paul, J. Cadle, and D. Yeates (eds.). 2014. "Business Analysis," BCS Learning and Development First Floor, Block D, North Star House, North Star Avenue, Swindon, SN2 1FA, UK, ISBN 978-1-78017-277-4.

Central Role of the Specification

The scope of a specification has an interplay with the standards that define best practice for the manufacturing sector or product class and this interplay can be central to product quality in the manufacturing industries.

One of products we can use in illustration is the long-term indwelling Copper T 380A intrauterine contraceptive device,[3] which is a Class III medical device in the EU[4] and FDA classifications[5]—see Figure 2.1.

The specification details the product requirements laid down by the WHO/UNFPA, based on the original Population Council specification.[6] This specification requires conformance to the related ISO 7439[7] product standard for copper-bearing contraceptive intrauterine devices—which is the wider product group and calls for the manufacturers to be independently certified to quality management standard ISO 13485 by accredited certification bodies.[8] The standard ISO 13485 is a medical device sector specific extension of the Quality Management foundation standard ISO 9001. The specification also requires using suppliers to have certification to other related to standards for operations such as sterilization, stability testing, and material qualification.

---

[3]World Health Organization (WHO) and United Nations Population Fund (UNFPA). 2016. "TCu380A Intrauterine Contraceptive Device (IUD) WHO/UNFPA Technical Specification and Prequalification Guidance 2016." https://www.unfpa.org/sites/default/files/resource-pdf/TCu380A_IUD_WHO_UNFPATechnicalSpec_Guidance_updated2017.pdf.

[4] See European Commission Dg Health and Consumer. "Cosmetics and Medical Devices—M Devices: Guidance Document—Classification of Medical Devices," European Commission Dg Health and Consumer Directorate B Unit B2. http://ec.europa.eu/DocsRoom/documents/10337/attachments/1/translations/en/renditions/native.

[5]US Food and Drug Administration. December 19, 2017. "Overview of Medical Device Classification and Reclassification." https://www.fda.gov/aboutfda/centersoffices/officeofmedicalproductsandtobacco/cdrh/cdrhtransparency/ucm378714.htm.

[6]See Population Council. "NDA 18–680 Application to FDA for CuT380A IUD," Population Council 1984.

[7]Ch 2.2 of UNFPA/WHO CuT380A specification.

[8]Ch 2.6 of UNFPA/WHO CuT380A specification.

PART NUMBER	DESCRIPTION	QTY.
1	TCu380A-Finished Product	1
2	Copper Collar	2
3	T-frame	1
4	Thread	1
5	Insertion Rod	1
6	Insertion Tube	1
7	Insertion Tube Flange	1
8	Copper Wire	1

Figure 2.1 Specification drawing of CuT380A[9]

The specification lists product material and performance characteristics and requires certification of compliance to specific standards for manufacturing systems and processes, such as sterilization and testing for biological qualification of starting materials.

The use of the medical device delivers value in contraception and family planning.[10] This added value is compared with the efficacy, cost, and other dimensions of alternative and comparable competitor products. There are protocols used to measure the efficacy and safety of medicines and medical devices and the specification cites the relevant "Cochrane Review" of the device's efficacy.[11]

Importantly it also specifies the acceptance criteria for statistical process control and acceptance sampling and testing.

---

[9]See WHO/UNFPA. "TCu380A Intrauterine Contraceptive Device (IUD), WHO/ UNFPA Technical Specification and Prequalification Guidance, 2016." UNFPA, 2016, 108 pages. https://www.unfpa.org/sites/default/files/resource-pdf/TCu380A_ IUD_WHO_UNFPATechnicalSpec_Guidance_updated2017.pdf.

[10]Annex 1 The Technical Basis Paper, of UNFPA/WHO CuT380A specification.

[11]See R. Kulier, P. O'Brien, F.M. Helmerhorst, M. Usher-Patel, and C. d'Arcangues. 2007. "Copper Containing, Framed Intra-uterine Devices for Contraception." *Cochrane Database of Systematic Reviews* no. 4, Art. No.: CD005347. doi:10.1002/14651858.CD005347.pub3.   https://www.cochranelibrary.com/cdsr/ doi/10.1002/14651858.CD005347.pub3/epdf/full.

There are risks associated with products and services and for this device they are related to the specification conformance of the device and the potential for clinical complications of pelvic infection and loss of protection through expulsion.

The medical device manufacturing quality assurance standard—ISO 13485: 2016, includes the requirement in the foundation standard for risk-based thinking and includes a requirement for documented risk management, with records, for product realization.[12]

The Sterility Assurance Level of 1×10^{-6} required for terminally sterilized medical devices is "the probability of a single viable microorganism occurring on an item after sterilization."[13] This is a quality measurement at the parts per million (ppm) level and can only be achieved by all round process management and assurance—in the language of the ISO 9001 standard "where the resulting output cannot be verified by subsequent monitoring or measurement."[14]

At the same time the tests for acceptance are drawn from sampling tables for attributes with acceptable Quality Levels based on sampling and testing final product samples. The sample testing and the acceptable quality levels that are specified can only discriminate down to 0.01 percent for yes/no type quality characteristics, or measurements, that is 1×10^{-4} or a $100 \times$ poorer a quality level than that specified for sterility. There are sampling tables for variables, but even with the greater discrimination they offer, the level of assurance could not be met.

There are some real paradoxes and apparent contradictions embedded in even national and international specifications where levels of quality claim to be verifiable by sampling methods that would consume the whole delivery to establish conformance.[15]

---

[12]ISO 13485. "ISO 13485:2016—Medical Devices—Quality Management Systems—Requirements for Regulatory Purposes." https://www.iso.org/search .html?q=13485, clause 7.1.

[13]See ISO 11137-2: 2006. "Sterilization of Health Care Products—Radiation—Part 2: Establishing the Sterilization Dose." https://www.iso.org/standard/62442.html, section 3.2.11.

[14]ISO 9001: 2008 clause 7.5.2; ISO 9001:2015 clause 8.5.1 f.

[15]ISO 28597: 2017. "Acceptance Sampling Procedures by Attributes—Specified Quality Levels in Nonconforming Items Per Million." https://www.iso.org/ standard/64630.html.

The foundation and related standards for Quality Assurance rightly focus on monitoring, measurement, analysis, and evaluation to establish the performance and effectiveness of Quality Management.

The example we have used applies to just about every discipline we could imagine. To know where we are and where must get to, we must define the starting and end points in a way that makes the journey possible and reveals the issues and challenges that we will have to face to get there.

Circular Economy

The impact of the consumer society on the environment with pollution and other destructive behaviors is now clear.

Current approaches to quality extend the product or service life cycle to beginning at the start of the supply chain with sustainable sourcing and reuse and finish with end of life accounting for avoiding waste and pollution and enabling closed loop recycling. Thus the journey has become longer and even more demanding.

These are reflected in the manufacturing environment that affects management systems at every level (see Figure 2.2).

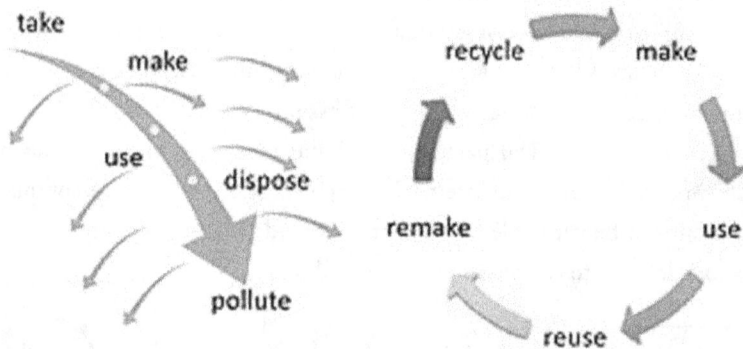

CC 3.0 Catherine Weetman 2016

Figure 2.2 Linear vs circular economy[16]

---

[16]See C. Weetman. December 3, 2016. "The Circular Economy Handbook for Business and Supply Chains: Repair, Remake, Redesign, Rethink." Kogan Page, 1 edition, 3, ISBN-10: 9780749476755, ISBN-13: 978-0749476755, 288 pages.

The effect of waste on the environment, climate emergency, short-age of raw materials, and clean manufacturing is summarized by the worldwide body—the Organization for Economic Co-Operation and Development:

"In recent years, the efforts of manufacturing industries to achieve sustainable production have shifted from end-of-pipe solutions to a focus on product life cycles and integrated environmental strategies and management systems. Furthermore, efforts are increasingly made to create closed loop, circular production systems and adopt new business models."[17]
Key findings[18]:

1. Practices for sustainable manufacturing have evolved
2. Eco-innovation seeks more radical improvements
3. Eco-innovation has three dimensions: targets, mechanisms, and impacts
4. Sustainable manufacturing calls for multi-level eco-innovations
5. Current eco-innovations focus mostly on technological development but are facilitated by nontechnological changes
6. Clear and consistent indicators are needed to accelerate corporate sustainability efforts
7. Improved benchmarking and better indicators would help deepen understand of eco-innovation
8. Integration of innovation and environmental policies is crucial for promoting eco-innovation
9. Creating successful eco-innovation policy mixes requires understanding the interaction of supply and demand

---

[17]OECD—Organisation For Economic Co-Operation and Development. "Sustainable Manufacturing and Eco-Innovation Framework, Practices and Measurement Synthesis Report." https://www.oecd.org/innovation/inno/43423689.pdf, and T. Machiba. "OECD Project on Sustainable Manufacturing and Eco-innovation," please contact: Senior Policy Analyst, Structural Policy Division, OECD Directorate for Science, Technology and Industry. e-mail: tomoo.machiba@oecd.org, Tel: +33 1 45 24 99 84, or visit www.oecd.org/sti/innovation/sustainablemanufacturing.
[18]Ibid.

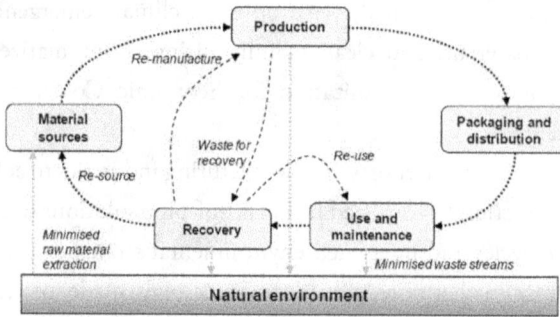

Figure 2.3 Closed loop production system[19]

The key findings highlight the scale of the changes and the challenges facing manufacturing and the management of the processes to achieve the goals of closed loop (Figure 2.3), circular production systems. The inclusion of environmental management standards in the management system becomes virtually essential.

Eco-Parks and a New Industrial Revolution

Recent advances build on pre-existing tools in an evolutionary manner and advances and the rate of development is exponential—like multiplying viruses! See Figure 2.4.[20]

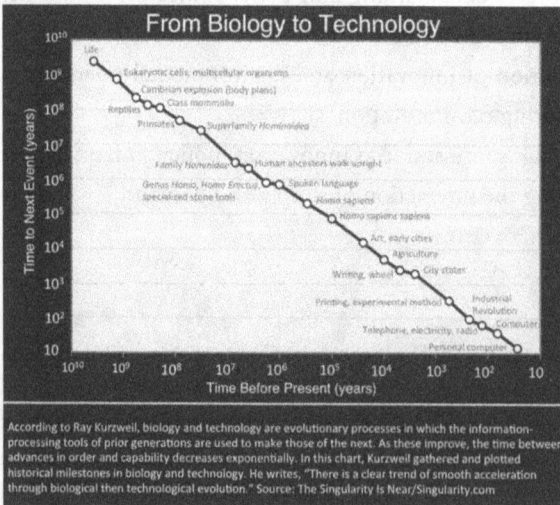

Figure 2.4 Accelerating change—from biology to technology

---

[19]Ibid.

[20]See R. Kurzweil. March 9, 2006. "The Singularity is Near," Duckworth, ISBN-10: 0715635611, ISBN-13: 978-0715635612, 683 pages.

The evolution in the manufacturing environment as a result of these changes opens up new opportunities for radical improvement and change and the integration of manufacturing back into the urban and agricultural environment.[21]

The progress from limiting pollution to closed loop production and the ability to place manufacturing back in the community is revitalizing the nature of society with fresh potential. See Figure 2.5.

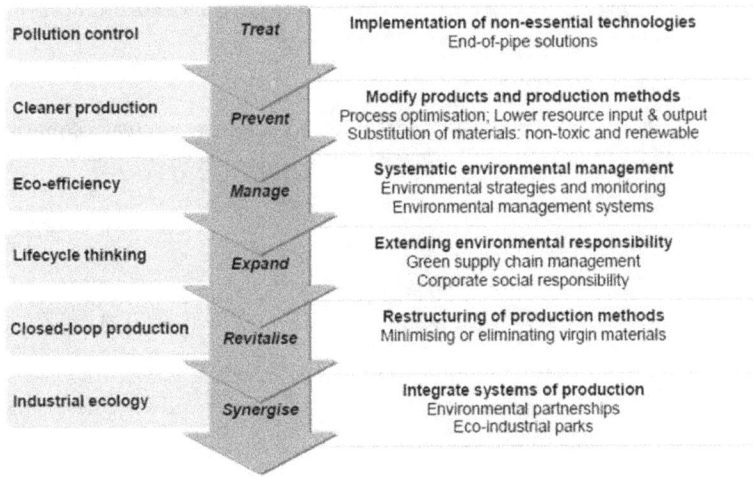

Pollution control	Treat	Implementation of non-essential technologies End-of-pipe solutions
Cleaner production	Prevent	Modify products and production methods Process optimisation; Lower resource input & output Substitution of materials: non-toxic and renewable
Eco-efficiency	Manage	Systematic environmental management Environmental strategies and monitoring Environmental management systems
Lifecycle thinking	Expand	Extending environmental responsibility Green supply chain management Corporate social responsibility
Closed-loop production	Revitalise	Restructuring of production methods Minimising or eliminating virgin materials
Industrial ecology	Synergise	Integrate systems of production Environmental partnerships Eco-industrial parks

Figure 2.5 The evolution of sustainable manufacturing concepts and practices OECD[22]

The Ellen McArthur Foundation highlights in its mission key parties and steps to enable the vision[23]:

- Learning
  - Developing the vision, skills, and mindsets needed to transition to a circular economy

---

[21]See OECD—Organisation for Economic Co-Operation and Development. "Sustainable Manufacturing and Eco-Innovation Framework, Practices and Measurement Synthesis Report." https://www.oecd.org/innovation/inno/43423689.pdf.

[22]See OECD—Organisation For Economic Co-Operation And Development. "Sustainable Manufacturing and Eco-Innovation Framework, Practices and Measurement Synthesis Report." https://www.oecd.org/innovation/inno/43423689.pdf.

[23]E. McArthur. "Our Mission is to Accelerate the Transition to a Circular Economy." https://www.ellenmacarthurfoundation.org/our-story/mission.

- Business
  - Catalyzing circular innovation and creating the conditions for it to reach scale
- Institutions, Governments, and Cities
  - Creating the enabling conditions for a circular economy to thrive
- Insight and Analysis
  - Providing robust evidence about the benefits and implications of the transition
- Systemic Initiatives
  - Transforming key material flows to scale the circular economy globally
- Communications
  - Engaging a global audience around the circular economy

These societal imperatives require that we must be better able to safely introduce new products and services as a result of the innovation and change that are required and that we can understand and articulate what we are doing across the whole of a product life cycle.

Technology Verification

Change is accelerating and some even believe we are heading to a singularity. But whether that is true we cannot wait along the normal timescales for the development of product and service standards and test methods to show that a development is safe. We must be able to independently validate and verify safe and effective technological change as part of the development. And so, Environment Technology Verification (ETV) is a global movement of which the EU ETV project[24] (Figure 2.6) and the resulting development of ISO 14034[25] are key foundations being used

---

[24]See EU Environment. "EU Environmental Technology Verification." https://ec.europa.eu/environment/archives/etv/, https://ec.europa.eu/environment/ecoap/etv/, and https://www.youtube.com/watch?v=UOkTDwiZnyg.
[25]See ISO 14034. "ISO 14034:2016 Environmental Management—Environmental Technology Verification (ETV)." https://www.iso.org/standard/43256.html.

by verification bodies in many places worldwide and supported by global verification initiatives.[26]

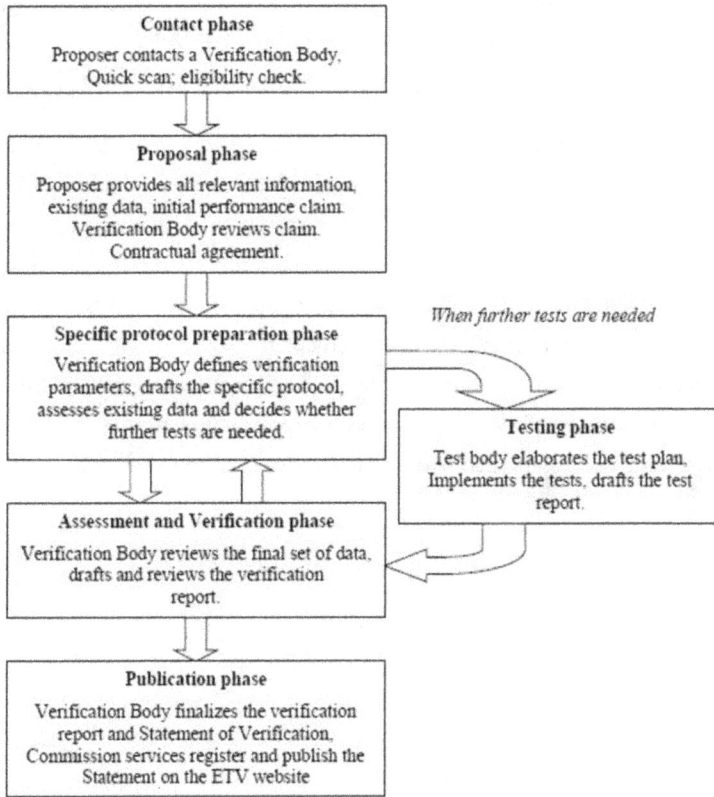

Figure 2.6 EU ETV pilot program phases[27]

The EU ETV General Verification Protocol is the schedule accompanying ISO 17020 to which Verification Bodies were accredited in the EU ETV Pilot Procedure, although they can now be accredited to ISO 14034.

The process of verification establishes the innovative product or service performance claim and the test methods before the test data is reviewed or the testing is performed, and the verification assessed and reported—see Figure 2.6.

---

[26]Verifiglobal. http://www.verifiglobal.com/en.

[27]See EU Environment, "EU Environmental Technology Verification pilot programme General Verification Protocol Version 1.2 – July 27th, 2016", http://etv.ios.edu.pl/sites/pliki/doc/en/eu_etv_gvp_rev2.pdf

This "up front" independent assessment is bringing into wider application the concepts and principles of prior study protocols and public post study reports that are already applied to pharmaceuticals and medical devices.

Life-Cycle Perspective and Analysis

A life-cycle perspective requires these principles to be applied to the whole of the product's life in an appropriate qualitative manner and a full analysis will look for an evidence-based assessment often with quantitative measures. A perspective will apply best practice in the most appropriate and practicable manner when full analysis is not practicable or appropriate. This is analogous to risk-based thinking and risk management that we consider below—see "Risk management and risk-based thinking" below. An application to the life cycle in respect of environmental innovation looks at how the new product or service adds value compared with some already established reference.

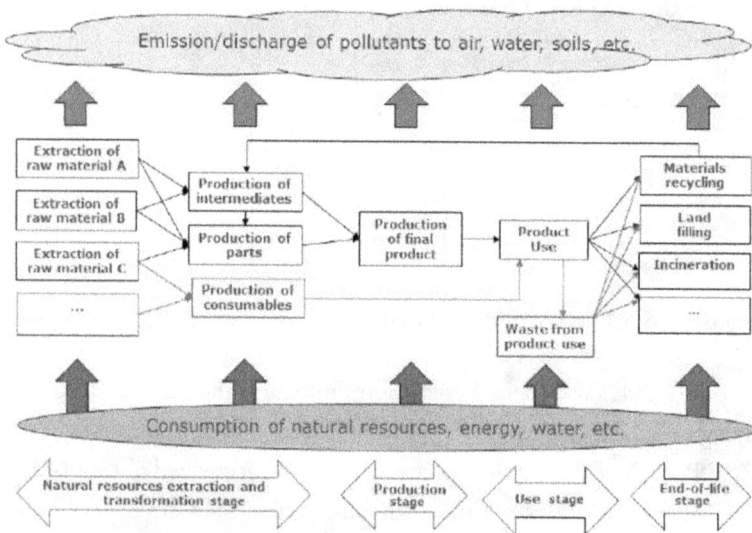

Figure 2.7 Life-cycle perspective of a product or service[28]

Figure 2.7 shows the life-cycle stages of a product or a process. The elements connected in black picture a simple product that does not require consumables for its operation and does not generate waste. The elements connected in red picture a more complex situation where the product

---

[28]Ibid.

(or process) requires consumables for its operation (e.g., filters, oil) and generate waste (e.g., wasted filters, waste oil). These elements may have to be taken into consideration in a life-cycle perspective of the technology.

Industry 4.0

The impact of information and digital technology is the latest in a series of advances that we consider in summary in Chapter 23, Quality in History and Time of War—see Figure 2.8, for changes in industry and quality approaches.

Aligned view of changes in industry and quality approaches

Period	Summary description	Quality	Summary description
Industry 1.0–Prior to 1890	+ Humans harness water and steam power to build industrial infrastructure. + Crude machines gain productivity over independent craft work. + Increased output is achieved using mechanical advantages. + Work focuses on performing tasks faster and more consistently. + Transportation/moving goods occurs more frequently.	Quality 1.0	+ Quality is assured through measurement and inspection. + Production volume is emphasized rather than quality. + Inspection does not focus on cost reduction, eliminating wastes, or loss and inefficiency. + Work conditions are not important; maximizing worker productivity takes precedence.
Industry 2.0–1890 to 1940	+ Electricity powers industrial machines. + Performance capability gains occur through application of new mechanisms. + Scale of automation becomes broader as motor size can be varied to fit specific circumstances.	Quality 2.0	+ Maximizing productivity continues to be the primary focus. + Adherence to standards that reflect the minimally acceptable quality level is prevalent. + Financial quality is measured based on scrap and rework. + Labor performance is used to measure productivity.
Industry 3.0–1940 to 1995	+ Computer power provided to workers to increase productivity. + Use of information and communication technology drives improvements. + Human participation in workplaces declines. + Stand-alone robotic systems replace manual work.	Quality 3.0	+ Quality is a business imperative. + Meeting customer requirements (customer satisfaction) is emphasized. + Continual improvement is applied. + Gains in productivity occur by stabilizing highly efficient processes, standardizing work and involving all workers in the activities that create quality. + Standardization activities (ISO 9001) and achieving business excellence through organizationwide assessment (such as the *Baldrige Criteria for Performance Excellence*) emerge.
Anticipated changes that will occur during Industry 4.0–1995 to present	+ Integrated cyber-physical interfaces automate working environments. + Automated processes deal with end-to-end systems. + Humans serve only in positions where human judgment cannot be automated and human interactions cannot be simulated. + Machines learn to learn (artificial intelligence).	Quality 4.0	+ Digitization is used to optimize signal feedback and process adjustment, and adaptive learning supports self-induced system corrections. + Quality shifts its control-oriented focus from the process operators to the process designers. + Machines learn how to self-regulate and manage their own productivity and quality. + Human performance is essential; the emphasis shifts from production to system design and integration with the business system.

Figure 2.8 Changes in industry and quality approaches[29]

Source: Watson, Gregory H., "The Ascent of Quality", Quality Progress, March 2019, pp 24-30, http://asq.org/quality-progress/2019/03/career-development/the-ascent-of-quality-40.html

[29]See G. H. Watson. March 2019. "The Ascent of Quality." *Quality Progress*, pp. 24-30. http://asq.org/quality-progress/2019/03/career-development/the-ascent-of-quality-40.html.

"The technology landscape is richer and more promising than ever before. In many ways, cloud computing, big data, virtual reality (VR), augmented reality (AR), blockchain, additive manufacturing, artificial intelligence (AI), machine learning (ML), Internet Protocol Version 6 (IPv6), cyber-physical systems, and the Internet of Things (IoT) all represent new frontiers. These technologies can help improve product and service quality, and organizational performance.

In many regions, the internet is now as ubiquitous as electricity. Components are relatively cheap. And a robust ecosystem of open-source software libraries means that engineers can solve problems 100 times faster than just two decades ago. This digital transformation is leading us toward connected intelligent automation: smart, hyperconnected agents deployed in environments where humans and machines cooperate—and leverage data—to achieve shared goals.

This isn't the world's first industrial revolution. In fact, it is its fourth—and the disruptive changes it will bring suggest we'll need a fresh perspective on quality to adapt to it" is how Nicole Radziwill introduces the opportunities and challenges of Industry 4.0.[30]
This is her summary of the impact on Quality:

"Quality 4.0: A fresh perspective

Quality 4.0 is the name given to the pursuit of performance excellence during these times of potentially disruptive digital transformation. It comes from 'Industry 4.0'—a term coined at Hannover Fair in 2011 to describe the fourth industrial revolution.

That event emphasized the increasing intelligence and interconnectedness of smart manufacturing systems. It reflected on the newest technological innovations, placing them in historical context and tracing the development of key technologies from the 1700s to the present.

During the first industrial revolution (late 1700s and early 1800s), innovations in steam and waterpower made it possible for production facilities to scale up and expand potential production locations. Earlier, manufacturing facilities had to be constructed along rivers so waterwheels could be used to generate power.

---

[30]See N. Radziwill. October 2018. "Let's Get Digital," *Quality Progress*, pp. 24-29. http://asq.org/quality-progress/2018/10/basic-quality/lets-get-digital.html.

By the late 1800s, the discovery of electricity and development of infrastructure enabled engineers to build machinery for mass production. Iron ore production increased, enabling machines themselves to be mass produced. In the United States, the expansion of railways made it easier to obtain supplies and deliver finished goods.

The widespread availability of reliable power sparked a renaissance in computing. Toward the end of World War II, digital computing started to emerge from its analogue roots. The third industrial revolution came at the end of the 1960s with the invention of the programmable logic controller. This made it possible to automate processes, such as filling and reloading tanks, turning engines on and off, and controlling sequences of events based on the state of the process and changing environmental conditions.

The World Economic Forum (WEF) has been keenly interested in these changes. In 2015, it launched a digital transformation initiative to coordinate research that would help anticipate the effects of these changes on business and society. WEF recognized that we've been actively experiencing digital transformation since the emergence of digital computing in the 1950s: first with mainframes, then client-server computing and PCs, followed by the advent of the internet and early e-commerce sites.

Mobile devices and cloud computing led to a convergence of services, as multiple customer touch points (phone, fax, web, and tablets) gradually blended into the single view of the customer that most organizations now have. Just 20 years ago, organizations were barely able to link your phone calls to customer service, emails, and web form queries. Now, it's taken for granted.

The first industrial revolution was characterized by steam-powered machines, and the second by electricity and assembly lines. Innovations in computing and industrial automation defined the third. The fourth industrial revolution brings us machine intelligence, pervasive computing, affordable storage and robust connectivity. How can we leverage them to improve quality and performance?"

The ASQ Future of Quality Report 2015 considers in depth many different aspects of Industry 4.0 and related scenarios.[31]

---

[31]American Society for Quality—ASQ. "The Future of Quality: Quality Throughout 2015 Future of Quality Report." https://asq.org/quality-resources/research/future-of-quality.

Radziwill summarizes the main changes as follows:

- "Production and availability of information: More information is available because people and devices are producing it at greater rates than ever before. Falling costs of enabling technologies, such as sensors and actuators, are catalyzing innovation in these areas.

- Connectivity: First and foremost, the introduction of IPv6—which defines how data are sent from one computer to another—has ensured that there will be enough addresses to locate the billions of devices that are expected to connect to the Internet. The information produced by these devices will be instantly accessible over the Internet. In addition, improved network infrastructure is expanding the extent of connectivity, making it more widely available and robust. And unlike the 1980s and 1990s, there are far fewer communications protocols that are commonly encountered, so it's a lot easier to get one device to talk to another device on your network.

- Intelligent processing: Affordable computing capabilities (and processing power) are available to analyze and interpret that information so it can be incorporated into decision making. High-performance software libraries for advanced processing and visualization of data are easy to find and, in many cases, easy to use. In the past, for example, software developers had to write their own code for even common tasks. Now, they can use open-source solutions that are battle tested by many.

- New modes of interaction: The ways in which we acquire and interact with information also are changing. In particular, new interfaces, such as AR and VR, expand possibilities for training and navigating a hybrid physical-digital environment with greater ease.

- New modes of production: 3D printing, nanotechnology, and gene editing are poised to change the nature and means of production in several industries. Technologies for augmenting or enhancing human performance (exoskeletons, brain-computer interfaces, and even autonomous vehicles, for example) also will open new mechanisms for innovation in production and distribution. New technologies, such as blockchain, have the potential to change the nature of production as well by challenging ingrained centralized perceptions of trust, control, consensus and value creation."[32]

---

[32]See N. Radziwill. October 2018. "Let's Get Digital," *Quality Progress*, pp. 24-29. http://asq.org/quality-progress/2018/10/basic-quality/lets-get-digital.html.

Watson identifies two main areas emerging in Industry 4.0[33]:

"There is a growing need for organizations to divide their data analytics resources into two compartments—developing strategic insights and market positions (data science) and managing daily routine operations (quality). This arrangement challenges the perception of the value of quality management and raises questions regarding the importance of 'little data analysis,' which focuses on real-time, data-based investigations of problems' causalities and ensuring consistent quality is produced by a stable process.

Many of the control mechanisms in this daily management system can be enabled through robotics or other types of automation that use sensor systems, data monitors, or telemetry. These systems are supported by AI systems that feed corrective action signals through an adaptive feedback mechanism for changing production system settings."[34]

The key components on Industry 4.0 are shown in Figure 2.9.

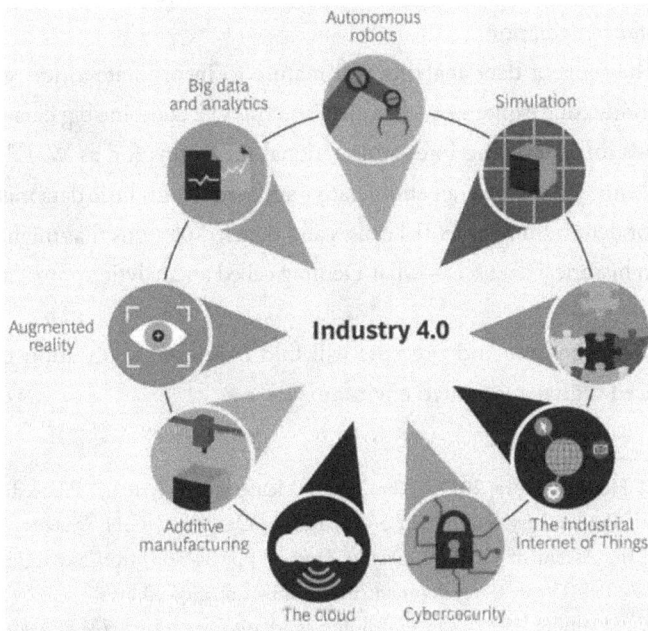

Figure 2.9 Nine technologies of Industry 4.0[35]

[33]G.H. Watson. March 2019. "The Ascent of Quality," *Quality Progress*, pp. 24-30. http://asq.org/quality-progress/2019/03/career-development/the-ascent-of-quality-40.html.
[34]Ibid.
[35]See Boston Consulting Group. "Embracing Industry 4.0 and Rediscovering Growth." https://www.bcg.com/capabilities/operations/embracing-industry-4.0-rediscovering-growth.aspx.

Greg Watson proposes the following three insights for the future of quality based on the technologies of Industry 4.0:

1. "The emphasis will shift from the operationally oriented task of creating and executing a quality strategy to more holistically applying quality as a strategy across the entire organization. Quality thinking will equal financial thinking in organizations' operational management systems, as demonstrated by and documented as the Toyota Management System, which goes beyond the well-known Toyota Production System.[36]

2. The distinction between quality professionals and data scientists will be replaced by a new approach that might be called 'collaborative analytics.' It will merge all continual improvement activities into an integrated, cross-functional, organization wide method driven by a structured, scientific approach to problem investigation, diagnosis, and remediation.

3. The tools of data analytics will mature to incorporate a new way of conducting exploratory data analysis. This will combine big data methods for identifying interesting rational subgroups (or, as W. Edwards Deming described, an enumerative approach) with little data methods for determining potential causes and detailed patterns that might exist in historical data sets—what Deming called an analytic approach."[37,38]

Basic principles and precepts will find continual application but in enhanced digital automated environments.

---

[36]See T. Horikiri. April 2017. "The Toyota Management System," Proceedings of the Fifth Productivity Summit in Sochi, Russia, Quoted in G.H. Watson. March 2019. "The Ascent of Quality," *Quality Progress*, pp. 24-30. http://asq.org/quality-progress/2019/03/career-development/the-ascent-of-quality-40.html.

[37]See W.E. Deming. 1975. "On Probability as a Basis for Action." *The American Statistician* 29, no. 4, pp. 146-62. Quoted in G.H. Watson. March 2019. "The Ascent of Quality," *Quality Progress*, pp. 24-30. http://asq.org/quality-progress/2019/03/career-development/the-ascent-of-quality-40.html.

[38]See G.H. Watson. March 2019. "The Ascent of Quality," *Quality Progress*, pp. 24-30. http://asq.org/quality-progress/2019/03/career-development/the-ascent-of-quality-40.html.

CHAPTER 3

Quality and Service Industries

What Is a Service Business or Organization?

The key difference between manufacturing and service industries is that there is no primary tangible direct output and there is no principal product inventory to stock and hold ready for sale.

A restaurant appears to be a hybrid where there is a product being consumed along with a service being provided. The (added) value is that customer does not need to prepare and clear up the meal.[1] A consensus appears to exist on it being a service business.

Training, maintenance, and test and calibration are examples of service businesses where the client brings themselves or provides the item to be maintained, tested, or calibrated.

Human agency is critical in both manufacturing and service industries or businesses. The modern versions of the standard keep a clear distinction so that there is no confusion in the applicability of the standard. Responsibility for the processes and the individual actions within a process, and competence in the process management and delivery of the outcomes are the same. What is generally different is the level and nature of the direct involvement of the individual in the creation and delivery of those outcomes.

Both manufacturing and service organizations will use products and include services. The scope of the services may extend to product delivery, installation, service, maintenance (including calibration), and repair and

---

[1]G.N. Kenyon and K.C. Sen. 2015. The Perception of Quality: Mapping Product and Service Quality to Consumer Perceptions. London: Springer-Verlag, 2.1 Understanding the demand landscape.

include the corresponding responsibilities of the organizations in their supply chain.

Internal and External Customers

But of critical importance is the recognition that customers do not just exist for the customer facing roles at the organizational interfaces—the paying customer for the product or service, but also within the organizational processes. The person next in line for what you make or the service you provide is your customer. The process perspective is vital and helps us to see that we are all linked not just by being responsible for chunks of a process but by providing goods and services to the next person to use them whether inside or outside our organization.

Going the Extra Mile and the Importance of Family

The role of the individual in the service delivery brings in new dimensions. There is a basic expectation of personal interaction in terms of clarity of communication, friendliness, and empathy. But there is the capacity to exceed expectations in terms of the personal interaction and the depth of service provided and bringing in what is known as "customer going the extra mile and the importance of family."

Interestingly the foundations for customer delight are laid within the organization in the reality of the family atmosphere that is built within the organization and in the degree to which your product and service become an asset to your customer.[2]

Especially when things go wrong, whether through our fault or not, then going the extra mile can transform and, where fault is involved and redeemed a situation can be transformed and loyalty and long-term relationships built—this is an example of breakthrough change in the most unpromising of circumstances.[3]

See also Chapter 20, Quality in the professions and vocations—quality, life, and service.

---

[2]H. Curtis. January 2010. "Back to Basics Customer Delight Two Key Elements to Ensure Customer Satisfaction," Quality Progress.

[3]K. Bemowski. February 1996. "Americans' Nostalgic Affair with Loyalty," Quality Progress, pp. 33-26.

CHAPTER 4

Quality, Risk, Opportunity, and Improvement

This chapter is one of the larger and more challenging ones but getting hold of the classic and foundational principles here is vital for a safe understanding and application of quality thinking.

Consistency and Variation

A main criterion of quality is consistent delivery to the requirements. Variation is the enemy of consistency. A consistent measurement outcome always yields the same result. A measure of consistency is the scatter or dispersion of results around some, assumed, true value. Perfect consistency can be represented by a single value on a chart, variation by a bell-shaped curve around the average or central value. If we weigh 10 screws on a balance, we expect to get the same result each time. If we notice any differences, it might be related to whether the last digit on the reading or the position of the needle on the scale leads us to record the result slightly differently. A stable process tends to come to rest on a central value that we can picture with a chart. The spread of results around that central value is a measure of the variation in the process and it could be the output we are measuring in either a measure of the product—weight of the loaf, or the service—waiting time at the checkout. As the results diverge more and more from the acceptable central value, we may find that the user is experiencing something they rate as unacceptable. We illustrate all of this in the rest of this chapter.

These concepts of variation and consistency occur very much more widely across the whole of life than we might first imagine. We meet them in areas where we know exactly what we feel and experience even if we find it difficult to measure or even express. We look for a consistent friendly and open response in people who are serving us or caring for us. We look for consistency in the relationships we have and call that faithfulness. When someone makes us a promise in a contract or deal, in respect of payment, or in a personal relationship such as marriage—keeping to those promises is called faithfulness. That is consistency and the opposite is variation or change without reason to do with us and the relationship.

Process Capability

One of the first questions we want to answer is—given that there is variation, what is the risk we might produce unacceptable products or provide an unacceptable service. No-one should knowingly take a risk to produce unacceptable products. The risks are there, they seem to be a fact of life, and we have to learn how to manage and reduce them so that variability is never out with the limits of acceptable product. We want to know how measurements on the product or service under normal circumstances will reveal that we have made or provided something that is unacceptable—that it is non-conforming or non-compliant.

We need to know something about the risk of us going beyond what is acceptable—the specification limit. We need to know how likely it is to find results far enough away from the mean value so that they transgress the specification limit and become nonconforming.

Normal Distribution and Standard Normal Distribution

The shape of the curve shows that more readings are closely gathered around the mean than there are as we get further away from the mean in either direction.

There is a greater probability of finding readings near the mean; we may never find one with the same value as the mean. There is an arithmetical or statistical measure of the way measurements are distributed, but the expectation is that most will be around the mean. The language of mathematics and statistics uses common sense terms and provides definitions and symbols by which these can share safely, explored, and shaped into sometimes counterintuitive discoveries that provide exciting tools to assist us in real-world tasks. Probability, distributions, and expectations are grounded in the real world of taking measurements in nature and society.

The normal distribution is one of many distributions that exist in nature and technology (and there are some very strange ones—I came across the Rosin-Rammler distribution in the milling of amalgam for dental fillings that was first discovered with coal. It is a double logarithmic distribution). The normal distribution is also called Gaussian[1] and is one of a group of bell-shaped distributions—but it is not alone in this. The normal distribution has many important properties. See Figure 4.1.

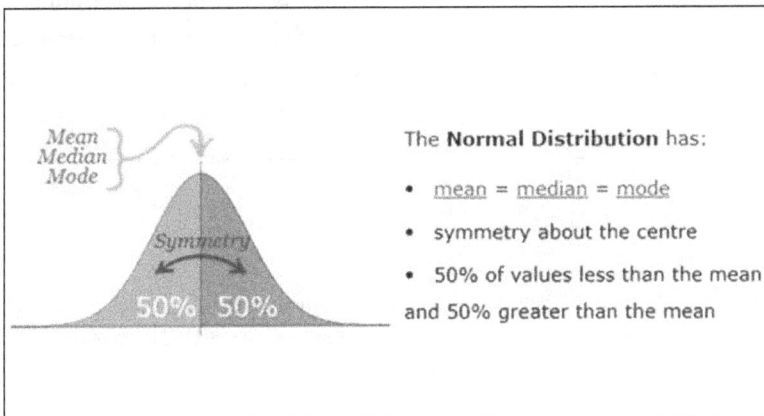

The **Normal Distribution** has:

- mean = median = mode
- symmetry about the centre
- 50% of values less than the mean and 50% greater than the mean

Figure 4.1 Properties of the normal distribution[2]

Mean is the arithmetic mean obtained by summing the observations and dividing by the number of observations; median is the most frequently occurring value, and mode is the middle value in an ordered list. The normal distribution is for measures that are continuously variable, i.e. not discrete such as 1 child, 2 children, 3 children—the previously normal atomic family of 2.3 children is hard and uncomfortable to picture!

---

[1]After Johann Carl Friedrich Gauss https://en.wikipedia.org/wiki/Carl_Friedrich_Gauss who discovered a family of functions of which the normal distribution is an important example.

[2]See Mathsisfun. "Normal Distribution." https://www.mathsisfun.com/data/standard-normal-distribution.html.

A standard normal distribution is one where the mean is 0 and the standard deviation is 1. "Every normal distribution is a version of the standard normal distribution whose domain has been stretched by a factor σ {sigma} (the standard deviation) and then translated by μ {mu} (the mean value)".[3] Given that every normal distribution is a scaled version of the standard normal distribution, they all share the same likelihood distribution in respect of finding measurements near to or further away from the mean value.

Likelihood and Normal Distributions

When we get to two standard deviations from the mean on each side of the mean we have covered approximately 95 percent of the distributions and there is only a 5 percent likelihood of finding readings or measurements outside these limits. So we can talk about a 95 percent confidence interval—see Figure 4.2.[4]

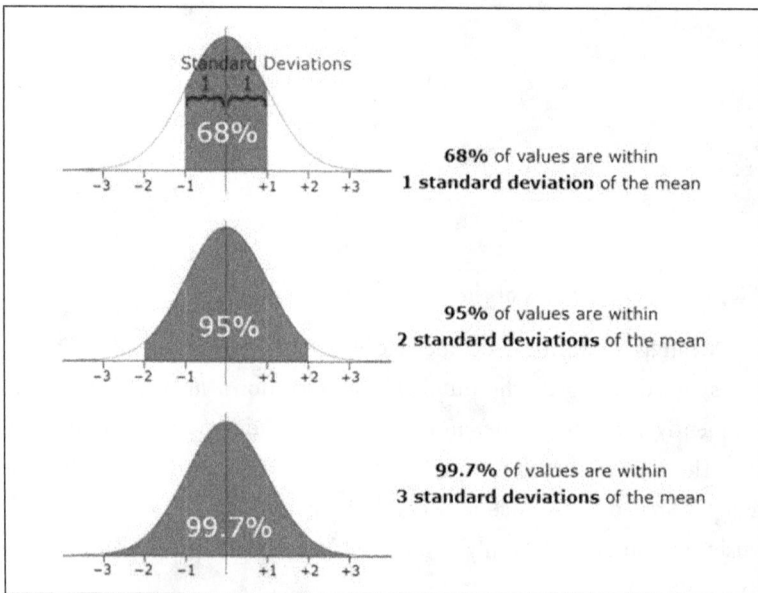

Figure 4.2 68–95–97 rule of 1–3 standard deviations
Source: Reber, Michael F., 2019, "In No Uncertain Terms", Quality Progress, May 2019, pp 18 – 24, http://asq.org/quality-progress/2019/05/continuous-improvement/in-no-uncertain-terms.html

---

[3]"Normal Distribution." https://en.wikipedia.org/wiki/Normal_distribution.
[4]See Mathsisfun. "Normal Distribution." https://www.mathsisfun.com/data/standard-normal-distribution.html.

Similarly, when get to 3 standard deviations, or 3σ (to use the Greek sigma symbol for standard deviation), we have covered approximately 99.7 percent, leaving only 0.3 percent likelihood of finding readings or measurements outside these limits. Reducing the percent back to a fraction by dividing by 100 we have a 1 in 0.003 or 1 in 3×10^{-3}. It is only when we get below $\pm 6\sigma$ that we are down to the approximately less than one in a million likelihood or confidence interval, of finding a reading or measurement – see Indices of process capability and Figure 4.3.

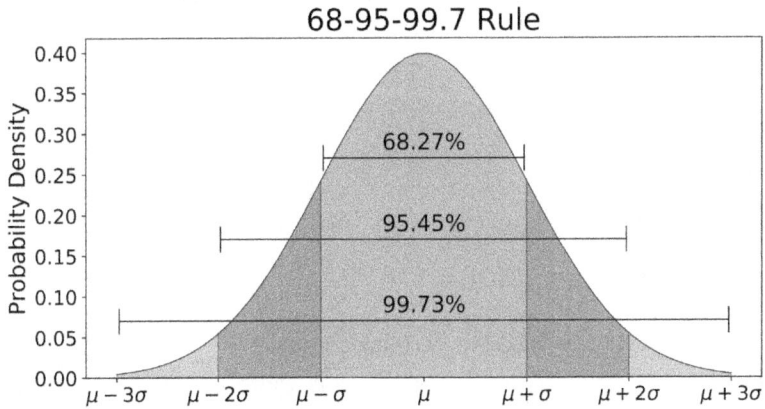

Figure 4.3 The coverage of 1–3 standard deviations of the normal distribution[5]

Coefficients of Variation

The measure of how much variation there is relative to the mean value is the standard deviation/mean value, and expressed as a percentage this would be multiplied by 100:

$$CV = \frac{\sigma}{\bar{x}}, \text{ or}$$

$$CV\% = \frac{\sigma}{\bar{x}} \times 100$$

Where σ is the population standard deviation and $\bar{x}$ arithmetic mean of the values whose dispersion you want to describe.

[5]See M. Galarnyk. "Explaining the 68-95-99.7 Rule for a Normal Distribution," *Towards Data Science*. https://towardsdatascience.com/understanding-the-68-95-99-7-rule-for-a-normal-distribution-b7b7cbf760c2.

σ, the population standard deviation, is the square root of sum of the differences between each value and the arithmetic mean,

$$= \sqrt{\left(\frac{\sum_{i=1}^{n}(x_i - x^-)^2}{n}\right)}\,^6.$$

The variance is the sum before the square root is taken

$$\sigma^2 = \sum_{i=1}^{n}(x_i - x^-)^2 / n\,.$$

The standard deviation of a sample you have taken, s, has already sacrificed 1 degree of freedom in estimating the sample mean $\bar{x}$ and so the

sample standard deviation $s^2 = \dfrac{\sum_{i=1}^{n}(x_i - x^-)^2}{n-1}$

This is used widely and can be replaced by a nonparametric statistic when appropriate.[7]

Indices of Process Capability

"The comparison is made by forming the ratio of the spread between the process specifications (the specification 'width') to the spread of the process values, as measured by six process standard deviation units (the process 'width').

We are often required to compare the output of a stable process with the process specifications and make a statement about how well the process meets specification. To do this we compare the natural variability of a stable process with the process specification limits. A process where almost all the measurements fall inside the specification limits is a capable process. This can be represented pictorially by the plot below—see Figure 4.4."[8]

---

[6]The is the population standard deviation. If we are taking the standard deviation of a sample then the unbiased estimator of the standard deviation has a divisor of n-1 rather than just n

[7]See M. Frank, M. Braginsky, V. Marchman, and D. Yurovsky. "Variability and Consistency in Early Language Learning," *The Wordbank Project*, Chapter 15 Variability and Consistency. https://langcog.github.io/wordbank-book/index.html.

[8]NIST/SEMATECH. "6.1.6. What is Process Capability?" e-Handbook of Statistical Methods. http://www.itl.nist.gov/div898/handbook/, https://www.itl.nist.gov/div898/handbook/toolaids/pff/pmc.pdf and https://www.itl.nist.gov/div898/handbook/pmc/section1/pmc16.htm.

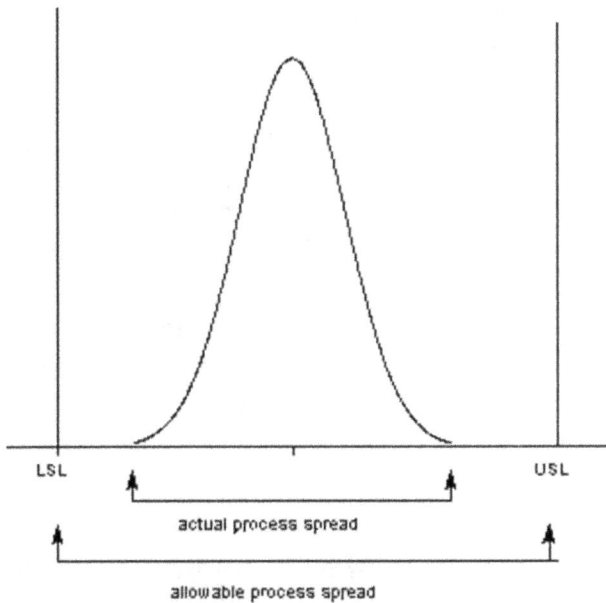

Figure 4.4 A capable process

The vitally important point to note is that this only looks as good as it is if you note that the mean of the actual distribution is centered over the specification mean. If the process wanders off toward either limit, then the probability of transgressing the limit increases. Therefore, although the bald C_p index is agnostic as regards the centering of the distribution, the other two take this into account. The indices proposed must also account for the relative nearness of the process distribution mean to the specification limits. Which is why the bald C_p index, although valuable in respect of potential process capability, is limited and potentially misleading in respect of actual process capability.

"There are several statistics that can be used to measure the capability of a process:

$$C_p, C_{pk}, \text{ and } C_{pm}$$

Most capability indices estimates are valid only if the sample size used is 'large enough.' Large enough is generally thought to be about 50 independent data values.

The C_p, $C_{pk.}$ and C_{pm} statistics assume that the population of data values is normally distributed. Assuming a two-sided specification, if μ and are σ the mean and standard deviation, respectively, of the normal data and USL, LSL, and T are the upper and lower specification limits and the target value, respectively, then the population capability indices are defined as follows:

$$C_p = \frac{USL - LSL}{6\sigma}$$

$$C_{pk} = min\left[\frac{USL - \mu}{3\sigma}, \frac{\mu - LSL}{3\sigma}\right]$$

$$C_{pm} = \frac{USL - LSL}{6\sqrt{\sigma^2 + (\mu - T)^2}}$$

where USL is the upper specification limit, LSL is the lower specification limit, σ is the process standard deviation, μ is the process mean, and T is the specification target value."[9]

However, if we are careful in ensuring that the process distribution is centered, then the bald C_p index is very revealing of two things:

1. How potentially good, low risk or relatively risk-free, the process is in respect of delivering conforming product;
2. How important it is to have highly capable processes and monitor them to ensure they remain centered.

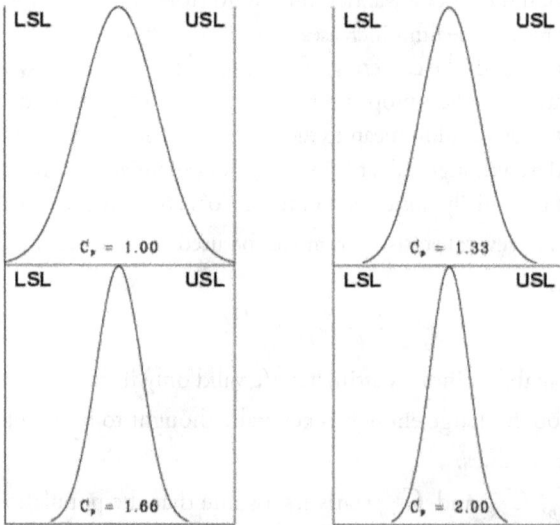

Figure 4.5 Plot showing Cp for varying process widths[10]

---

[9]Ibid.
[10]Ibid.

This can be expressed numerically in Table 4.1:

Table 4.1 Specification range reject likelihood[11]

USL–LSL	6σ	8σ	10σ	12σ
Cp	1.00	1.33	1.66	2.00
Rejects	0.27%	64 ppm	0.6 ppm	2 ppb
% of spec used	100	75	60	50

Note: The 3.4 ppm limit for 6σ arises because there is an allowance for a 1.5σ drift so the value being used lies between the 8σ and the 10σ values.

where ppm = parts per million and ppb = parts per billion. Note that the reject figures assume that the distribution is centered at μ.[12]

Risk as Likelihood

"You cannot inspect quality into a product"[13]—100 percent inspection may still be practised for some high-end luxury brand products, but where sampling and testing (Figure 4.6) are possible and appropriate then that is a way to proceed for final verification before distribution and delivery.

Acceptance Sampling	Hypothesis Testing
Acceptable quality level (AQL) $\theta = \theta_0$ Lot tolerance percent defectives (LTPD) $\theta = \theta_1$	Hypothesis $\theta = \theta_0$ Alternative $\theta = \theta_1$
Allowable number of defectives c	Critical value c
Producer's risk α of rejecting a lot with $\theta \leq \theta_0$	Probability α of making a Type I error (significance level)
Consumer's risk β of accepting a lot with $\theta \geq \theta_1$	Probability β of making a Type II error

Figure 4.6 Acceptance sampling and hypothesis testing[14]

Here is an example from manufacturing and any organization verifying incoming product of how risk as likelihood is the first way we encounter risk. We also take a sideways look at how wide is the application of the principles involved.

---

[11]Ibid.

[12]Ibid.

[13]Quote of Harold F Dodge used by W Edwards Deming in "Out of the Crisis."

[14]See E. Kaçmaz. "Acceptance Sampling," *PowerPoint*. http://ceng.eskisehir.edu.tr/emrekacmaz/%C4%B0ST252/icerik/25.6-Acceptance-Sampling.pptx.

Suppose someone as producer takes a sample from a lot before delivery, or as a customer takes a sample after delivery, and takes several readings how likely are we to find a reading or measurement that will cause us concern about the product we have in front of us?

What quality level are we looking for—say 0.65 percent defective, the acceptable quality level or 0.65 percent AQL? Is there an expectation that in the worst case—knowing that we have variation to deal with, a different larger but still small proportion of defects, e.g. misshapes, might be acceptable—say 5 percent and we will abbreviate this to 5 percent LQ—limiting quality level?

Our assumption is that the lot conforms—this is our working hypothesis—our "null" hypothesis.

We want to test and accept the lot if our sample results allow us to.

We take a sample of a certain size, say n items, from a lot of size N, where N is greater than > or much greater than >>, the number of items, n, to be taken as a sample and decide what, for the sample we have taken and the acceptable quality level we would accept for the lot as a whole, is the maximum number of defects, c, we will accept.

The first important finding to note is for effective discrimination of the risks involved that the proportion of the lot size N that we take is of no real significance at all, if it is not greater than 100 percent. What is important is the size of the sample "n" that we take.

We want a high probability that the manufacturer will accept the lot if the quality is at or better than the agreed acceptable quality level and a low risk, α, that they will falsely reject the lot if the sample appears to contain more nonconforming items than is acceptable but the lot is in fact at or better than the agreed acceptable quality level.

Conversely, as a customer, we want a high probability that we will reject the lot if the sample is worse than the agreed acceptable quality level and a low risk, β, that we will falsely accept the lot if the sample appears to contain less nonconforming items than is acceptable but the lot is in fact at or worse than the agreed acceptable quality level.

We have four parameters—AQL, n, c, and LQ and we need to see how the probability of acceptance changes as the proportion of actual defectives in the population increases and we move from 100 percent acceptance to 0 acceptance or complete rejection, from acceptance of good product by the producer to protection from poor quality for the consumer.

A form of statement for generalized hypothesis testing, taken from the background of clinical trials, is:

"In any formal statistical test of the null hypothesis (the statement that a population parameter is equal to a specific value), there are two possible types of error. Type 1 or alpha error has occurred if the investigator rejects the null hypothesis when it is true. For example, an experimental treatment is declared an advance over standard treatment when it is not. Type 2 or beta error has occurred if the null hypothesis is not rejected when it is false. In this case, the investigator concludes that the experimental treatment is no different from the standard when it actually is. The two types of error can be conceptualized, respectively, as the consumer's risk and the producer's risk. In many reports of clinical trial methodology, it is the producer's risk that is emphasized. It is understandable why producer's risk would be of concern to authors of clinical studies. There are, however, numerous potential sources of consumer's risk."

So we can see that this vital concept is central to the scientific method and of great practical importance in many, many areas of life including, as we shall see below in Figure 4.6., the law and justice!

Ideal and Typical OC Curves with α and β Risks

We can calculate this relationship by one of several statistical models[15] and the results are ideal and typical OC curves with α and β risks (Figure 4.7):

This curve shows that at the AQL there is a risk, α, that we shall reject the lot N based on the sample of n with acceptance number c defectives because of the random occurrence of more than c defectives in the sample.

At the other end of the curve there is a risk, β, that the consumer will accept a poor lot with more than c defectives in it because of the random occurrence of less than c defectives in it.

---

[15]Binomial—ignoring N, hypergeometric—using N, and Poisson.

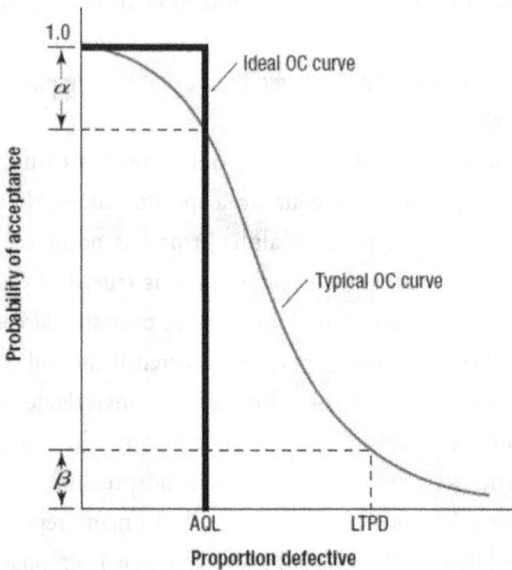

Figure 4.7 Ideal and typical OC curves with α and β risks[16]

Lot Tolerance Percent Defective (LTPD) is a form of LQ.

A first response is to say "we should 100 percent inspect" but even this is fraught with issues, quite apart from any time and cost considerations, because 100 percent inspection is certainly not perfect if reliant on human inspectors.

As we increase the size of the sample and maintain the acceptance number, we improve the discrimination of the operating characteristic both reducing α and the limiting quality.

We[17] used one of the operating curve statistical models[18] to calculate the different discrimination of a family of five operating characteristic curves, see Table 4.2, of differing n and c but similar n/c relationships for the medical device discussed in Chapter 2.

---

[16]See Pearson. "Acceptance Sampling Plans," *Pearson MyLab Operations Management.* https://www.pearsonmylabandmastering.com/global/myomlab/ and https://wps.prenhall.com/wps/media/objects/7117/7288732/65767_28_SuppG.pdf.

[17]Potter, WD and Paul Hayes, unpublished work for United Nations Family Planning Association (UNFPA).

[18]Binomial—ignoring N, using the cumulative binomial distribution function in Excel.

Table 4.2 Varying sample size and reject number for a given AQL and LQ

Sample size	Nonconforming products	Equivalent AQL	P_a at the AQL	P_a at LQ
20	0	0.65	87.8	59
125	2	0.65	95.1	36.6
200	3	0.65	95.7	23.4
315	5	0.65	98.2	17.1
500	7	0.025	98.2	5.2

The risks here are simple probabilities of accepting a good product when it is true—and not, as the producer and accepting bad when it is not true—or when it is. Risk here is likelihood or probability.

The sample issues we have discussed here have wider application as Table 4.3 shows.

Table 4.3 The analogy between judge's decisions and statistical tests[19]

Judge's decision	Statistical test
Innocence: The defendant did not commit crime	Null hypothesis: No association between Tamiflu and psychotic manifestations
Guilt: The defendant did commit the crime	Alternative hypothesis: There is association between Tamiflu and psychosis
Standard for rejecting innocence: Beyond a reasonable doubt	Standard for rejecting null hypothesis: Level of statistical significance (à)
Correct judgment: Convict a criminal	Correct inference: Conclude that there is an association when one does exist in the population
Correct judgment: Acquit an innocent person	Correct inference: Conclude that there is no association between Tamiflu and psychosis when one does not exist
Incorrect judgment: Convict an innocent person.	Incorrect inference (Type I error): Conclude that there is an association when there actually is none
Incorrect judgment: Acquit a criminal	Incorrect inference (Type II error): Conclude that there is no association when there actually is one

---

[19]See A. Banerjee, U.B. Chitnis, S.L. Jadhav, J.S. Bhawalkar, and S. Chaudhury. July to December 2009. "Hypothesis Testing, Type I and Type II Errors." *Industrial Psychiatry Journal* 18, no. 2, pp. 127-31. https://www.ncbi.nlm.nih.gov/pmc/articles/PMC2996198/.

Making Inferences

We are making inferences from the data about the underlying distribution and then from the information we derive from applying that model what this is telling us about a real world situation—a product delivery conforms to requirements and is ready to be used, or not - and there will be a delay, loss, and possibly other consequences.

Distributions

We are using statistical models—probability distributions, to understand the world around us. We need to be confident that we have selected the right model and validated our choice by confirmatory checks that it is the right selection. We may need to look at all the sample data gathered in the recent past and check that the probability distribution selected is the right one.[20]

Sampling

We generally take samples to make an inference, often an estimate, of some measure—or measures, of the population—this can be a sample from a lot or batch of product. This is something we see when an election is called and the different parties want to make an estimate of where the populace, or different sections, stand on issues and voting intentions.

The sampling method, or protocol, is critical to getting a representative sample from which a safe estimate may be made.

The errors and uncertainty in the most widely recognized sampling methods from materials sampling to signal digitization can be very significant indeed. "Cone and quartering" is a recognized method for taking a sample of granular materials but it is very poor at taking a representative sample and mechanical sample splitters such as the spinning riffler are preferred.[21]

---

[20]The are well documented checks for the appropriateness of using a "normal" distribution function see E.Limpert, and W.A. Stahel, 14 Jul 2011, "Problems with Using the Normal Distribution – and Ways to Improve Quality and Efficiency of Data Analysis", Plos One, https://journals.plos.org/plosone/article?id=10.1371/journal .pone.0021403 and https://www.ncbi.nlm.nih.gov/pmc/articles/PMC3136454/

[21]See M. Campos-M. January 2017. "Applications of Quartering Method in Soils and Foods." *Int. Journal of Engineering Research and Application* 7, no. 1(Part -2), pp. 35-39. https://www.ijera.com/papers/Vol7_issue1/Part-2/F0701023539.pdf.

The two key concerns in sampling are that a sample should be representative and random. If there is not a single homogeneous population, if it is heterogeneous, then you need to understand as much as possible about the heterogeneity and sample representativity. These might be different strata or areas of gaseous, liquid, or particulate flow, different groups of people, or other forms of heterogeneity. You might want to protect against being presented with the best examples and chose to take your own and so ignore the top easy ways to access layers. If there is any possibility that the lot or batch still reflects a process and time sequence, then taking individual samples at random, using a random number generator, will minimize the risk of accidentally harmonizing with a pattern of variability and underestimating the true variability in the sample.

There is an assumption that methods once standardized can be routinely applied. An authoritative guide on sampling makes it clear that this is not always a safe assumption: "Unlike the assumption that is often made for estimates of uncertainty for an analytical method, an estimate for one sampling protocol for one batch of material should not be assumed as automatically applicable to any subsequent batch of material. For example, depending on the sampling target, the degree of heterogeneity (i.e. inhomogeneity) may have changed substantially. There will be a need, therefore, for routine monitoring of key parameters of sampling quality to examine and update estimates of uncertainty for subsequent batches."[22]

There are no shortage of methods for sampling but relatively little actual estimation of their, undoubtedly significant and possibly very large, contribution to measurement uncertainty—as the CITAC observes: "Sampling protocols have been written to describe the recommended procedure for the sampling of innumerable types of material and for many different chemical components. These protocols are sometimes specified in regulation or in international agreements. These procedures rarely identify the relative contributions of sampling and chemical analysis to the combined

---

[22]See M.H. Ramsey, S.L.R. Ellison, and P. Rostron (eds.). 2019. *Measurement Uncertainty Arising from Sampling: A Guide to Methods and Approaches.* Eurachem/EUROLAB/ CITAC/Nordtest/AMC Guide. ISBN (978-0-948926-26-6). https://www. eurachem.org/index.php/publications/guides/musamp and https://www.eurachem. org/images/stories/Guides/pdf/UfS_2007.pdf.

uncertainty."[23] A situation that was confirmed to me at the time of writing[24] by the head of laboratory of a public water utility in the UK , and separately by a Professor of Industrial Statistics within the EU ETV Technical Working group.

Process Stability

Using standard deviations to assess process sampling risk assumes a stable process with only the causes of "common" variation which are normally attached to it.

Sometimes the lack of stability indicates that some special cause is happening—our average weight is increasing or decreasing.

Sometimes that change is expected, and its absence would be worrying—the child's weight and height are not changing as expected under the anticipated growth mechanisms.

Sometimes a change away from the norm could be wonderful…taking us to a better place of performance.

"Control charts are used to check for process stability. In this context, a process is said to be 'in statistical control' if the probability distribution representing the quality characteristic is constant over time. If there is some change over time in this distribution, the process is said to be 'out of control.' This traditional definition of 'statistical control' has been generalized over the years to include cases for which an underlying statistical model of the quality characteristic is stable over time. These useful generalizations include, for example, regression, variance component, and time series models.

For continuous quality characteristics, specification limits are often given in practice. An item is considered to be 'O.K.' if the value of its quality characteristic is within the specification limits and 'not O.K.' otherwise. Deming (1986) and many others have argued that meeting specification limits is not sufficient to ensure good quality and that the variability of the quality characteristics should be reduced such that,

[23]See Section 1.5.4, M.H. Ramsey, S.L.R. Ellison (eds.). *Measurement Uncertainty Arising from Sampling: A Guide to Methods and Approaches.* Eurachem, EUROLAB, CITAC, Nordtest and the RSC Analytical Methods Committee. ISBN (978-0-948926-26-6). https://www.eurachem.org/index.php/publications/guides/musamp and https://www.eurachem.org/images/stories/Guides/pdf/UfS_2007.pdf.
[24]August 2019.

as Deming (1986, p. 49) describes it, 'specifications are lost beyond the horizon.'

Thus, for many quality characteristics, quality improvement corresponds to centering the probability distribution of the quality characteristic at a target value and reducing variability. Taguchi (1981, p. 14) advocated reduction of variability until it becomes economically disadvantageous to reduce it further. To use a control chart such as the X-chart to monitor the process mean or the R-chart to monitor variability, samples are taken over time and values of a statistic are plotted. For the type chart introduced by Shewhart (1931, 1939), an out-of-control signal is given by the chart as soon as the statistic calculated from a sample falls outside control limits. These limits are usually set at ± 3 standard errors of the plotted statistic from a centerline at its historical average value. The formula for the calculation of the standard error is usually based on a distributional assumption, e.g., the binomial model for a p-chart used to monitor proportions. The resulting control limits are referred to as 'three-sigma' limits. Other rules are also used for signaling an out-of-control situation based on 'non-random' patterns on the chart. Many of these patterns are given in the Western Electric Handbook (1956)."[25]

Risk as Likelihood and Consequence

Risk diverges from being just likelihood when it comes to business risk and the two are covered by different definitions in the key standards on risk derived from the related ISO guide:

Risk is framed as just uncertainty, but commonly accepted practice and general understanding is that it is what the note to the definition suggests—a combination of likelihood and consequence:

"2.1 Risk: effect of uncertainty on objectives

NOTE 1 An effect is a deviation from the expected—positive and/or negative.

NOTE 2 Objectives can have different aspects (such as financial, health and safety, and environmental goals) and can apply at different levels (such as strategic, organization-wide, project, product, and process).

---

[25]See W.H. Woodhall. October 2000. "Controversies and Contradictions in Statistical Process Control." *Journal of Quality Technology* 32, no. 4. http://asq.org/pub/jqt/past/vol32_issue4/qtec-341.pdf.

NOTE 3 Risk is often characterized by reference to potential events (2.17) and consequences (2.18), or a combination of these.

NOTE 4 Risk is often expressed in terms of a combination of the consequences of an event (including changes in circumstances) and the associated likelihood (2.19) of occurrence.

NOTE 5 Uncertainty is the state, even partial, of deficiency of information related to, understanding or knowledge of an event, its consequence, or likelihood. [ISO Guide 73:2009, definition 1.1]"[26]

Likelihood, by contrast, is defined as follows:

"2.19 Likelihood: chance of something happening

NOTE 1 In risk management terminology, the word 'likelihood' is used to refer to the chance of something happening, whether defined, measured or determined objectively or subjectively, qualitatively or quantitatively, and described using general terms or mathematically (such as a probability or a frequency over a given time period).

NOTE 2 The English term 'likelihood' does not have a direct equivalent in some languages; instead, the equivalent of the term "probability" is often used. However, in English, 'probability' is often narrowly interpreted as a mathematical term.

Therefore, in risk management terminology, 'likelihood' is used with the intent that it should have the same broad interpretation as the term 'probability' has in many languages other than English. [ISO Guide 73:2009, definition 3.6.1.1]"

Uncertainty and Risk and Opportunity

The foundation ISO standard on management systems did something innovative and strong when it included "opportunity" in the same heading as risk as the positive consequence of uncertainty: "6.1 Actions to address risks and opportunities."[27] I first met this when working with a Risk Consulting company on an Integrated Management System for a client and fifteen years ago that sounded quite innovative—though entirely logical!

Here is the helpful introduction in the standard to "opportunity and risk" in the section on "risk-based thinking": "Opportunities can arise as a result of a situation favourable to achieving an intended result, for example, a set

---

[26]See ISO 31000:2009, "Risk Management—Principles and Guidelines."
[27]See ISO 9001:2015, "Quality Management Systems—Requirements."

of circumstances that allow the organization to attract customers, develop new products and services, reduce waste or improve productivity. Actions to address opportunities can also include consideration of associated risks. Risk is the effect of uncertainty and any such uncertainty can have positive or negative effects. A positive deviation arising from a risk can provide an opportunity, but not all positive effects of risk result in opportunities."[28]

Risk Management and Risk-Based Thinking

Very often we apply principles before full formal application and the EU ETV project introduced a "Life Cycle Perspective" that was intended to stop short of full, and necessarily more formal quantitative, life cycle analysis. The increased formality and rigour are readily deduced from the name. In the same way "risk-based thinking" (Figures 4.8 and 4.9) as specified in the base quality management standard[29] is intended to require the use of risk management principles, and this will be assessed at audit by certification bodies for independently audited organizations, rather than full risk management.

The standard is explicit on this distinction: "Although 6.1 specifies that the organization shall plan actions to address risks, there is no requirement for formal methods for risk management or a documented risk management process. Organizations can decide whether or not to develop a more extensive risk management methodology than is required by this International Standard, e.g. through the application of other guidance or standards."[30]

Risk and Loss, Likelihood and Impact

In both risk-based thinking and risk management there is an underlying process structure through to the realization of risk. There are risk "sources" which contain the potential for "events", and there are "causes" which are the actual triggers for "events" which are risks, or opportunities that are realized.[31] The event gives risk to the consequences (see Figure 4.9).

---

[28]See section 0.3.3 in ISO 9001:2015, "Quality Management Systems—Requirements."
[29]See sections 0.3.3 and 6.1 in ISO 9001:2015, "Quality Management Systems—Requirements."
[30]See Annex A.4 ISO 9001:2015, "Quality management systems—Requirements."
[31]For a fuller treatment, see section 2.3 in "Risk Management Guidelines—Companion to AS/NZ ISO 31000:2009," SA/SNZ HB 436:3013. https://www.standards.org.au/standards-catalogue/sa-snz/publicsafety/ob-007/sa--snz-hb--436-2013.

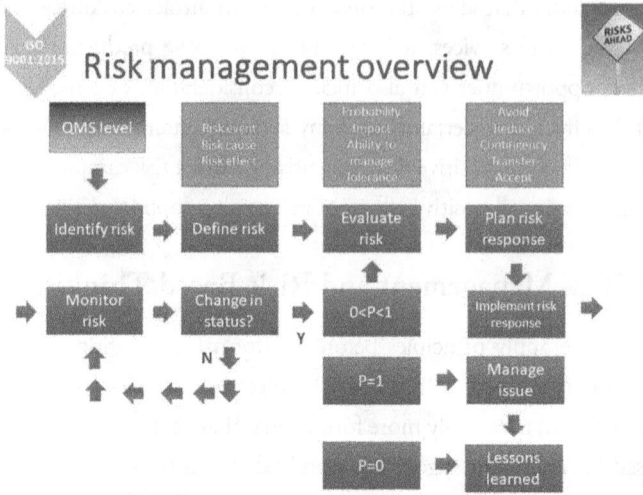

Figure 4.8 What is risk-based thinking?[32]

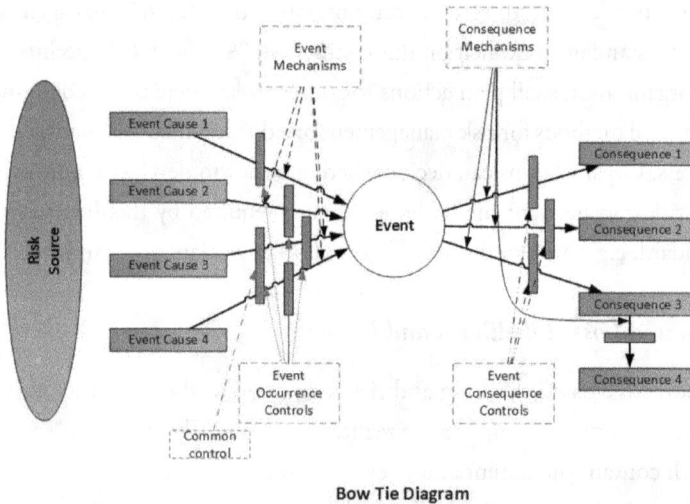

Bow Tie Diagram

Figure 4.9 From risk source to consequence—Bowtie diagram

[32]See R. Green and C. MacNee. 2015. "Implementing ISO 9001:2015—9001:2015 Transition Training," CQI and IRCA, Implementing ISO 9001:2015 Training Course.

The risk assessment process is subjective but results in measurements are quantitative. Likelihoods are assessed and entered, and corresponding impacts or consequences result in a combined risk score.

These assessments at their simplest can be purely qualitative as the example in Table 4.4 shows.

Table 4.4 Risk matrix table[33]

Areas	Risks	Likelihood	Impact	Controls
Reputation	A real or perceived link or association between the charity and terrorist activity damages the charity's reputation.	Low	High	• Draw up detailed partnership agreements • Review partner's governance structures • Review project audit and monitoring, including field visits • Include an impact and risk assessment for all projects • Take references and contact other affiliates of the partner for recommendations • Request standard documentation and invoices • Check the consolidated list of designated individuals and entities (see Chapter 1 of toolkit)
Financial/criminal	Financial loss, fraud, money laundering, terrorist financing.	Medium	High	• Clear responsibilities and segregation of duties • Scheme of delegation

(continued)

---

[33]See "Tool 4: Risk Management—Risk Matrix," Charity Commission for England and Wales, in Compliance Toolkit: Protecting Charities from Harm, Chapter 2 Charities: due diligence, monitoring and verifying the end use of charitable funds. https://assets.publishing.service.gov.uk/government/uploads/system/uploads/attachment_data/file/550692/Tool_4.pdf in https://www.gov.uk/government/publications/charities-due-diligence-checks-and-monitoring-end-use-of-funds.

Table 4.4 Risk matrix table (continued)

Areas	Risks	Likelihood	Impact	Controls
Financial/ Criminal	Failure to comply with UK, international, or local regulations.	High	Medium	• Developing and implementing a fraud policy • Purchases and tender controls, Reconciliations of cash book to petty cash and bank, expenses procedures, and authorization limits
	Exchange rate losses or gains.	Medium	Medium	• Monitor exchange rate losses or gains and review impact on expenditure and income • Use appropriate bank accounts and procedures
	Funds or assets provided are not used for the intended project or misappropriated.	Low	Medium	• Quarterly project financial reviews and project reports • Documented financial procedures • Regular budget monitoring and forecasting and grant management
Security	Risk to staff and/or beneficiaries. Obstacles to the effective delivery of services. Areas of conflict, political instability, hostile government.	High	High	• Country-specific security risk assessment • Crisis management policy and procedures • Health and safety and security training

These qualitative scores provide the data for the matrix—see Figure 4.10.

Risk Matrix

An alternative hybrid—mixed quantitative and qualitative matrix is provided—see Figures 4.10 and 4.11

QUALITY, RISK, OPPORTUNITY, AND IMPROVEMENT   49

Risk assessment matrix				
Severity Probability	Catastrophic	Critical	Marginal	Negligible
Frequent	High	High	Serious	Medium
Probable	High	High	Serious	Medium
Occasional	High	Serious	Medium	Low
Remote	Serious	Medium	Medium	Low
Improbable	Medium	Medium	Medium	Low
Eliminated	Eliminated			

Figure 4.10 Qualitative risk matrix

		LIKELIHOOD				
		A	B	C	D	E
CONSEQUENCE SEVERITY	5	Medium	Medium	High	High	High
	4	Low	Medium	Medium	High	High
	3	Low	Low	Medium	Medium	High
	2	Low	Low	Low	Medium	Medium
	1	Low	Low	Low	Low	Low
	0	OK	OK	OK	OK	OK

Figure 4.11 Quantitative and qualitative risk matrixes

Risk Management

Once the risks that fall on or above the action level threshold have been decided, then the four strategies that are commonly accepted come into play and the appropriate one needs selection for each risk.

"There are four basic strategies that can be applied to manage a recognized risk. These strategies can be identified as the four T's:

1. Transfer the financial consequences to third parties or share it. In this context, for example, through the terms or conditions of a partnership agreement or grant that enables the charity to claw back the grant or payment in certain situations.

2. Terminate the activity giving rise to the risk completely. In this context, for example, by refusing the grant or not accepting the project or stopping a particular activity or service.

3. Treat the risk through effective management. In the context of giving grants or supporting projects, the best way to manage risk is to carry out proper due diligence and act on its results, ensuring there is suitable and regular reporting. Other ways of managing specific risk include making grants in smaller amounts conditional on certain events happening, or satisfactory reporting and auditing, or making an initial grant first and making it easy to terminate this.

4. Tolerate the risk as one that cannot be avoided if the activity is to continue. An example of this might be where trustees take out an insurance policy that carries a higher level of voluntary excess or where the trustees recognize that in an emergency the main concern is to get aid to those who need it. Not all risks can be avoided entirely. The general approach is that the greater the risk, the more that trustees need to do to be able to demonstrate that they have discharged their duty to manage it."

However, this is vast simplification. There is a whole management support system that is effectively called into play. In just the same way as is needed for effective quality management and one that is very closely analogous.

There is a cycle to the risk assessment cycle (Figure 4.12) that should flow into appropriate implementation of risk management.

The key standard on risk management provides a fuller statement of the whole management context.

This is a PDCA cycle and the references in the diagram are to the sections of the ISO 31000 standard.

The risk assessment cycle

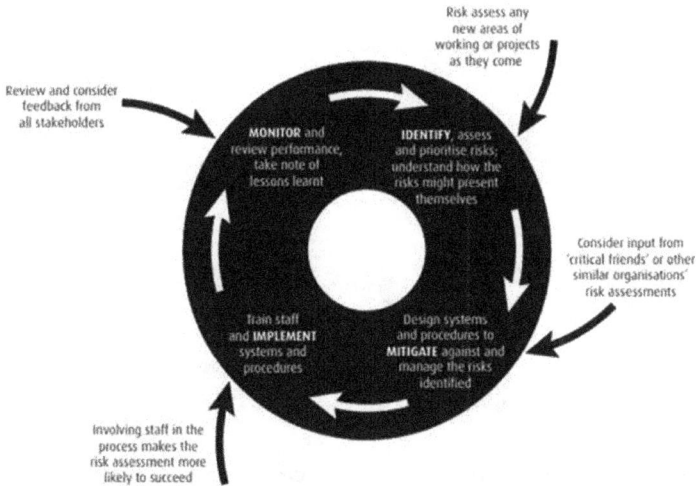

Figure 4.12 Risk assessment cycle[34]

The framework for managing risk (see Figures 4.13 and 4.14) wraps around the central risk management process and again the references in the diagram are to the sections of the ISO 31000 standard.

There is a valuable handbook to the standard to help in its implementation.[35]

A government-sponsored initiative provided a table of the possible approaches to risk identification—see Appendix, pp.188–189, Examples of opportunity and risk management approaches and their main uses.[36]

---

[34]See Charity Commission for England and Wales, "Tool 1: Risk Management— The Risk Assessment Cycle," Charity Commission for England and Wales, In Compliance Toolkit: Protecting Charities from Harm, Chapter 2 Charities: due diligence, monitoring and verifying the end use of charitable funds. https://assets.publishing.service.gov.uk/government/uploads/system/uploads/attachment_data/file/550688/Tool_1.pdf   in   https://www.gov.uk/government/publications/charities-due-diligence-checks-and-monitoring-end-use-of-funds.

[35]"Risk Management Guidelines—Companion to AS/NZ ISO 31000:2009," SA/SNZ HB 436:3013. https://www.standards.org.au/standards-catalogue/sa-snz/publicsafety/ob-007/sa--snz--hb--436-2013.

[36]See "Sigma Opportunity and Risk Guide," The SIGMA Project—Sustainability Integrated Guidelines for Management. https://www.scribd.com/document/356655959/Sigma-Risk-Opportunity.

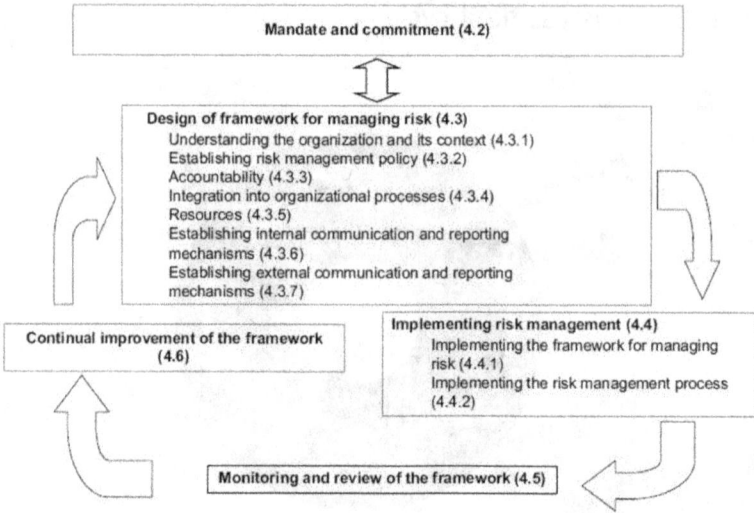

Figure 4.13 Relationship between the components of the framework[37]

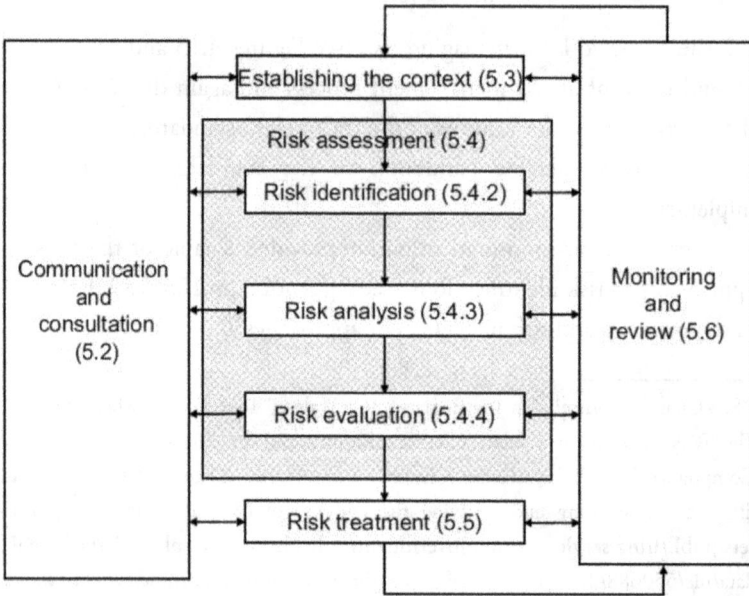

Figure 4.14 Risk management process[38]

---

[37]See ISO 31000:2009, "Risk Management—Principles and Guidelines."
[38]Ibid.

Risk Avoidance

Taormina relates the importance of risk avoidance at the start of this seminal article: "Before I became an expert witness, I was oblivious to the reality that process variability could lead to catastrophic fires, injury, loss of property, and death. My realization of this led to the thesis that our traditional approach to proactive quality management was fundamentally flawed. Those who employ tools such as failure mode and effects analysis (FMEA) uncover potentially detrimental process inconsistencies in their investigations. Those who mine prognosis and assessment of risk scales (PAR) for improvement ideas are seldom proactive enough to be effective for risk avoidance. Rarely is preventive action a result of an epiphany or flash of genius. Nor are PARs typically the result of cognitive risk investigations. Even more uncommon is a formal program of foreseeable risk implemented as an immutable and proactive cultural mandate. The trigger for implementing a mandate of risk avoidance is too often the outcome of a product or service being involved in a massively costly failure or some human tragedy."[39]

Risk exists even when it is not visible as events and the state of business well-being needs a different diagnostic approach to examine the health of a business. "Foreseeable risk is a systematic diagnostic method that examines the health of a business using proven tools of process analysis, performance to standards, business metrics and management system effectiveness. Used proactively, foreseeable risk is a roadmap for organizations to achieve peak health and wellness. Used as a forensic tool, it provides documented evidence of the standard of care and foreseeable risk measured against quantifiable standards of performance. For enlightened business leaders, foreseeable risk is a strategy for achieving peak performance while immunizing the organization from products liability and organizational negligence. By virtually eliminating product defects and

---

[39]See T. Taormina. November 2019. "Risk Avoidance—Clearing a Safe Path—A Breakthrough Approach to Avoid and Evade Risk," *Quality Progress*, pp. 16-25. http://asq.org/quality-progress/2019/11/risk-management/clearing-a-safe-path.html.

service errors, organizations can achieve unparalleled pinnacles of customer service and defect avoidance."[40]

Taormina goes to outline the implications of this vital contribution to
risk management in these steps:

- Foreseeable risk—implementation;
- Adopting the avoidance paradigm;
- The tools of foreseeable risk;
- Action items.

He concludes with a call to action.[41]

Tows Analysis

Finding a practical approach to "risk-based thinking" for the new
management standards that do not require "formal risk management" can be a fraught and difficult affair, particularly when external
certification bodies are involved as evidenced by the discussions in
LinkedIn.[42]

The common thread running through the discussion is that (all) you
need is to have "identified the risk and opportunities and have a corresponding action ...."

---

[40]Ibid.

[41]Ibid.

[42]Formal Risk Management and ISO 9001:2015, Jesson de los Santos, CLSSBB,
IE Certified Lean Six Sigma Black Belt & Trainer | ISO9001,14001, OHSAS
18001 Consultant | Management Consultant | Speaker. https://www.linkedin.
com/groups/1268337/1268337-6280582540738813953?midToken=AQEWC
CpRh3waLA&trk=eml-b2_anet_digest_of_digests-hero-12-view%7Ediscussio
n&trkEmail=eml-b2_anet_digest_of_digests-hero-12-view%7Ediscussion-null-
22wpuq%7Ej6lzhq06%7E4r-null-communities%7Egroup%7Ediscussion&lipi=urn
%3Ali%3Apage%3Aemail_b2_anet_digest_of_digests%3BAEVQXAhAS1mE3ke%
2BVWlTjw%3D%3D.

One example of this that predates the ISO 9001:2008 standard is TOWS analysis where a conventional SWOT analysis is complemented with actions responding to the risks and opportunities represented in the Johari window of internal strengths and weaknesses vs external threats and opportunities.[43]

Here is a summary of the Weihrich approach from Ravanavar and Charantimath[44] (Table 4.1) and see Table 4.5:

Table 4.5 TOWS strategic alternatives matrix[45]

	Internal strengths (S)	Internal weaknesses (W)
External opportunities (O)	SO: *"Maxi-Maxi" Strategy* Strategies that use strengths to maximize opportunities	WO: *"Mini-Maxi" Strategy* Strategies that minimize weaknesses by taking advantage of opportunities
External threats (T)	ST: *"Maxi-Mini" Strategy* Strategies that use strengths to minimize threats	WT: *"Mini-Mini" Strategy* Strategies that minimize weaknesses and avoid threats

Here is an example of application from the original paper (Figure 5)—see Table 4.6 in the next page.

---

[43]The TOWS Matrix—A Tool for Situational Analysis, Heinz Weihrich, Professor of Management, University of San Francisco, 1982.

[44]G.M. Ravanavar and P.M. Charantimath."Strategic Formulation Using Tows Matrix—A Case Study." G.M. Ravanavar, Professor & Dean (Academic), Bahubali College of Engineering, Shravanabelagola-573135, India; Dr. P.M. Charantimath Professor, KLS Institute of Management Education & Research, Belgaum-590011, India. http://ijrdonline.com/Journal/1344316744strategic.pdf; http://blog.oxford-collegeofmarketing.com/2016/06/07/tows-analysis-guide/.

[45]See H. Weihrich. "The TOWS Matrix—A Tool for Situational Analysis." https://www.academia.edu/34211017/The_TOWS_Matrix_A_Tool_for_Situational_Analysis.

Table 4.6 Application of the TOWS matrix to Volkswagen—This illustrative analysis covers the period from late 1973 to early 1975

	Internal strengths:	Internal weaknesses:
	1. Strong R & D and Engineering 2. Strong Sales and Service Network 3. Efficient Production/Automation Capabilities	1. Heavy Reliance on One Product (Although Several Less Successful Models were Introduced) 2. Rising Costs in Germany 3. No Experience with U.S. Labor Unions if Building Plant in the USA.
External Opportunities: (Also Consider Risks)	**SO:**	**WO:**
1. Growing Affluent Market Demands More Luxurious Cars with Many Options	1. Develop and Produce Multiproduct Line with Many Options, in Different Price Classes (Dasher, Scirocco, Rabbit, Audi Line) (O1 S1 S2)	1. 1. Develop Compatible Models for Different Price Levels (Ranging from Rabbit to Audi Line) (O1 W1)
2. Attractive Offers to Build an Assembly Plant in the USA.	2. Build Assembly Plant Using R & D, Engineering, and Production/Automation Experience (O2 S1 S3)	2. To Cope with Rising Costs in Germany, Build Plant in USA., Hiring U.S. Managers with Experience in Dealing with U.S. Labor Unions (O2 W2 W3)
3. Chrysler and American Motors Need Small Engines	3. Build Engines for Chrysler and AMC (O3 S3)	
External Threats:	**ST:**	**WT:**
1. Exchange Rate: 2. Devaluation of Dollar in Relation to Deutsche Mark (DM) 3. 2. Competition from Japanese and U.S. Automakers 4. 3. Fuel Shortage and Price	1. Reduce Effect of Exchange Rate by Building a Plant in the USA. (T1 T2 S1 S3) 2. Meet Competition with Advanced Design Technology—e.g., Rabbit (T2 T3 S1 S2) 3. Improve Fuel Consumption Through Fuel Injection and Develop Fuel-Efficient Diesel Engines (T3 S1)	**A.** Overcome Weaknesses by Making Them Strengths (Move Toward OS Strategy) 1. Reduce Threat of Competition by Developing Flexible Product Line (T2 W1) **B.** Possible Options *not* Exercised by VW: 1. Engage in Joint Operation with Chrysler or AMC 2. Withdraw from U.S. Market

An example of an application to a small- to medium-sized laboratory supplies business is provided—see Appendix, pp. 195–197 Example TOWS Analysis.

Limits to Risk Management—Adulteration and Corruption

When Archimedes ran through the streets, without even his bathrobe, shouting "Eureka" it wasn't because he had discovered an important scientific principle he could publish in the top scientific journal of the day! It was because he had discovered how to prove that his sponsor's crown was not pure gold and had been adulterated with silver.[46]

Most, if not all, the chemicals receipts incoming verification I was responsible for in charge of at the dental chemicals laboratory started with some form of identity and purity test—usually a melting point test. Medical device testing I am presently engaged with has largely moved away from any live animal testing and even the in-vitro replacement tests are being replaced with more sensitive high pressure liquid chromatography (HPLC) testing where a test can be compared with a reference sample of known identity and purity. The sampling theory we discussed earlier originated in the need to verify the integrity of delivered grain shipments.[47]

Poor quality can be detected and prevented but there are limits as to the protection offered against wilful intent. The term "adulteration" is a legal term meaning "the act of making food or drugs worse in quality by adding something to them"[48] and it has other links we shall explore later. But the essential point is that there is a basis of trust irrespective of whether quality differences are just the effect of common random differences or, possibly, more significant ones due to special causes.

Improvement

Improvement is a consequence of the obverse of risk—opportunity, but it is more than that. Improvement is a possible action at the end of the

[46]See R. Ross. April 26, 2017. "Eureka! The Archimedes Principle," LiveScience/Pure Science, Future US, Inc. 11 West 42nd Street, 15th Floor, New York, NY 10036. https://www.livescience.com/58839-archimedes-principle.html and Pollo, Marcus Vitruvius, "The Ten Books on Architecture–Book IX Introduction." https://www.math.nyu.edu/~crorres/Archimedes/Crown/Vitruvius.html.
[47]See Wikipedia. "SGS S.A." https://en.wikipedia.org/wiki/SGS_S.A.
[48]See Cambridge Dictionary. "Adulteration," https://dictionary.cambridge.org/dictionary/english/adulteration.

PLAN–DO–CHECK–ACT cycle (Figures 4.15 and 4.16), but it is more even than that. It is even more than needing to improve when aiming to do it right we fail and need to correct and prevent it from happening again.

Needs and expectations change. New ways of doing things, new technologies make improvement possible. Not just an incremental improvement from the present situation, but a breakthrough to an entirely different position or level.

Incremental and Breakthrough

Incremental change and improvement take the system as it is and corrects, maintains, develops, and looks for improvement and change based on the status quo. Breakthrough improvement can start from several positions. There can be a critical look at the mix of added value core operations and other non-added value transport, wait, communication, and other activities. The advent of new technologies opens possibilities of re-engineering the process and other "green field" thinking.

Continual or Continuous Improvement

"The terms **continuous improvement** and **continual improvement** (Figure 4.15) are frequently used interchangeably, but the main difference between the terms is time:

Dictionary	Continual	Continuous
Dictionary.com	*adjective* 1. Of regular or frequent recurrence; often repeated; very frequent. 2. Happening without interruption or cessation; continuous in time.[1]	*adjective* 1. Uninterrupted in time; without cessation. 2. Being in immediate connection or spatial relationship.[2]
Merriam-Webster	*adjective* 1. Continuing indefinitely in time without interruption. 2. Recurring in steady, usually, rapid succession.[3]	*adjective* 1. Marked by uninterrupted extension in space, time or sequence. 2. *Of a function*: having the property that the absolute value of the numerical difference between the value at a given point and the value at any point in a neighborhood of the given point can be made as close to zero as desired by choosing the neighborhood small enough.[4]
Oxford	*adjective* 1. Forming a sequence in which the same action or event is repeated frequently. 2. Having no interruptions.[5]	*adjective* 1. Forming an unbroken whole; without interruption. 2. Forming a series with no exceptions or reversals. 3. *Mathematics* (of a function) of which the graph is a smooth unbroken curve, i.e. one such that as the value of x approaches any given value a, the value of f(x) approaches that of f(a) as a limit.[6]

Figure 4.15 Common dictionary definitions of continual and continuous improvement

Source: Reber, Michael F., 2019, "In No Uncertain Terms", Quality Progress, May 2019, pp. 18–24, http://asq.org/quality-progress/2019/05/continuous-improvement/in-no-uncertain-terms.html

But some quality practitioners make the following distinction:

Continual improvement: A broader term preferred by W. Edwards Deming to refer to general processes of improvement and encompassing "discontinuous" improvements—that is, many different approaches, covering different areas.

Continuous improvement: A subset of continual improvement, with a more specific focus on linear, incremental improvement within an existing process. Some practitioners also associate **continuous improvement** more closely with techniques of statistical process control.[49]

The distinction between the terms reflects the issues of breakthrough—reflected to a preference for "continual" improvement, and "continuous"—reflects the assumption of mainly incremental improvement.

Improvement and Business Performance

There is a firm belief that the product and service quality directly affects the bottom line—see Chapter 14, Quality, costs, and the bottom line below and particularly—Speaking the language of management, and—Quality and the bottom line.

Plan-Do-Check-Act

Whether it is incremental or breakthrough improvement, risk management or any other process an organization employs, the phases of the process can be mapped onto the PDCA cycle.

The PDCA cycle seems almost to be simplistic—an oversimplification. But as a key open source free integrated management system standard shows,[50] it can be applied at all levels of an organization. And as the standard points out, the cycles at the lower levels are more dynamic and cross linked.

But more than just the application scope of the PDCA cycle, the standard shows how the cycle can be deconstructed into 12 elements.

---

[49]Excerpted from "In No Uncertain Terms," *Quality Progress.* See M. F. Reber. May 2019. "In No Uncertain Terms," *Quality Progress*, pp. 18-24. http://asq.org/quality-progress/2019/05/continuous-improvement/in-no-uncertain-terms.html.

[50]See "Management System Specification and Guidance MSS 1000:2014," *CQI Integrated Management SIG*. https://www.integratedmanagement.info/mss-1000.

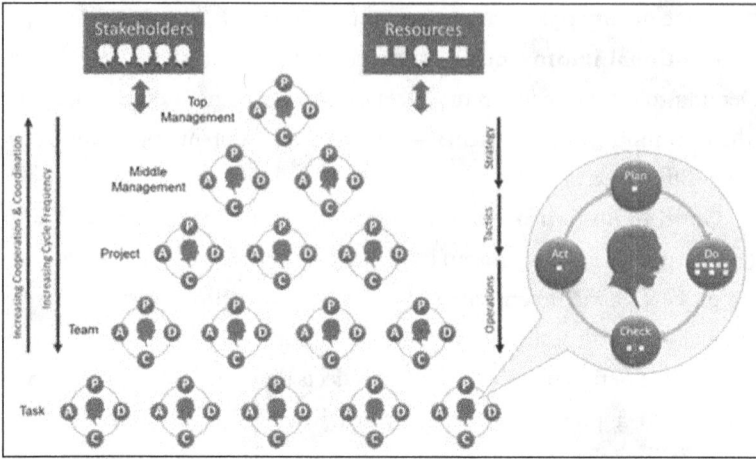

Figure 4.16 Universal Plan–Do–Check–Act throughout an organization[51]

These elements the standard describes as follows:

"Plan

Element 1 covers the analysis and synthesis processes required before the execution of the tasks or processes. It includes foundation planning, strategic planning, formulation of policy and objectives, identification of applicable legislation and standards, and prospect and risk assessment.

Do

Elements 2 to 9 comprise eight elements, each defining a specific area requiring management control and guidance. Elements, 2 to 5, cover personnel, commerce, data, energy and matter, and suppliers, and represent the five general ingredients of an organization's structures and processes.

---

[51]See "Management System Specification and Guidance MSS 1000:2014," *CQI Integrated Management SIG.* https://www.integratedmanagement.info/mss-1000.

Element 6 covers the normal structures and associated normal processes that deliver the purpose of the organization. Element 7 covers contingency structures and processes that need to be initiated when normal structures and normal processes become dysfunctional or abnormal situations need to be managed. Element 8, the final one within this group, covers the systematic management of temporary and permanent change including changes to the management system.

Check

Elements 10 and 11 address reactive and proactive management processes. Element 10, reactive investigation, involves the reporting and analysis of internal and external events, including near misses so that the organization may learn from them. Element 11, planned monitoring, involves activities such as audits, inspections, and benchmarking, and are used to confirm that the 'Plan' has been implemented, is being complied with and is delivering its intended performance. Both of these elements are important, complementary, and provide data for lagging and leading key performance indicators.

Act

Element 12 covers the review of all aspects of the organization's performance and the assignment of actions to drive continual improvement and alignment with its stakeholders evolving needs and expectations."[52]

The history of the PDCA cycle illustrates this.[53]

---

[52]See "Management System Specification and Guidance MSS 1000:2014," *CQI Integrated Management SIG.* https://www.integratedmanagement.info/mss-1000.

[53]An Introduction to the PDCA Cycle Webcast, Part 1. http://asq.org/2011/07/continuous-improvement/intro-to-pdca-1.html.

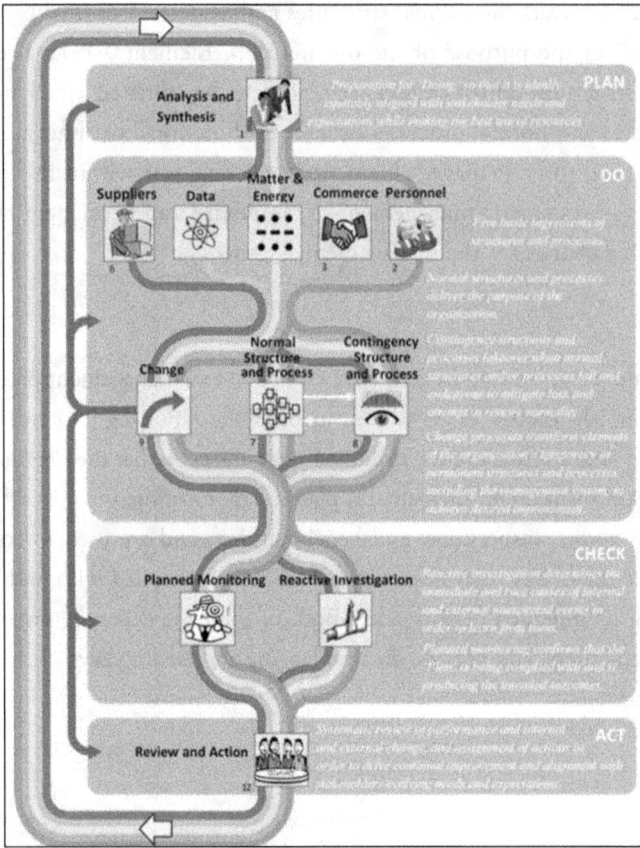

Figure 4.17 Universal Plan–Do–Check–Act Twelve Element Structure[54]

Juran Trilogy Planning, Control, Improvement

The elder statesman of quality who, along with others, made such a monumental and foundational contribution post World War II and right up to the beginning of this century (he died in 2008) laid the foundation for PDCA in his approach of planning, control, and improvement (Figure 4.18).

---

[54]See "Management System Specification and Guidance MSS 1000:2014," *CQI Integrated Management SIG*. https://www.integratedmanagement.info/mss-1000.

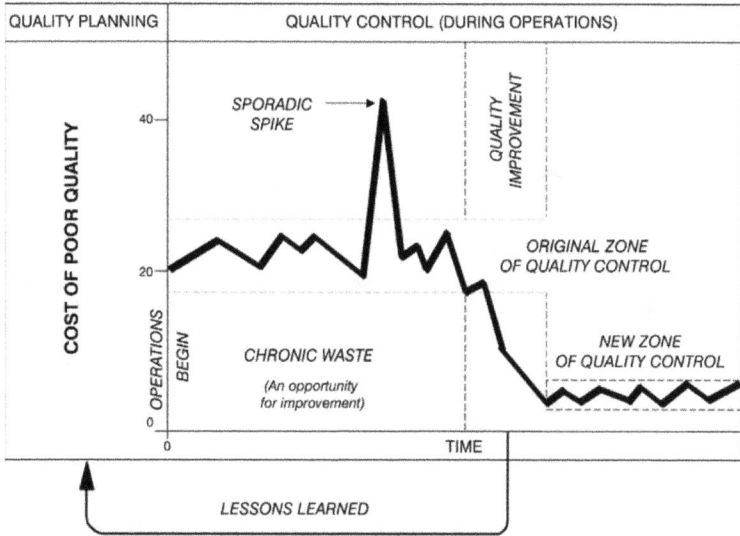

Figure 4.18 Juran—planning, control, and improvement[55]

The concept explains how to move from "quality control" through "quality improvement" to new levels of performance and predates the ascendance of PDCA and underpins it. See Chapter 14 Quality, costs, and the bottom line for more background on the cost of poor quality.

---

[55]See J.M. Juran. "The Juran Trilogy: Quality Planning." https://www.juran.com/blog/the-juran-trilogy-quality-planning/.

CHAPTER 5

Quality and the Individual

The language used in connection with people and quality can be off putting. Addressing other members of staff as "human resources"—and departments dealing with the people involved in an organization are often called that, which doesn't sit easily with many.

We are certainly deeply involved and central to many aspects of quality and will continue to be so whatever contributions artificial intelligence and robotics make to our future.

Our behaviours and attitude largely determine the look, feel, and success of service industries—as long as competence is present. Competence can't be traded off against anything else. We may engineer out aspects of direct human control and involvement in manufacturing processes, but the inevitable and necessary human interfaces limit the extent of that automation.

People are central to quality and a fishbone analysis of the factors in any organizational process rightly includes our contribution.

When providing a service we are forming a relationship and touching another human life—see Chapters 3—Going the extra mile and the importance of family and Chapter 19—Touching lives. There is "giving and receiving" involved. But we can't put ourselves forward for this until we are equipped with the personal tools to do this, principally the competencies, skills, experience, knowledge and any necessary physical resources, and with the right understanding and attitude.

Personal Quality

At the outset, before anything else, we need to be equipped with the competence, skills, experience, and knowledge; and the understanding, attitudes, and behaviours that are necessary to complement the more cerebral requirements.

Competence

To establish competence—a "can-do" ability, we must have the opportunity to demonstrate this safely under supervision and be assessed and signed off by a competent person authorized to sign people as competent.

But before we get to that point, we need to know what competencies are required for the roles we are expected to fulfil. Job descriptions typically list the competencies required but often the process context of the responsibilities and the competencies required is lacking.

Here is a definition of competencies and the rationale for their use from a leading safety-critical international organization[1]:

"What Are Competencies?

A competency is generally defined as a combination of skills, knowledge, attributes, and behaviours that enables an individual to perform a task or an activity successfully within a given job. Competencies are observable behaviours that can be measured and evaluated, and thus are essential in terms of defining job requirements and recruiting, retaining, and developing staff.

Why Use Competencies?

Competencies enable the staff of an organization to have a clear understanding of the behaviours to be exhibited and the levels of performance expected to achieve organizational results. They provide the individual with an indication of the behaviours and actions that will be valued, recognized, and rewarded.

Using a competency framework enables an organization to successfully align its staff's skills, capabilities, and knowledge with organizational priorities, resulting in business improvement and efficiencies.

---

[1] See IAEA, The International Atomic Energy Authority. "The Competency Framework—A Guide for IAEA Managers and Staff," International Atomic Energy Agency, Vienna International Centre, PO Box 100, A-1400 Vienna, Austria. Telephone: +43 (1) 2600-0, Facsimile +43 (1) 2600-7. https://www.iaea.org/sites/default/files/18/03/competency-framework.pdf.

Therefore, a well-structured and well-defined competency framework plays a key role in accomplishing an organization's goals in line with its mission and mandate.

More specifically, competencies ensure that:

- Clear expectations are set and staff members are guided as to how they can assume and reinforce behaviours in line with the organization's mission, culture, and goals.
- A shared language is created to describe what is needed and expected in the work environment, thereby providing for reliable and high-quality performance delivery.
- The various facets of human resources management can be integrated, enhancing consistency in human resources planning, recruitment, learning and development, and performance management, and thereby contributing to the streamlining of human resources operations and ultimately to efficiency gains.
- Skills gaps are addressed, strengths are further developed, and requirements for career progression are clarified.
- Staff mobility, organizational change, and shaping of the organizational culture are fostered."

Their list of competencies (Table 5.1) is split into core and functional competencies and it is clear that the core competencies relate to behaviours as well as skills:

Core Competencies

- Communication
- Teamwork
- Planning and Organizing
- Achieving Results

Functional Competencies

- Leading and Supervising
- Analytical Thinking

Table 5.1 Technical/scientific credibility competencies[2]

	Individual contributor		Manager	Senior manager
	Associate	**Specialist**		
DEFINITION	Acquires and applies new skills	Ensures that work is in compliance	Provides guidance and advice in his/her area of expertise on the application of scientific/professional methods, procedures and approaches.	Demonstrates vision, expertise and resourcefulness in developing strategies, seizing good opportunities, mastering challenges and risks, and addressing issues relevant to the program's goals.
	to remain up to date in his/her area of expertise. Reliably applies knowledge of basic technical/scientific methods and concepts.	With internationally accepted professional standards and scientific methods.		
	.	Provides scientifically/technically accepted information that is credible and reliable.		

[2]See IAEA, The International Atomic Energy Authority. "The Competency Framework—A Guide for IAEA Managers and Staff," International Atomic Energy Agency, Vienna International Centre, PO Box 100, A-1400 Vienna, Austria. Telephone: +43 (1) 2600-0, Facsimile +43 (1) 2600-7. https://www.iaea.org/sites/default/files/18/03/competency-framework.pdf.

INDICATORS	Applies knowledge of basic technical/scientific methods and tools; • Provides reliable technical/scientific information and data; • Stays informed about current knowledge developments in his/her area of expertise and acquires new skills to keep up to date; • Proposes new procedures and techniques in response to changing needs in his/her area of work.	• Provides authoritative technical/scientific advice in his/her area of expertise; • Is recognized in the academic and international communities in his/her area of expertise; • Carries out or leads technical/scientific endeavors adopting the latest trends and practices; • Carries out peer reviews of work performed by colleagues; • Ensures that work adheres to accepted technical standards and scientific methods, and to the applicable Agency's regulations, rules and policies; • Produces work that is accepted and recognized for its credibility and trustworthiness based on best practice, professional theories and standards.	• Keeps abreast of the latest developments in the field of his/her expertise; • Provides authoritative advice to senior management in his/her area of expertise; • Guides operational practices and advises senior management on the validity of technical and scientific methods and procedures in the achievement of programmatic outputs; • Acts as a technical/scientific resource and supports the development of new skills by colleagues; • Encourages team members to publish articles in peer-reviewed publications and to make presentations at scientific/technical meetings, in compliance with the Agency's regulations, rules and policies.	• Is recognized in the academic and/or international communities for his/her expertise; • Demonstrates vision and identifies emerging issues relevant to the Agency's mandate by providing strategic advice to the Director General on scientific/technical programs; • Identifies trends and opportunities and defines risk mitigation strategies in line with Department/Division's programmatic needs and priorities in compliance with the Agency's regulations, rules, and policies.

- Knowledge Sharing and Learning
- Judgment/Decision-Making
- Technical/Scientific Credibility
- Change Management
- Commitment to Continuous Process Improvement
- Partnership Building
- Client Orientation
- Persuasion and Influencing
- Resilience"[3]

The competencies are differentiated by different roles and these competencies are high-level statements that could be attached to specific top-level process responsibilities but would need complimenting with activity-specific competencies.

This is just one example of competency, there are others and bigger—but still not exhaustive lists.[4]

The example process flowchart (see Appendix, pp. 190–193, Example Process Flowchart) has "Service" creating a RAMS (Risk Assessment and Method Statement) in the "Authorization to Work" phase. This requires a wide mix of competencies, and some of them linked to a depth of knowledge and experience related to the technologies, industry or commercial sector, best practice, and regulations.

Authorizing a person for a role requiring specific competencies will need to draw on the references, qualifications, and other evidence that

---

[3]See IAEA, The International Atomic Energy Authority. "The Competency Framework—A Guide for IAEA Managers and Staff," International Atomic Energy Agency, Vienna International Centre, PO Box 100, A-1400 Vienna, Austria. Telephone: +43 (1) 2600-0, Facsimile +43 (1) 2600-7. https://www.iaea.org/sites/default/files/18/03/competency-framework.pdf.

[4]See Office of Financial Management. "Competency Examples with Performance Statements," Washington State Office of Financial Management, P.O. Box 43113, Olympia, WA 98504-3113, Administration, Phone: 360-902-0555, Email: ofm.administration@ofm.wa.gov. https://www.google.co.uk/url?sa=t&rct=j&q=&esrc=s&source=web&cd=19&cad=rja&uact=8&ved=2ahUKEwiOwaugw-nkAhUUTBUIHb4iDnQQFjASegQICRAC&url=https%3A%2F%2Fofm.wa.gov%2Fsites%2Fdefault%2Ffiles%2Fpublic%2Fshr%2FStrategic%2520HR%2FWorkforce%2520Plannin g%2FCompetencyExamples.doc&usg=AOvVaw1JVptqUz1WrStj52zFWkfJ.

they bring with them to the role and the organization—which should be appropriately validated with properly authorized copies of certifications[5], and a balance judgment on how many of these need to be demonstrated on the job, exercising the role in the specific organization. The context of each organization and the procedures, protocols, equipment, environment, and other resources will all be factors in the person's ability to achieve and demonstrate the competencies they claim.

Identifying the Need for Training and Ensuring Opportunity

Even if we bring a complete set of well-proven competencies and the need to validate these within the organization is minimal, there will still be a need for a level of induction training to become familiar with the context for the use of the competences.

There will also be, very likely, specific procedures and equipment familiarization to get specific experience on and be signed off for independent or semi-independent operations.

Then there may be competency gaps to be filled and specific evidence of the effectiveness of training to be demonstrated and signed off.

The training needs to follow best practice and be explicitly aimed at delivering on-the-job competencies in an assessable manner in the specific organizational context,[6] given that then the complete training experience needs defining.

There are further steps beyond training to achieve mastery[7] which open whole new dimensions of challenge and opportunity—see Chapter 1

---

[5]See "Competent People" in R.D. Reid. November 2017. "Standard Issues—IATF 16949—Navigating Difficult Requirements—An in-depth Look at Process Control, One of the Most-cited IATF 16949 Requirements," *Quality Progress*, pp. 63-65. http://asq.org/quality-progress/2017/11/standards-issues/navigating-difficult-requirements.html.

[6]See "Training Requires Controls" in P. E. Boyers. May 2017. "Back to Basics—Maintaining Knowledge—How ISO 9001:2015 Is Helping Organizations Remember Their Future," *Quality Progress*, p. 64. http://asq.org/quality-progress/2017/05/back-to-basics/maintaining-knowledge.html.

[7]See D. Kachoui. April 2018. "Personal Improvement—Becoming A Master—Do You have What it Takes to Achieve Mastery?" *Quality Progress*, pp. 38-43. http://asq.org/quality-progress/2018/04/career-development/becoming-a-master.pdf.

Improvement and PDCA, and excellence the destination, which are central to personal improvement and achievement of excellence.

Performance Appraisal

One of the inputs into defining training needs is "Performance Appraisal"—a review, with interview, between a job holder and their manager—with review also from above, of the individual's performance in the role against role description and previous objectives.

W. Edwards Deming was one of a group of leading quality practitioners and thinkers post World War II who led a revolution that started as a result of the changes needed to industrial practices under the pressure of war and the rebuilding of society and manufacturing capacity in Japan post World War II. His 14 points recognize human aspects which no one previously, or since, had been anywhere near as successful in bringing to the fore—see Table 5.2.[8]

Although the 14 points do not directly touch on Performance Appraisal his opposition was firm: "Evaluation of performance, merit rating, or annual review…The idea of a merit rating is alluring. The sound of the words captivates the imagination: pay for what you get; get what you pay for; motivate people to do their best, for their own good. The effect is exactly the opposite of what the words promise."[9]

And "The first step in a company will be to provide education in leadership. The annual performance review may then be abolished."[10]

The central issue is that individual is part of a system and the performance of the individual reflects both their position in the system, their interaction with the system, and the performance of the system.[11]

---

[8]See R.D. Moen and C.L. Norman. June 2016. "Quality History—Always Applicable Deming's System of Profound Knowledge Remains Relevant for Management and Quality Professionals Today," *Quality Progress*, pp. 46-53. http://asq.org/quality-progress/2016/06/basic-quality/always-applicable.pdf.

[9]See W.E. Deming. August 11, 2000. *Out of the Crisis*, 1st ed. (Cambridge, MA: MIT Press), p. 101, ISBN-10: 978-0-2625-4115-2, ISBN-13: 978-0-2625-4115-2.

[10]Ibid.

[11]See R. D. Moen. November 1989. "The Performance Appraisal System: Deming's Deadly Disease," *Quality Progress*, pp. 62-66.

Table 5.2   Evolution of Deming's 14 points

Point	Early 1982 (handout)	1986 (Out of the crisis)
1	Innovate and allocate resources to fulfill the long-range needs of the company and customer, rather than short-term profitability.	Create constancy of purpose toward improvement of product and service.
2	Discard the old philosophy of accepting defective products and defective workmanship.	Adopt a new philosophy.
3	Eliminate dependence on mass inspection for quality.	Cease dependence on mass inspection.
4	Reduce the number of suppliers for the same item. Demand and expect suppliers to use statistical process control and to furnish evidence thereof.	End the practice of awarding business on the basis of price tag alone.
5	Use statistical techniques to identify the two sources of waste: system 85% and local faults 15%; constantly strive to reduce this waste.	Improve constantly and forever the system of production and service.
6	Institute better job training with the help of statistical methods.	Institute training.
7	Provide supervision with the use of statistical methods. The aim of supervision should be to help people do a better job.	Adopt and institute leadership.
8	Reduce fear throughout the organization by encouraging open, two-way communication.	Drive out fear.
9	Reduce waste by putting together as a team the people who work on design, research, sales, and production.	Break down barriers between staff areas.
10	Eliminate use of goals and slogans in an attempt to increase productivity.	Eliminate slogans, exhortations, and targets for the workforce.
11	Examine closely the impact of work standards. Do they consider quality or help anyone do a better job?	Eliminate numerical quotas for the workforce. Eliminate numerical goals for people in management.
12	Institute rudimentary statistical training on a broad scale.	Remove barriers that rob people of pride of workmanship.
13	Institute a vigorous program for retraining people in new skills to keep up with changes in materials, methods, design of product, and machinery.	Encourage education and self-improvement for everyone.
14	Make maximum use of statistical knowledge and talent in your company.	Take action to accomplish the transformation.

Moving away from performance appraisal enables a move to better management not based on a short-term view based on conformance around variances and expressed in an adversarial relationship and towards long-term continual improvement in a cooperative manner aimed at reducing common cause variance and eliminating special cause variance.[12]

While believing performance appraisal can improve performance and provide fair and defensible rewards, there is an argument to avoid the traps including rivalry, politics, and fear by decoupling them from arbitrary numbers and coupling them to customer expectations, teamwork, balanced holistic criteria generated in a participative manner. The argument is that they can be done in the right way to benefit all.

Appreciative Inquiry

Appreciative inquiry offers a positive alternative to performance appraisal.[13] "Appreciative inquiry is an approach to thinking that works from the propositions of affirmative action and visions of the possible, rather than problem solving, finding what is wrong and looking for difficulties."[14]

The contrast with problem-solving performance appraisal is clear when it is described like this: "Appreciative Inquiry (AI) is a way of looking at organizational change which focuses on identifying and doing more of what is already working, rather than looking for problems and trying to fix them. It makes rapid strategic change possible by focusing on the core strengths of an organization and then using those strengths to reshape the future.

AI is a participative learning process (Figure 5.1) to identify and spread best practice. It is also a way of managing and working that encourages trust, reduces defensiveness and suspicion, and helps to establish strong working relationships quickly."

---

[12]Ibid., and R. Starcher. December 1992. "Mismatched Management Techniques," *Quality Progress*, pp. 49–52.

[13]See L. Waters, and M. White. 2015. "Case Study of a School Wellbeing Initiative: Using Appreciative Inquiry to Support Positive Change." *International Journal of Wellbeing* 5, no. 1, pp. 19–32. doi:10.5502/ijw.v5i1.2.

[14]See G. Cox. "Appreciative Enquiry," New Directions Ltd., 26a Downleaze, Bristol BS9 1LZ, UK, +44 (0)117 968 1451 (UK), +44 (0)7753 626284.

DEFINITION
Topic to work on

DISCOVERY
What's already working?

DELIVERY
Action planning

"Positive Core"

DREAM
Overall vision

DESIGN
Options to make it happen

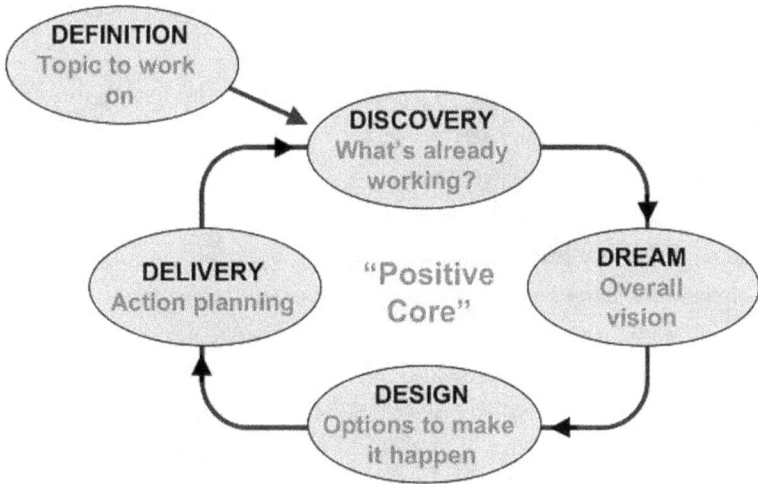

Figure 5.1 AI change process[15]

Complete packs of prepared material are available for use for "anyone who wishes to use an appreciative inquiry approach to support service improvement or redesign."[16]

Leadership and the Individual

Deming stresses the importance of leadership as a means of replacing performance review: "The first step in a company will be to provide education in leadership. The annual review may then be abolished. Leadership will take its place" and the leader instead of being a judge will be a

---

[15]See Coaching Leaders. "What is Appreciative Enquiry," Coaching Leaders Ltd, Registered in England No: 344576, 6 Station View, Hazel Grove, Stockport, England, SK7 5ER, andy@coachingleaders.co.uk, 0844 284 6372, +33 (0) 5 55 35 64 72. https://coachingleaders.co.uk/what-is-appreciative-inquiry/.

[16]See Scottish Social Services Council. "Appreciative Inquiry Resource Pack," Scottish Social Services Council Compass House 11 Riverside Drive Dundee DD1 4NY, Tel.: 0345 60 30 891 Fax: 01382 207215, Email: enquiries@sssc.uk.com, www.sssc.uk.com, http://learn.sssc.uk.com/pluginfile.php/1874/mod_resource/content/1/Appreciative%20Inquiry%20resource%20pack131a.pdf?id=653, http://learn.sssc.uk.com/course/view2770.html?id=67.

colleague, counselling and leading his people on a day to day basis, learning from and with them."[17]

The emphasis moved from management to leadership in ISO 9001:2015 and we consider this in more depth later—see Chapter 13, Quality Management—Leadership.

But this role behaviour is one we can all adopt when required: "every human being is a leader in some part of his or her life—because leadership is an influence process. We believe that anytime you seek to influence the thinking, behaviour, or development of someone in your personal or professional life, you are taking on the role of a leader."[18]

Troy put it very clearly in respect of quality professionals in particular: "the quality professional, wherever he or she may be and at whatever level of management, must be a leader to be effective. The quality professional at work somewhere in the quality field is not an artist alone at the canvas. That professional is bringing insight, tools, principles, and personal example to someone—to some crew, team, or section; to a business unit; or to something even bigger, such as a hospital, a federal agency, or a school system.

This task is going to be bigger than the sole person, perhaps much bigger. It will involve other people, with all of their complexities, strengths, weaknesses, hopes, and fears. So whatever our quality professional is working on, it is going to take leadership to get the job done."[19]

There is clear evidence that quality activities management must embrace both left brain activities with objective measurement and decision making and right brain issues of relationships, values, beliefs, and emotions. This has been recognized in the foundation management standard and it includes everyone in the organization.

---

[17]See W.E. Deming. August 11, 2000. *Out of the Crisis*, 1st ed. (Cambridge, MA: MIT Press), ISBN-10: 978-0-2625-4115-2, ISBN-13: 978-0-2625-4115-2.

[18]See K. Blanchard and P. Hodges. 2005. *Lead Like Jesus*. Nashville, TN: Thomas Nelson, ISBN 10:0-8499-1872-3 and K. Blanchard, P. Hodges, and P. Hendry. *Lead Like Jesus Revisited*, Published in Nashville, Tennessee, by W Publishing, an imprint of Thomas Nelson, ISBN: 978-0-7180-7725-9.

[19]B. Troy. "Is Every Quality Professional a Leader?" Quality in Mind for The Global Quality Community, *ASQ Blog*. http://asq.org/blog/2014/11/every-quality-professional-a-leader/.

Shame and Guilt, Is and Ought

Deming's 14 points, the weaknesses of a narrow performance appraisal, the promise and potential of appreciative enquiry and the recognition of the role and all-pervasive responsibility for leadership point to the contribution and importance of values, relationships, and emotion in quality as in life.[20]

The appropriation of these value characteristics into the quality dialogue has to examine such fundamental issues as "guilt" and "shame" which affect and determine the degree of self-regulation of individuals in marginal situations and the differences that can exist in these in different cultures.[21]

The author and TED speaker Brene Brown has valuable material to help in this area.[22]

Personal Change and Improvement

"Values, priorities, goals, plan, and do"[23]—makes up a planned approach to personal quality improvement. Placing emphasis on values and priorities provides the opportunity to include a strong work–life balance. Planning over the weekend avoids the Monday morning panic and pressured environment when values and priorities may be put at risk. The "do" phase includes weekly and longer-term review. The links to a PCDA applied to oneself are clear.

Forsha applies the quality principles coming from Crosby, Deming, Juran and others to personal change and applies a PDCA like quality improvement process to the issue of meeting personal requirements and involving in a constant gradual process of continuous improvement. Knowing why you want to change and being able to test through, say the 5 whys, is of central importance. But you must get to the point of

---

[20]See C.P. Alexander. November 1989. "The Soft Technologies of Quality," *Quality Progress*, pp 24 28.

[21]See L.S. Dillon. October 1990. "Can Japanese Methods be Applied in the Western Workplace," *Quality Progress*, pp. 27-30.

[22]See B. Brown, March 2012, "Listening to Shame", https://www.ted.com/talks/brene_brown_listening_to_shame

[23]J.V. Kovach. April 2018. "The Path to Personal Quality," *Quality Progress*, p. 16. http://asq.org/quality-progress/2018/04/career-coach/the-path-to-personal-productivity.html.

accepting the need for change and deciding that there is a need to act covering the three steps—identifying the need for change, securing the motivation, and acting. The same tool set we apply within our organizational settings can be deployed for personal change. This lays a foundation for (renewed) self-respect, establishing (or re-establishing) personal integrity, and letting that flow into the all-important relationships through which you can function within a team and organization. All the lessons of personal change are put to the test in the real world of organizations and relationships and the behaviours that we adopt.[24]

---

[24]See H.I. Forsha. January to May 1992. "The Pursuit of Quality Through Personal Change Pts 1–5," *Quality Progress*, also Brown (William C.) Co, U.S. February 1, 1992, ISBN-10: 0873891406, ISBN-13: 978-0-8738-9140-0.

CHAPTER 6

Quality and the Team

Pulling Together in the Same Direction

Any organization can be likened to a human with corporate will and memory and members contributing to the functioning of the body.

A well-coordinated body is a healthy body where all the members function in response to the head.

The effective team must have everyone pulling in the same direction.

The foundation management standard, and the standards built on it, all stress the importance of everyone knowing just how their contributions contribute to meeting the customer requirements and any supporting statutory and regulatory requirements.[1]

Organizational roles and responsibilities are defined to enable, sustain, and support the properly coordinated processes that working together deliver that "secure profitable future" that is the business organization's aim.

The team members also need to share, accept, and express the common business aim, shared values, and agreed performance standards and team priorities.[2]

---

[1]See 5.1.1 h), 5.1.2 d), 5.2.2 d), 5.3 d), in ISO 9001:2015, "Quality Management Systems—Requirements."

[2]See Renault Institute of Quality Management. "Renault Quality Dealership Programme Step 9—How to Improve Teamwork," The Rivers Office Park, Denham Way, Maple Cross, Rickmansworth, Hertfordshire, WD3 9YS, +44 (0) 1923 69 72 69, rnc.info@rnconsulting.co.uk

Profiles and Team Roles

The personality type model suggests that there are personal strengths and weaknesses centered around our position on four scales[3]:

- Introversion vs. Extraversion
- Sensing vs. iNtuition
- Thinking vs. Feeling
- Judging vs. Perceiving

These are given single-character abbreviations and the 16 personality types resulting from different combinations are expanded with examples. Additionally, research showed that teams had role types that greatly aided high performance:[4]

- Resource investigator
- Team worker
- Evaluator
- Finisher
- Shaper
- Coordinator
- Implementor
- Finisher

Using these in the different stages of a team process, project, or task and in the context of the team formation issues that may arise can greatly assist performance

Experience shows that people can have more than one style and fulfil more than one team role based on innate or learned abilities and recent

[3]See Truity, "Myers & Briggs' 16 Personality Type Profiles," Truity Psychometrics LLC, 1300 Clay Street, Suite 600, Oakland, CA 94612-1247, (415) 223-3151. https://www.truity.com/page/16-personality-types-myers-briggs.

[4]See Belbin. "The Nine Belbin Team Roles," Belbin, 3-4 Bennell Court, West Street, Comberton, Cambridge, CB23 7EN, UK. Tel +44 (0) 1223 264975, https://www .belbin.com/about/belbin-team-roles/.

and longer-term experience. It can be a matter of choice to exercise these depending on the team needs and situation.

We may need space and time to adjust our way of thinking to introduce new perspectives to be able to think outside the situations we box ourselves into. Activities like group discussion, case study discussion, critical incident discussion, and others can facilitate reflective learning that opens new possibilities.[5]

---

[5]See J.R. Dew. July 2015. "Best Practices—Turning on the Light Bulb—Critical Reflection Needed to Get Everyone to Understand and Embrace Quality," Quality Progress, pp. 30-34. http://asq.org/quality-progress/2015/07/basic-quality/turning-on-the-light-bulb.pdf.

CHAPTER 7

Quality and the Community

Interested Parties, Stakeholders, and People

The scope of those affected by the quality aims and objectives clearly includes the communities in which they operate and wider society as well.

Corporate Social Responsibility[1]

The modern vision of business philanthropy was stated by the UK Government early this century: "Today, corporate social responsibility goes far beyond the old philanthropy of the past–donating money to good causes at the end of the financial year–and is instead an all-year round responsibility that companies accept for the environment around them, for the best working practices, for their engagement in their local communities and for their recognition that brand names depend not only on quality, price, and uniqueness but on how, cumulatively, they interact with companies' workforce, community, and environment. Now we need to move toward a challenging measure of corporate responsibility where we judge results not just by the input but by its outcomes: the difference we make to the world in which we live, and the contribution we make to poverty reduction."[2]

As another government document expressed it "business doesn't exist in isolation, simply as a way of making money. Your employees depend

[1]See M.J. Epstein and K.O. Hanson. August 2005. "Praeger Perspectives—The Accountable Corporation vol. 3 Corporate Social Responsibility." Praeger Publishers, ISBN-10: 027598494X.
[2]See UK Gov DTI. May 2004. "Corporate Social Responsibility—A Government Update," First published. Department of Trade and Industry. www.dti.gov.uk/DTI/ Pub 7201/1k/05/04/NP. URN 04/1112. www.csr.gov.uk.

on your business. Customers, suppliers, and the local community are all affected by you and what you do. Your products, and the way you make them, have an impact on the environment.

Corporate social responsibility (CSR) takes all this into account and can help you create and maintain effective relationships with your stakeholders. It isn't about being "right on" or mounting an expensive publicity exercise. It means taking a responsible attitude, going beyond the minimum legal requirements and following straightforward principles that apply, whatever the size of your business."[3]

Epstein provides essential material for further study on the history and development, moves toward implementation, the challenges, and paths to success and the emerging next steps in the volume on Corporate Social Responsibility in the Praegar Perspectives.[4]

Triple Bottom Line

The urgency of needing to measure the contribution to wider society was understood by key business leaders.

"The phrase 'the triple bottom line' was first coined in 1994 by John Elkington, the founder of a British consultancy called 'SustainAbility'. His argument was that companies should be preparing three different (and quite separate) bottom lines. One is the traditional measure of corporate profit—the 'bottom line' of the profit and loss account. The second is the bottom line of a company's 'people account'—a measure in some shape or form of how socially responsible an organization has been throughout its operations. The third is the bottom line of the company's "planet" account—a measure of how environmentally responsible it has been. The triple bottom line (TBL) thus consists of three Ps: profit, people, and planet. It aims to measure the financial, social, and environmental performance of the corporation over a period of time. Only a company

---

[3]See Business Link. February 6, 2009. "Grow Your Business Guidebook," Business Link.
[4]See M.J. Epstein and K.O. Hanson. August 2005. "Praeger Perspectives–The Accountable Corporation vol 3 Corporate Social Responsibility." Praeger Publishers, ISBN-10: 027598494X.

that produces a TBL is taking account of the full cost involved in doing business."[5]

However, it is clear the urgency that Hindle felt has not been realized in practice and he now asks for a rethink.[6] He concludes that "Triple Bottom Line has failed to bury the single bottom line paradigm." Although "TBL's stated goal from the outset was system change—pushing toward the trans-formation of capitalism. It was never supposed to be just an accounting sys-tem. It was originally intended as a genetic code, a triple helix of change for tomorrow's capitalism, with a focus was on breakthrough change, disrup-tion, asymmetric growth (with unsustainable sectors actively side-lined), and the scaling of next-generation market solutions. It 'needs a new wave of TBL innovation and deployment' but at a different pace and scale."

Elkington contributes a whole chapter on the triple bottom line in the Praegar Perspectives volume on Corporate Social Responsibility.[7]

Taguchi and Loss to Society

Genichi Taguchi is another of those quality practitioners whose contribu-tions have hugely advanced practice and thinking. His work on robust parameter design is based on his total quality philosophy and his loss function. He saw that loss begins with all departure from the specification aim value and not just when the specification limits are reached. This loss just gets bigger the further from the central aim value by the square of the difference—a statistic already in common use and one particular—and common, choice of all the possible loss functions (Figure 7.1).[8]

---

[5]See T. Hindle. April 5, 2012. "Triple Bottom Line in The Economist Guide to Management Ideas and Gurus," Main edition, Economist Books, ISBN-13: 978-1-8466-8607-8.

[6]See J. Elkington. "25 Years Ago I Coined the Phrase 'Triple Bottom Line.' Here's Why It's Time to Rethink It." https://hbr.org/2018/06/25-years-ago-i-coined-the-phrase-triple-bottom-line-heres-why-im-giving-up-on-it.

[7]See M.J. Epstein and K.O. Hanson. August 2005. "Praeger Perspectives—The Ac-countable Corporation vol 3 Corporate Social Responsibility." Praeger Publishers, ISBN-10: 027598494X.

[8]See 1.2 in P.G. Hoel, S.C. Port and C.J. Stone. 1971. *Introduction to Statistical Theory* (Boston, MA: Houghton Mifflin Company), ISBN: 0-395-24498-6.

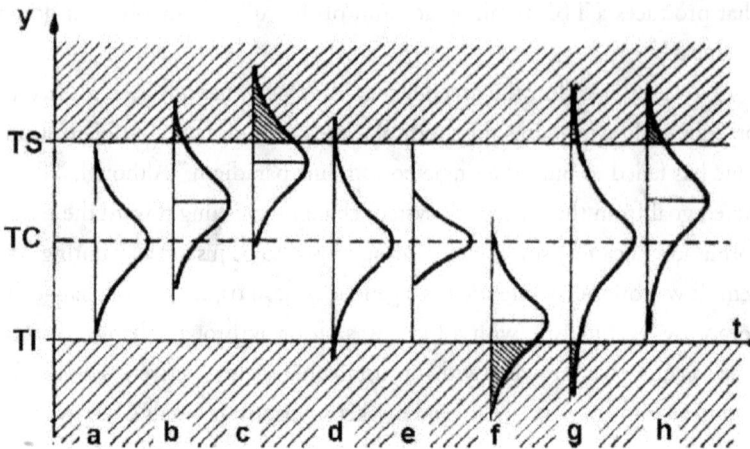

Figure 7.1 *Optimal and other distributions*[9]

"The loss to society could occur due to causes such as rework, waste of material, customer dissatisfaction, warranty costs, and additional money the customer has to spend in using a less-than-ideal product: in short, all expenses imparted to society due to the producer shipping that product."[10]

Community and Quality

Corporate social responsibility often results in some people from organizations being released for work on community projects with benefits in both directions.

People are also using the skills and experience to work with others in their communities to build quality improvement initiatives in the

[9]See C. Denes and M. Țîțu. June 2017. "Taguchi's Quality Loss Function and Experimentation Plan Used In (author—Wire Electrical Discharge Machining) WEDM," Nonconventional Technologies Review 2017, Romanian Association of Nonconventional Technologies Romania, http://www.revtn.ro/index.php/revtn/article/view/182/128.

[10]See P. Gamage, N.P. Jayamaha, and N.P. Grigg. 2017. "Acceptance of Taguchi's Quality Philosophy and Practice by Lean Practitioners in Apparel Manufacturing." *Total Quality Management*, 28, no. 11, pp. 1322-38, doi:10.1080/14783363.2015.1135729.

community. The success of the efforts of Madison WI forms a model of what can be done[11] and has resulted in a handbook on how to proceed.[12]

Community Development Trusts[13] and Community Benefit Societ-ies[14] are examples, in the United Kingdom, of other community-based initiatives that can be central in building community and achieving im-provement goals.

Related initiatives in areas like open data are being used to facilitate related aims in cities like Bristol.[15]

Building Capabilities and Releasing Vision

Governments provide for the welfare of citizens to varying degrees, and the quality of life and care in the community is strongly related to the state provisions. These vary greatly around the world and the capabilities of those welfare provisions have been severely tested in the latest severe acute respiratory syndrome coronavirus (SARS-CoV-2)-producing coronavirus disease (COVID-19).[16] The performance, achievements, capability, and costs of these state provisions are kept under review. The achievements include eradication of worldwide pandemic diseases such as the feared small pox, the virtual eradication of diseases such as tuberculosis, and the prospect of bringing diseases like malaria to the same state. But as medical technology advances, populations expand and age, and expectations rise,

---

[11]See G.E.P. Box, L.W. Joiner, S. Rohan, and F. Joseph Sensebrenner. May 1991. "Quality in the Community: One City's Experience," *Quality Progress*, pp. 57-63.

[12]See F. Voehl. "Recovering Prosperity Through Quality: Community Quality Coun-cils Operating System Guidebook." https://www.comminit.com/africa/content/recovering-prosperity-through-quality-community-quality-councils-operating-sys-tem-guideb.

[13]See Development Trusts Association Scotland (DTAS). https://dtascot.org.uk/.

[14]See Community Shares. "Cooperative and Community Benefit Societies." https://communityshares.org.uk/about-cooperative-and-community-benefit-societies.

[15]See Bristol City Council. "Our Data Bristol Initiative." https://www.bristol.gov.uk/doc-uments/20182/0/Our+Data+Bristol.pdf/6c41ae6b-5146-8c15-68cd-a3ac28277c9f.

[16]See WHO. "Naming the Coronavirus Disease (COVID-19) and the Virus That Causes It." https://www.who.int/emergencies/diseases/novel-coronavirus-2019/technical-guidance/naming-the-coronavirus-disease-(covid-2019)-and-the-virus-that-causes-it.

then costs spiral and the system is stressed, the assumptions are tested, and the design is carefully examined.

I am deeply indebted to a very challenging recent publication for an in-depth assessment of design flaws in the UK Welfare State and National Health Service.[17] The architect of the UK Welfare State, Sir William Beveridge, published two further reports[18] in addition to the 1942 report on which the UK based the 1948 legislation.[19] He was concerned "he had missed and limited the power of the citizen and of communities."[20] The mounting costs and budgetary pressures have led to careful management of service delivery of outcomes provided for us rather than the creation of "solutions that start with people and the relationships between them."[21] The deficiency-oriented, needs-directed delivery of carefully managed and budgeted, relatively well-defined and circumscribed, fixed service solutions is relatively inflexible, one in which costs are driven down, quality of meeting real needs is sacrificed, spending on face-to-face delivery is dwarfed by the costs of managing the service, and all too many fall through the cracks (Figure 7.2). [22] There is a deep need for improvement, and it is increasingly being sought and found in the complementary capability approach that looks at what individuals and groups can bring to the table as

---

[17]See Cottam, Hilary. May 2, 2019. *Radical Help: How We Can Remake the Relationships between Us and Revolutionise the Welfare State Paperback* (London, UK: Virago).

[18]See Beveridge, William. October 7, 2015. *Full Employment in a Free Society (Works of William H. Beveridge): A Report (The Works of William H. Beveridge)*, 1st ed. (Abingdon, UK: Routledge) and Beveridge, William. January 20, 2011. *Beveridge and Voluntary Action in Britain and the Wider British World* (Manchester, UK: Manchester University Press).

[19]See Beveridge, William. 1942. "Social Insurance and Allied Services," His Majesties Stationery Office (HMSO).

[20]See p. 45, "The Welfare State." In *Radical Help: How We Can Remake the Relationships between Us and Revolutionise the Welfare State Paperback*, ed. Hilary Cottam (London, UK: Virago).

[21]Ibid., p. 46.

[22]For Figure 7.2 See p. 196, Cottam, Hilary. May 2, 2019. *Radical Help: How We Can Remake the Relationships between Us and Revolutionise the Welfare State Paperback* (London, UK: Virago).

skills, experiences, abilities, and competences. The alternative asset-based approach is very closely allied to, and another version of, the appreciative inquiry introduced as more effective alternative to the deficiency-based approach of performance appraisal (see Chapter 5, Quality and the Individual – Performance Appraisal – Appreciative Inquiry).

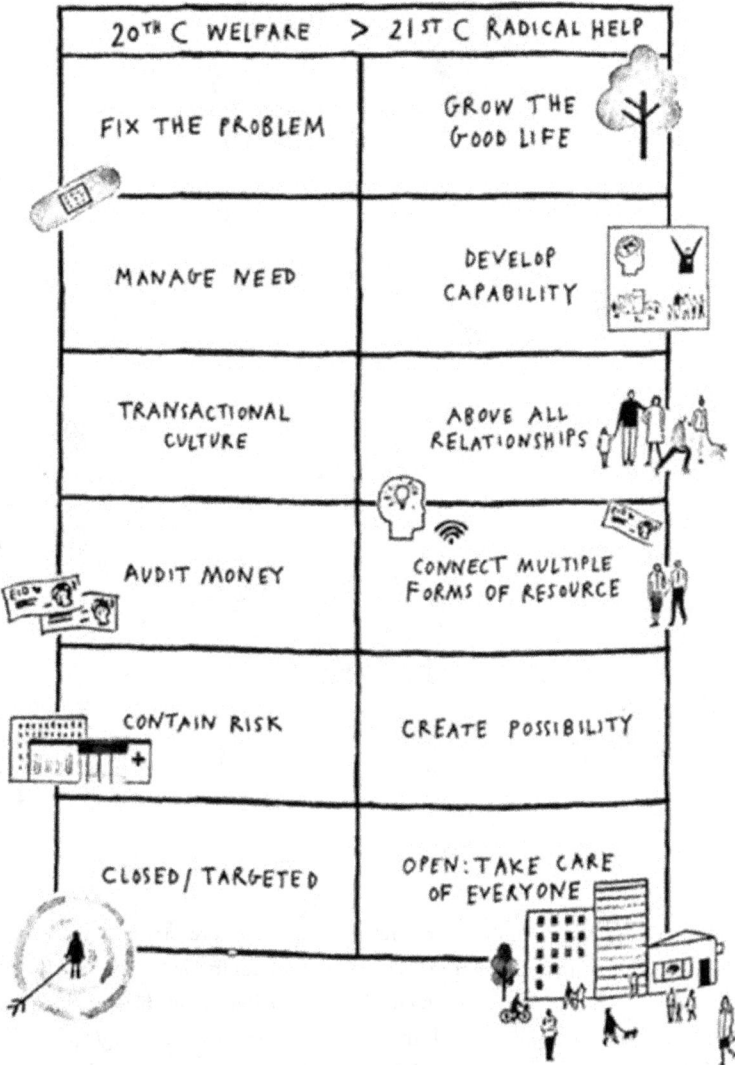

20TH C WELFARE	> 21ST C RADICAL HELP
FIX THE PROBLEM	GROW THE GOOD LIFE
MANAGE NEED	DEVELOP CAPABILITY
TRANSACTIONAL CULTURE	ABOVE ALL RELATIONSHIPS
AUDIT MONEY	CONNECT MULTIPLE FORMS OF RESOURCE
CONTAIN RISK	CREATE POSSIBILITY
CLOSED / TARGETED	OPEN: TAKE CARE OF EVERYONE

Figure 7.2 Deficiency-based versus capability growth approaches

Examples, case studies, and guides to employing community development using an asset-based approach are easy to find in both the United States and the UK.[23]

---

[23]See just these two carefully selected references, many more can easily be found— Croydon, "Community Connectors Asset Based Community Development (ABCD)," *Pilot Project Report.* https://www.croydon.gov.uk/sites/default/files/articles/downloads/abcd-reportsum.pdf and https://www.nurturedevelopment.org/wp-content/uploads/2016/01/Croydon-ABCD-full-report.pdf and Kretzman, John P., and John L. McKnight. December 31, 1998. *Building Communities from Inside Out: A Path toward Finding and Mobilizing a Community's Assets* (Chicago, IL: ACTA Publications).

CHAPTER 8

Quality, Health and Safety, and the Environment

Standalone or Integrated?

The management of quality covers many overlapping requirements and varies across the sectors of business and society. The obvious burden of having separate stand-alone management systems has been recognized and addressed in many ways.

The PAS 99 standard was the first Integrated Management System (IMS) standard (Figure 8.1),[1] closely followed by the Small Business Standard which was published by the Management Consultant Register of the Chartered Quality Institute.[2]

The Integrated Management Systems standard MSS 1000[3] is a full open source standard.

A management system must enable an organization to meet the several major universal commitments of:

- Quality;
- Health and Safety;
- Environment;
- Finance.

---

[1]See BSI. "PAS 99 Integrated Management Systems," BSI. https://www.bsigroup.com/en-GB/pas-99-integrated-management/.

[2]See Yumpu. "The Small Business Standard—Chartered Quality Institute." https://www.yumpu.com/en/document/view/4363996/the-small-business-standard-chartered-quality-institute.

[3]See "Management System Specification and Guidance MSS 1000:2014," *CQI Integrated Management SIG*. https://www.integratedmanagement.info/mss-1000.

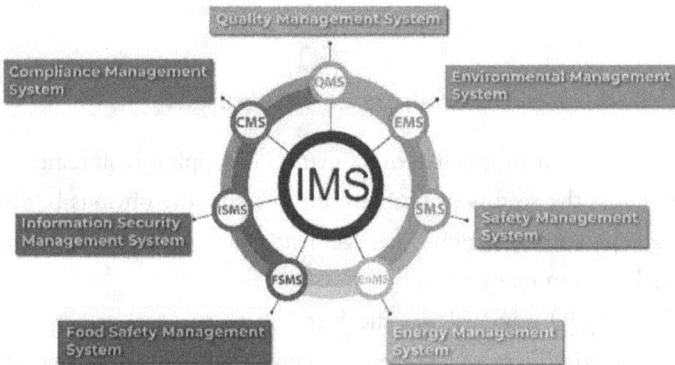

What is an Integrated Management System?

An Integrated Management System (IMS) integrates all of an organization's systems and processes into one complete framework, enabling an organization to work as a single unit with unified objectives.

Quality Management System
Compliance Management System
Environmental Management System
Information Security Management System
Safety Management System
Food Safety Management System
Energy Management System

QMS EMS CMS ISMS IMS SMS FSMS EnMS

$$IMS = QMS + EMS + SMS + EnMS + FSMS + ISMS$$
(etc)

Figure 8.1 What is an Integrated Management System?[4]

The evolution and development of these imperatives has resulted in parallel and separate streams and systems for all four. But the commonality, and the separation from the often-perceived overriding priority of financial management, has allowed a measured of integration to occur for the first three under the acronym "QHSE,"[5] which is now recognized in

[4]See Standards Store. "What is an Integrated Management System?" https://integrated-standards.com/articles/what-is-integrated-management-system/.

[5]See Fortis. "Fortis' Integrated Quality, Health, Safety, and Environmental Management System Implementation." http://asq.org/mining/ming_news/2014/10/safety/fortis-integrated-quality-health-safety-and-environmental-system-implementation.pdf; P. Lendrich. 2014. "QHSE Programs Ensuring Quality for Australian Businesses," Gastoday.com.au. https://web.a.ebscohost.com/ehost/pdfviewer/pdfviewer?vid=2&sid=8c542d5a-9433-42ab-ba17-32ef529cbc13%40sdc-v-sessmgr03; SGS. "QHSE Management." https://www.sgs.com/-/media/global/documents/flyers-and-leaflets/sgs-ind-wind-qhse-a4-en-10.pdf.

the international management standards. The integration of these three also provides a foundation that can reach well beyond the initial scope.

Quality, Safety and Environment Go Together

The reason they go together is much, much more than management convenience and commonality of the system elements.

Quality failures can, and sadly many times have, lead directly to safety disasters, serious injury, and loss of life. These together blight the human and physical environment–Chernobyl, Bhopal, Piper Alpha, Deep Water horizon and many, many others of smaller scale yet just as devastating to the lives affected.[6]

"The takeaway lessons from these, and other incidents, cover many issues":

From a pipeline valve failure exasercbated through lack of foresight on obtaining permission to flare from stakeholders who had concern over migrating birds:

- Engage Stakeholders and Prioritise
- Expect the 'Unexpected'
- Ensure Safety 'Wins'

From a major facility investment that failed after a multi million pound scoping investment:

- Understand ALL the Business Risks
- Use Competent People and Processes
- Defer to Expertise

From Piper Alpha[7] with the loss of 167 lives:

- Utilize Competent Plant, People, and Processes Plus Quality Principles
- Safety is much more important than Production
- Good Leaders Defer To Expertise

---

[6]Taken from a CQI branch presentation by Tim Ingram—See T. Ingram. "Project Risk Management." http://www.strategic-safety-consultants.com.
[7]See YouTube. "Piper Alpha." https://www.youtube.com/watch?v=Nwbw5PHZnqk.

From a major gas explosion that wiped out a house with the loss of four lives because the pipe records had failed to show that older metal pipe was still outside the premises:

- Consider Minor Errors with Major Consequences
- Consider Data Quality and Validity
- Stay 'Close' To The Consequences

From a national utility safely making a critical process change affecting the whole network:

- Apply Proactive Risk Management
- Be Thorough and Apply Rigorous Quality Controls
- Consider Your Stakeholders"[8]

The 2012 Olympics stand out in a number of ways, starting with the headline of no fatalities during construction (Figure 8.2). The abstract of a summary paper from Civil Engineers following the games has this abstract: "The workforce on the Olympic Park site in east London peaked at 12,000 and a total of 30,000 people will have worked on the project through its lifetime. Through careful planning, implementation of strategies with a proven track record, and clear leadership, the Olympic Delivery Authority managed to achieve an accident frequency rate comparable to the average for all British employment, significantly better than the construction sector. The project's health program also provided a degree of care and campaigning not previously experienced in construction."[9]

---

[8]All of the above, and the introduction to the Olympics 2012, came from a presentation at the East of Scotland CQI Branch—see—T. Ingram. "Project Risk Management." http://www.strategic-safety-consultants.com.

[9]See abstract to H. Shiplee, L. Waterman, K. Furniss, R. Seal, and J. Jones. May 2011. "Delivering London 2012: Health and Safety." *Proceedings of the Institution of Civil Engineers—Civil Engineering* 164, no. 5, pp. 46-54, ISSN: 0965-089X|E-ISSN: 1751-7672. https://www.icevirtuallibrary.com/doi/10.1680/cien.2011.164.5.46.

What Do These Represent?

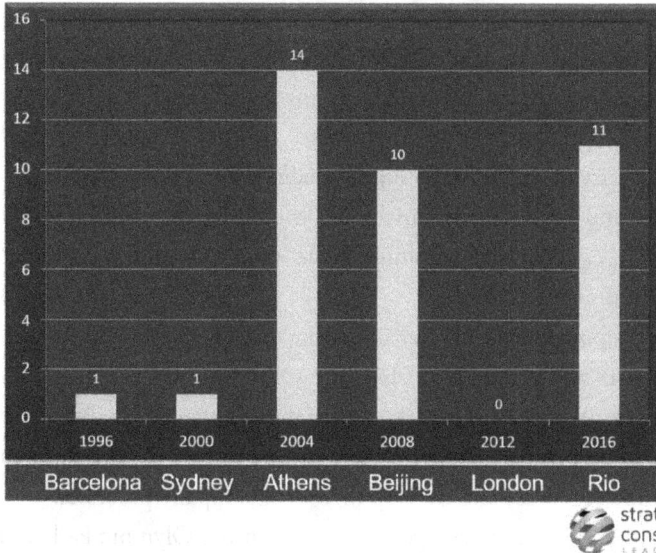

Figure 8.2 *Olympics construction fatalities*[10]

The experience was distilled into key messages by the UK Health and Safety Executive (HSE) and reported:

"The Olympic Park project has demonstrated that it is possible and feasible to develop high standards of health and safety, and a culture that supports this aspiration, within the construction sector.

Safety culture was measured using a modified version of the Health and Safety Laboratory's Safety Climate Tool (SCT). Scores for contractors working on the Olympic Park project were higher than the SCT 'all industry' dataset.

The Olympic Delivery Authority (ODA) and its delivery partner played a key part in the development of a positive safety culture on the Olympic Park. They communicated their expectations clearly from the outset, requiring all Tier 1 contractors (i.e. primary contractors with overall responsibility for individual projects) to subscribe to the same Health, Safety and Environment (HS&E) Standard and regular reporting by Tier 1 Chief Executives to the ODA Board on HS&E performance.

---

[10]See T. Ingram. "Project Risk Management." http://www.strategic-safety-consultants.com.

A number of elements contributed to the development of an effective safety culture on the Olympic Park site, including:

- The strategic role of the ODA across the Park, with safety being set as a priority and integrated into the companies from the outset through standards and requirements.
- The clarity throughout the supply chain of the organizational standards and requirements, including the desire for cultural alignment (i.e. consistent commitment to the same Health Safety & Environment standard).
- The empowerment of Tier 1 contractors to develop their own processes and systems to deliver the ODA's objectives. The ODA focused on engaging contractors, enabling them to develop their own good practice and drive their own performance. This allowed contractors to use and develop their own company processes.
- Recognition of the prestige of working on the Olympic Park and striving for excellence in all activities, including health and safety.
- The scale of the project and the length of the construction phase meant that there was sufficient time for initiatives to become embedded, and could be tailored to ensure their efficacy and success.
- Belief by workers in the genuine commitment within organizations, as the message was consistent and reiterated across the Olympic Park over time.

Through discussion with a sample of workers, supervisors, and managers, HSL identified a wealth of good practice that had been implemented on site in relation to the eight factors of the SCT. This was distilled into eight case studies, one focusing on each of the factors. The research provides evidence that it is possible, through engagement, worker involvement, and organizational commitment, to develop a strong safety culture.

The good practice identified in the case studies, plus the broader findings of the research, provide valuable learnings for the construction sector and wider industry as a model for making safety integral to 'how we do things around here'".[11]

---

[11]See Key Messages on page iii in N. Healey and C. Sugden. 2012. "Safety Culture on the Olympic Park," Research Report RR942, Health and Safety Executive, Health and Safety Laboratory, Harpur Hill, Buxton, Derbyshire SK17 9JN. http://www.hse .gov.uk/research/rrpdf/rr942.pdf.

These principles apply to striving for excellence in all aspects of Quality, Health and Safety and the Environment.

Additional case studies follow the links between quality and safety in the Deepwater Horizon blowout where buckled pipe, failed batteries, and miss wired solenoid lead to inability to shear the pipe and seal the well following the blowout.[12]

The Piper Alpha blowout (Figure 8.3) exhibits how a small beginning with serious contributory factors can cascade into something catastrophic, and deadly!

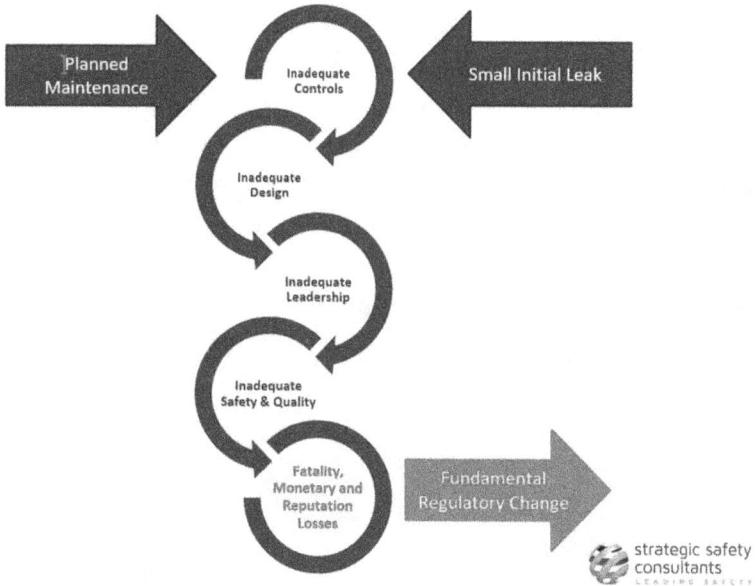

Figure 8.3 Piper alpha factor sequence[13]

Annex SL and Management System Integration

The issue of management system integration impacts directly on the structure and language of the main body of standards. The International Standards Organization (ISO), jointly with the International Electrotechnical Commission (IEC), developed, as part of their procedures for the

---

[12]See YouTube. "Deep Water Horizon." https://www.youtube.com/watch?v=9NQ8LehUWSE.

[13]See T. Ingram. "Project Risk Management." http://www.strategic-safety-consultants .com.

technical work and principles and rules for the structure and drafting of ISO and IEC documents, appendix 2 on High level structure, identical core text, common terms and core definitions and appendix 3 on Guidance on high level structure, identical core text, common terms and core definitions. These are termed "normative"—which means they must be followed, and in earlier versions were part of annex SL—whence the common usage reference.[14]

This means that integration is facilitated through a common structure and language across the whole family of management standards.

Society Imperatives

The structure and language simplification and increased clarity assists in the development of management systems for organization in more challenging situations such as those concerned with resettling refugees and seeing them progress into flourishing.[15] In just about every example and case study you see the organization has information systems providing support for the core processes quite apart from the information demands that quality management places on the organization. The scope of application encompasses all QHSE aspects, and many more!

---

[14]See IEC. "ISO/IEC DIR 1:2019 Edition 15.0 Consolidated with IEC SUP:2019 Edition 13.0—Procedures for the Technical Work–Procedures Specific to IEC." https://www.iec.ch/members_experts/refdocs/iec/isoiecdir1-consolidatediecsup%7Be d15.0.RLV%7Den.pdf.

[15]See R. Thickpenny. September 2019. "Protecting Society," Quality World, pp. 14-19.

CHAPTER 9

Quality and Information Technology

There are two main aspects that we aim to touch on here:

- The use of IT in achieving quality;
- The achievement of quality in IT.

As the first is somewhat more straightforward we will tackle that first.

Software for QA and QC

Early Beginnings

The American Society for Quality (ASQ), (previously the American Society for Quality Control—ASQC), has since the early 1980s produced a directory of software designed for quality assurance (QA) and quality control (QC) although now it is little more than a special advertising section.[1]

The impetus for this was the release of an open source disk operation system with the IBM Personal Computer when it, and its compatibles competitors, enabled quality practitioners in management positions with modest budgets to acquire the IT hardware and software resources to produce stand-alone systems for QA and QC, in many cases by their own endeavours.

---

[1]See American Society for Quality—ASQ. June 2017. "2017 Software Showcase & Directory," *Quality Progress*. http://asq.org/quality-progress/2017/06/software-quality/asqs-2017-software-showcase-directory.pdf.

The systems they created, or that were created for them, and the markets they represented covered all the components of the quality management system. QA and QC software has a strong base in document management which has separately also become a major business software sector.

Current Situation

The software for QA and QC now exists in a very different IT environment from where it started. The most important difference is that there are many very mature and excellent systems running the core processes of businesses and organizations—many of which cover processes and data of great interest and importance to QA and QC management. In order to have an integrated management system, it is vital that data is safely shared across the many software systems. A secondary, but very important and beneficial, difference is the development of the Internet and the impact of cloud computing and Software as a Service (SAAS) which vastly improves and greatly enhances team working.

Widening the Developer Base

In this environment and with the growth in the breadth and depth of the whole IT tool set and environment, despite the obvious vital importance of having skilled and experienced IT experts guiding and producing effective, safe, and secure software, the major software provider worldwide has made it possible to go back to the development roots of QA and QC software and promotes the contribution from Citizen Developers as well as Pro Developers—see Figure 9.1.[2]

The components promoted offer the promise of developing apps without writing codes.

For the foundation component, the PowerApps element, a good knowledge of an Excel-like code is all that is required—so the competent Power User is in safe territory building on all the safeguards built into the supporting and surrounding layers (see Figure 9.2).

---

[2]See S. Pant. "Dive Into PowerApps: Building Apps That Mean Business Without Writing Code," Presentation, Channel 9. https://channel9.msdn.com/Events/Ignite/2016/BRK3326-TS.

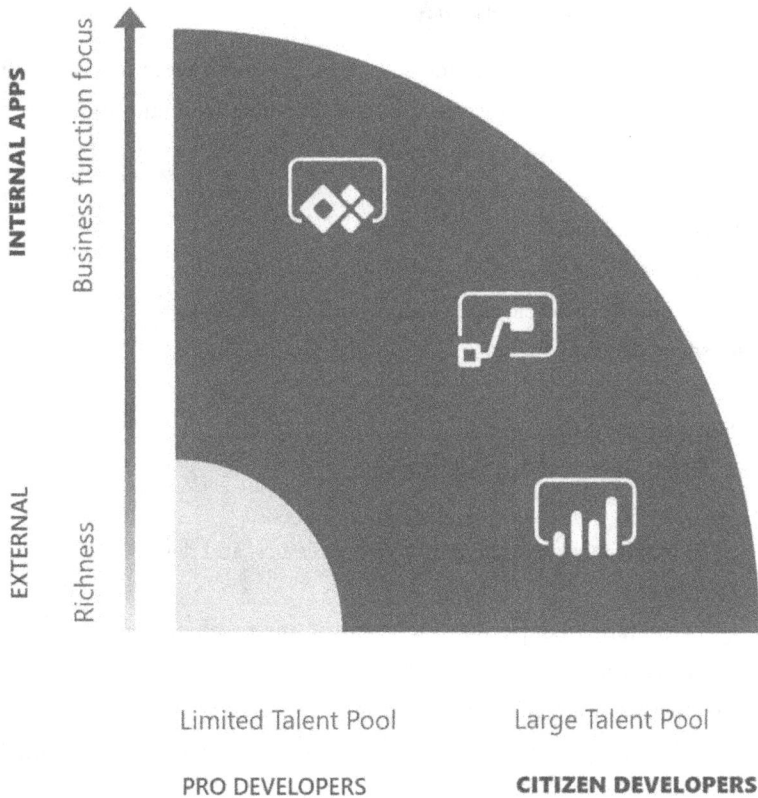

Figure 9.1 Build useful apps without writing codes

Figure 9.2 Key components for developing apps

Making safe connections with data from core process software is possible with the best of breed scalable databases with the "view"connections offered by all the major software providers conforming to the common foundations of database query languages—SQL. This opens the linking potential across the potential data and information silos in an organization and is one element at the foundation of the "big data" concept and practice.

"Why Is Big Data Important?

The importance of big data doesn't revolve around how much data you have, but what you do with it. You can take data from any source and analyse it to find answers that enable

1. cost reduction,
2. time reduction,
3. new product development and optimized offerings, and
4. smart decision-making.

When you combine big data with high-powered analytics, you can accomplish business-related tasks such as:

- Determining root causes of failures, issues, and defects in near-real time.
- Generating coupons at the point of sale based on the customer's buying habits.
- Recalculating entire risk portfolios in minutes.
- Detecting fraudulent behaviour before it affects your organization."[3]

Statistical Engineering

The systematic integration of statistical concepts, methods, and tools—often with other relevant disciplines—to solve important problems sustainably has given rise to the discipline of Statistical Engineering (Figure 9.3).[4]

"Statistical engineering is about solving big problems sustainably using statistical methods in thoughtful and responsible ways—typically by integrating multiple methods and even multiple disciplines. It is about engineering solutions."

---

[3]See SAS. "Big Data—What It Is and Why It Matters." https://www.sas.com/en_gb/insights/big-data/what-is-big-data.html.

[4]See L.A. Jones-Farmer and R.W. Hoerl. May 2019. "A Unified Approach," *Quality Progress*, pp. 48-51. http://asq.org/quality-progress/2019/05/statistics-spotlight/a-unified-approach.html.

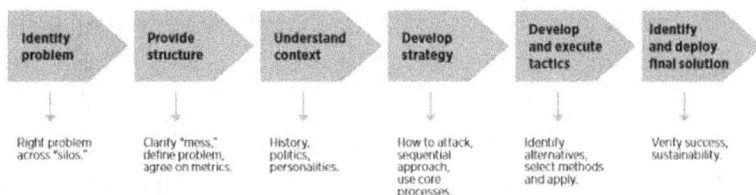

Figure 9.3 Typical phases of a statistical engineering project[5]

Source: Jones-Farmer, L. Allison and Roger W. Hoerl, "A Unified Approach", *Quality Progress*, May 2019, pp 48 – 51, http://asq.org/quality-progress/2019/05/statistics-spotlight/a-unified-approach.html

Artificial Intelligence and Expert Systems

As early as 1990 the possibilities of artificial intelligence and expert systems contributing directly to the management of quality were identified. The potential for linking customer requirements to lower level substitute quality characteristics or means in quality function deployment is a powerful example. The input is from human experience, the limits are sound programming, and the caution is the vital importance of careful testing. But given normal safeguards, the potential is significant.[6]

Software for QA and QC is still centrally about the system elements defined in the common standards but that is clearly more a statement of where things are today rather anything about the developments being delivered or just around the corner.

Software Quality

Summary

The quality of software is no different an issue, in principle, to any other product. The design and development phases are standard—requirements, design, implement, test, release, and support. This is also an expression of a software life cycle as it is a cycle that can be iterated as requirements change and are added.

---

[5]Ibid.

[6]See R.J. Braun. February 1990. "Turning Computers into Experts," *Quality Progress*, pp. 71-75.

The experience of the quality of software is almost universal and generally poor[7]. The reliability and usability of software affect travelers, online bankers, and others. The lack of access to, and the unwillingness to access, digital resources has added to the exclusion of the poor and exacerbated areas of poverty and ease of use appropriate to all users is one important aspect.[8]

The nature and scale of the issues faced in generating reliable software in a timely economic manner are huge and the failures manifest.

A central issue apparent in the early days was, and still is, that "computer programming is perceived as an art and not a measurable science" and as a result implementing the effort required to implement effective quality management is perceived as "monumental."[9]

The central product is dense computer language code of varying levels of normal readability which is then compiled into machine readable digital words (computer bytes of hexadecimal code). The understanding of the significance of a line or block of code depends on the diligence of the author in adding explanation to the code—commenting, all of which is stripped out at compilation and so adds no overhead in execution.

Even more significant factors that affect the quality of software can be hidden—the customer requirements can change dramatically around the product. Following a time as a hardware quality engineer I then started as a hardware and software engineer in a company making dedicated word processing systems when the market was switching to the open software architecture of the IBM PC and its compatibles and the "quote of the day" on the company network on the day the first redundancies were

---

[7]See M. Rodríguez, M. Piattini and C.M. Fernández. September 2015. "Software Quality—A Hard Look at Software Quality—Pilot program Uses ISO/IEC 25000 Family," *Quality Progress*. http://asq.org/quality-progress/2015/09/software-quality/a-hard-look-at-software-quality.pdf.

[8]See Low Incomes Tax Reform Group. "Digital Exclusion," Published by the Low Incomes Tax Reform Group of The Chartered Institute of Taxation (Charity Registration No. 1037771), 1st Floor, Artillery House, 11-19 Artillery Row, London, SW1P 1RT. ISBN: 978-1-8992-1837-0. https://www.litrg.org.uk/sites/default/files/digital_exclusion_-_litrg_report.pdf.

[9]J. Powers. July 1993. "TQM in Software Development Organizations," *Quality Progress*, pp. 79-80.

announced was that the new flagship product would "not be an IBM PC compatible"!

Software Quality Engineering

ISO produced what is effectively an added layer—a schedule, on "development, supply, installation and maintenance of computer software" for the foundation quality standard.[10] The latest version of this schedule is just entitled "Software Engineering."[11] Software engineering is about the "establishment and use of sound engineering principles" to control software cost, reliability, and efficiency and was first described as such in 1968.[12]

The eight software engineering principles identified early in the emergence of the discipline:

1. Define the software development life cycle (SDLC);
2. Specify the interfaces (make sure the parts will fit together);
3. Plan the testing early (plan to test it before you build it);
4. Review the design (check the design before you commit yourself);
5. Manage the configuration (changes must be kept under control);
6. Manage the quality (make sure you deliver the right quality);
7. Measure products and processes (learn from your mistakes and do better next time);
8. Define the quality policy (know where you are going).[13]

---

[10]See ISO. "ISO 9000-3:1997—Quality Management and Quality Assurance Standards—Part 3: Guidelines for the Application of ISO 9001:1994 to the Development, Supply, Installation and Maintenance of Computer Software." https://www.iso.org/standard/26364.html.

[11]See ISO. "ISO/IEC/IEEE 90003:2018—Software Engineering—Guidelines for the Application of ISO 9001:2015 to Computer Software." https://www.iso.org/standard/74348.html.

[12]See P. Naur and B. Randell. January 1969. "Software Engineering—Report on a Conference," Sponsored by the NATO SCIENCE COMMITTEE Garmisch, Germany, 7th to 11th October 1968, Scientific Affairs Division NATO Brussels 39 Belgium. http://homepages.cs.ncl.ac.uk/brian.randell/NATO/nato1968.PDF.

[13]See B. Hambling. "Managing Software Quality—ISO 9000 3 in an Iterative World," pp. 7, 8, McGraw-Hill, Shoppenhangers Road, Maidenhead, Berkshire SL 2QL, 01628 23432, ISBN-10: 007709039X, ISBN-13: 978-0-0770-9039-5.

Step 3—Plan the testing early (plan to test it before you build it) is not unlike the requirement to publish a clinical study protocol which declares before the study starts what it is you are seeking to investigate, and why, and how you will test and answer your null and alternative hypotheses so that you cannot fit the test criteria to the results after the event. That is the core of the scientific method.

Software Lifecycle Processes

"All the notes are present, even if they are not in the right sequence."[14] The latest version of the ISO schedule to ISO 9001 on Software Engineering, and the companion ISO/IEC/IEEE document on software lifecycle processes, provide an insight into the current best practice,[15] and sequence matters.

The software development life cycle comes in two distinct flavours—linear and spiral. The linear model importantly has discrete steps each of which is signed off before the other is started.

These, in Figure 9.4, are both essentially linear software development life cycles (SDLCs) even if the 'V' shape emphasizes 'a play of two halves' and the central nature of the 'Code' step.

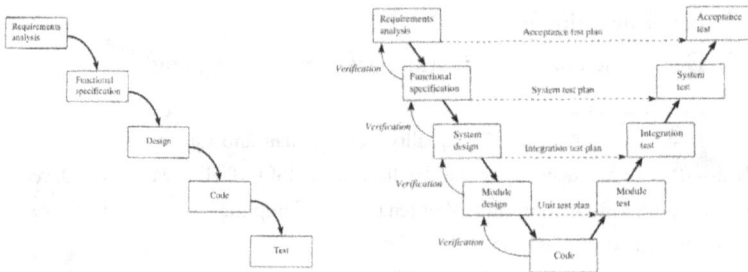

Figure 9.4 Waterfall and V linear SDLCs

[14]BBC. "The Morecambe and Wise Show, Christmas 1971 Featuring Andre Previn." https://www.bbc.co.uk/programmes/b00gw1d0.
[15]See ISO. "ISO/IEC/IEEE 90003:2018—Software Engineering—Guidelines for the Application of ISO 9001:2015 to Computer Software." https://www.iso.org/standard/74348.html; and ISO/IEC/IEEE, "ISO/IEC/IEEE 12207:2017(en)—Systems and Software Engineering—Software Life Cycle Processes." https://www.iso.org/obp/ui/#iso:std:iso-iec-ieee:12207:ed-1:v1:en.

Figure 9.5 Spiral SDLC

The spiral SDLC (Figure 9.5) points to multiple deliveries and under-pins rapid application development (RAD) involving both prototype and repeated cycles.

There is a perceived tension between quality, time, and cost and if there are ways for the testers and users to see and handle the application at as early a stage as possible—rapid application development (RAD)—then there are significant potential benefits.

The currently most well-known of the RAD techniques is 'Agile'. In Agile "all potential product features are placed into a feature backlog and prioritized for development, with the highest value features being developed first. Agile teams execute time-boxed work periods, typically called sprints, to develop these features. These sprints typically range from two to four weeks. Each agile team is composed of a small group of multi-disciplined developers that are focused on the continual delivery of valuable software. Within each team there is a Product Owner who is the voice of the customer, prioritizes the feature backlog, and accepts the de-livery of each feature. There is also a person that facilitates team meetings and eliminates blocking issues that are inhibiting team progress. Within the Scrum methodology, this person is called the Scrum Master. There is a regular cadence of meetings within each sprint. The sprint commences with a Sprint 'Kickoff' Meeting that determines what features the team will develop within the sprint. There are Daily 'Standup' Meetings where the team reviews progress, identifies any blocking issues, and assigns work to be performed next. A Sprint Completion Meeting is held at the end of each sprint to review, with customers and users outside of the agile team, the actual delivery of the features that were developed during the sprint. Within the agile team, a Sprint Retrospective Meeting is also held where the team can identify and address potential improvements to team performance."[16]

Quality Attributes

Trade-offs are also necessary between the key characteristics of software[17]:

- Functionality
- Reliability
- Usability
- Efficiency
- Maintainability
- Portability
- Compatibility
- Security

These characteristics are defined in ISO standards starting with ISO 9126—starting in 1991, now replaced by ISO 25010:2014[18] and are expanded with sub characteristics (Figure 9.6).[19]

---

[16]See J.D. Morgan. 2019. "It's No Longer Enough to Simply Be Agile," Presented at the 6th Annual University of Maryland Project Management Symposium, College Park, MD, in May 2019; Published in the *PM World Journal* VIII, no. VI, July 2019.
[17]See D. Spinellis. April 3, 2006. "Code Quality—The Open Source Perspective," Addison-Wesley Professional; 1st edition, Pearson Education Inc. 2006, Rights and Contracts, 57 Arlington Street, Suite 300, Boston MA 02116. ISBN 0-321-16007-8.
[18]See ISO, "ISO/IEC 25010:2011—Systems and Software Engineering—Systems and Software Quality Requirements and Evaluation (SQuaRE)—System and Software Quality Models."
[19]See M. Rodríguez, M. Piattini and C.M. Fernández. September 2015. "Software Quality—A Hard Look at Software Quality—Pilot Program Uses ISO/IEC 25000 Family," *Quality Progress*. http://asq.org/quality-progress/2015/09/software-quality/a-hard-look-at-software-quality.pdf.

Product quality model							
Functional suitability	Performance efficiency	Compatibility	Usability	Reliability	Security	Maintainability	Portability
Functional completeness Functional correctness Functional appropriateness	Time behavior Resource use Capacity	Coexistence Interoperability	Appropriateness recognizability Learnability Operability User-error protection User-interface aesthetics Accessibility	Maturity Availability Fault tolerance Recoverability	Confidentiality Integrity Nonrepudiation Accountability Authenticity	Modularity Reusability Analyzability Modifiability Testability	Adaptability Installability Replaceability

Figure 9.6 *Software characteristics and sub characteristics*
Source: Rodríguez, Moisés, Mario Piattini and Carlos Manuel Fernández, "Software Quality - A Hard Look at Software Quality - Pilot program uses ISO/IEC 25000 family ", Quality Progress, 2015 September, http://asq.org/quality-progress/2015/09/software-quality/a-h

Reprinted with permission from *Quality Progress* © 2015 ASQ, www.asq.org
All rights reserved. No further distribution allowed without permission.

Quality Requirements and Evaluation

The requirements and the way they will be evaluated need specification and linking up. At the top of the v SDLC and descending these will include:

- Critical success factors;
- Business performance measures;
- Acceptance criteria
- Key performance factors.

In order to facilitate reuse at every stage of the SDLC the objects and methods need careful definition and clear representation. At every level, and in many overlapping approaches, efforts are made for natural language, clarity and easy assimilation—which is where pictures score heavily, and careful definition is vital. Early efforts to address these issues resulted in Data Flow Diagrams and Data Dictionaries which still have their place and value[20] (see Appendix, page 194 Example Section of Data Flow Diagram for PowerApps documentation). These have been complemented with Object Oriented Objects and Methods that enable linking of classes and instances and defining the descriptors that are necessary and sufficient. Diagramming techniques complement these and other tools and enable linking of input requirements and output deliveries in the software development life cycle.

---

[20]C. Gane and T. Sarson. July 1977. "Structured Systems Analysis: Tools & Techniques." McDonnell Douglas.

Diagramming and Definition

Describing how the users interact with the system and what they require from it is aided by "Use cases" which can be diagrams, but even more effectively just text based.[21]

Use cases and use case diagrams are one element of the much wider toolset in the unified modeling language (UML), which is the de facto standard for modeling the business process and the architecture used to implement it in software.[22]

Integrating Risk in the SDLC

The development of software security has to be integrated into the SDLC as Table 9.1 from an early version of the key guide of the National Institute of Science and Technology.[23]

---

[21]See K. Bittner and I. Spence. 2003. "Use Case Modelling," Addison-Wesley Professional; Pearson Education Inc. 2006, Rights and Contracts, 57 Arlington Street, Suite 300, Boston, MA 02116. ISBN: 0-201-70913-9; and A. Cockburn. 2003. "Writing Effective Use Cases," Addison-Wesley Professional; Pearson Education Inc. 2001, Rights and Contracts, 57 Arlington Street, Suite 300, Boston, MA 02116. ISBN: 0-201-70225-8.

[22]See H. Erikson, and M. Penker. *Business Modeling with UML* (Hoboken, NY: John Wiley), 200, ISBN 0-47129551-5.

[23]See G. Stoneburner, A. Goguen, and A. Feringa. July 2002. "Risk Management Guide for Information Technology Systems—Recommendations of the National Institute of Standards and Technology," NIST Special Publication 800-30, Computer Security Division Information Technology Laboratory National Institute of Standards and Technology, Gaithersburg, MD 20899-8930 1Booz Allen Hamilton Inc. 3190 Fairview Park Drive Falls Church, VA 22042. https://www.ucop.edu/information-technology-services/initiatives/resources-and-tools/sp800-30.pdf.

Table 9.1 Integration of risk management into the SDLC[24]

Phase	Characteristics	Support from risk management activities
Phase 1—Initiation	The need for an IT system is expressed and the purpose and scope of the IT system is documented	Identified risks are used to support the development of the system requirements, including security requirements, and a security concept of operations (strategy)
Phase 2—Development or Acquisition	The IT system is designed, purchased, programmed, developed, or otherwise constructed	The risks identified during this phase can be used to support the security analyses of the IT system that may lead to architecture and design trade-offs during system development
Phase 3—Implementation	The system security features should be configured, enabled, tested, and verified	The risk management process supports the assessment of the system implementation against its requirements and within its modeled operational environment. Decisions regarding risks identified must be made prior to system operation
Phase 4—Operation or Maintenance	The system performs its functions. Typically the system is being modified on an ongoing basis through the addition of hardware and software and by changes to organizational processes, policies, and procedures	Risk management activities are performed for periodic system reauthorization (or reaccreditation) or whenever major changes are made to an IT system in its operational, production environment (e.g., new system interfaces)
Phase 5—Disposal	This phase may involve the disposition of information, hardware, and software. Activities may include moving, archiving, discarding, or destroying information and sanitizing the hardware and software	Risk management activities are performed for system components that will be disposed of or replaced to ensure that the hardware and software are properly disposed of, that residual data is appropriately handled, and that system migration is conducted in a secure and systematic manner

Quality by Design

It has long been an aim to define the requirements in a way that generates executable code thus providing a way to radically shorten the SDLC

[24]Ibid.

and one of the first examples was higher order—mathematically proven software that arose from a review of the errors in the Apollo moon shot software.[25] Today that same drive is expressed in Model Driven Architecture.[26] The aim is to use models, and principally UML models that can be machine processed.[27]

The use of Quality Function Deployment to link requirements down to architecture, code, criteria, and test[28] is something we will pick up again (see Quality Function Deployment (QFD)).

The diagramming tools used in system definition and modelling include cross functional flowcharts which will consider in Deployment for Quality and Quality Management.

There are other approaches such as "DevOps"[29] where "small teams of developers independently implement their features, validate the correctness in a production-like environment and have their code deployed into production quickly, safely, and securely" working with "Development, Testing and Operations." The base of DevOps is (Figure 9.7) a "pipeline which is executed each time a software developer commits and merges software code updates into Configuration Management (CM)" the automated pipeline is initiated and if successful proceeds to delivery into production.

---

[25]See Higher Order Software in J. Martin and C. McLure. "Structured Techniques for Computing," 2 Vols., Savant Research Institute, 2 New Street, Carnforth, Lancs, LA5 9BX, Tel 0524 734505 (has an analysis of the errors found in Apollo 10 software) and A. Fabio. "Margaret Hamilton Takes Software Engineering To The Moon And Beyond." https://hackaday.com/2018/04/10/margaret-hamilton-takes-software-engineering-to-the-moon-and-beyond/.

[26]See D.S. Frankel. 2003. *Model Driven Architecture—Applying MDA to Enterprise Computing* (Hoboken, NY: Wiley Publishing), ISBN 0-47131920-1; and H. Erikson and M. Penker. *Business Modeling with UML* (Hoboken, NY: John Wiley), 200, ISBN 0-47129551-5.

[27]See H. Erikson and M. Penker. *Business Modeling with UML* (Hoboken, NY: John Wiley), 200, ISBN 0-47129551-5.

[28]See W.C. Pai. 2002. "A Quality-Enhancing Software Function Deployment Model," Information Systems Management Summer. https://web.b.ebscohost.com/ehost/pdfviewer/pdfviewer?vid=0&sid=812d07b5-ad7a-4e90-bd77-6b87c68caa1e%40pdc-v-sessmgr02.

[29]See J.D. Morgan. 2019. "It's No Longer Enough to Simply Be Agile," Presented at the 6th Annual University of Maryland Project Management Symposium, College Park, MD, in May 2019; Published in the *PM World Journal* VIII, no. VI, July 2019.

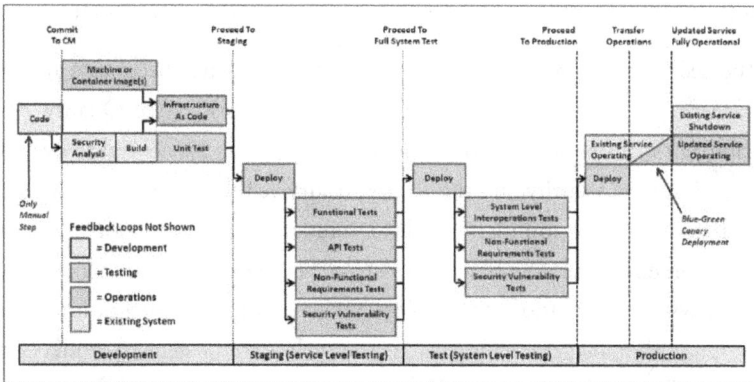

Figure 9.7 A DevOps pipeline is the automated execution of software initially constructed by the three disciplines[30]

Testing and Correcting

The boundaries are being extended. Carnegie Mellon reports work on "automated code repair." "Finding security flaws in source code is daunting; fixing them is an even greater challenge. We are creating automated tools that can repair bugs automatically or that prompt developers for more information to make effective repairs."[31]

Industry 4.0 and IOT and AI

Information Technology

Information Technology (IT) is a very significant change agent and has delivered many innovative breakthrough improvements and sees its skills in business analysis as a major business change agent.[32] The communication, data handling, processing, work flow, reporting, and many other elements are central to business now and we have commented how far the pendulum has swung to the detriment of those who find it hard to engage with the digital economy.

---

[30]See J.D. Morgan. 2019. "It's No Longer Enough to Simply Be Agile," Presented at the 6th Annual University of Maryland Project Management Symposium, College Park, MD, in May 2019; Published in the *PM World Journal*, VIII, no. VI, July 2019. https://pmworldjournal.com/article/its-no-longer-enough-to-simply-be-agile.

[31]See Carnegie-Mellon University. "Automated Code Repair." https://www.sei.cmu .edu/research-capabilities/all-work/display.cfm?customel_datapageid_4050=4555.

[32]See D. Paul, J. Cadle, and D. Yeates (eds.). 2014. "Business Analysis," BCS Learning and Development First Floor, Block D, North Star House, 3North Star Avenue, Swindon, SN2 1FA, UK, ISBN 978-1-78017-277-4.

Information Security Management Systems and Cybersecurity

The security of information management systems has become a major concern. Security is listed as a software characteristic (see Quality Attributes). Information security management systems are central to overall organizational security and the ability to survive the threats both internal and external. The foundational ISO standard for information security management systems is based on Annex SL (see annex sl and management system integration) to enable management system integration.[33]

The risk management approach is very close to the general model (see section Risk as likelihood and consequence and Figure 4.12 From risk source to consequence—Bowtie diagram) but with a major difference in that the threats are exploiting vulnerabilities and these are included in a very well-documented risk management process.[34]

An earlier version of the key National Institute of Science and Technology (NIST) Risk Management Guide for Information Technology Systems[35] has a very useful flowchart for IT risk management (see the risk-assessment methodology flowchart in Figures 9.8 and 9.9), which also links to the table showing the risk-management activities in each of the SDLC phases (see Table 9.1, Integration of Risk Management into the SDLC).

There is a more than sufficient toolset for ISMS risk assessment and Yang proposes how these can be used to provide a unified method for developing and evaluating an integrated system for information security

[33]See ISO. "ISO/IEC 27001:2013 Information Technology—Security Techniques—Information Security Management Systems—Requirements."

[34]See NIST. September 2012. "NIST Special Publication 800-30 Revision 1 Guide for Conducting Risk Assessments," Computer Security Division Information Technology Laboratory National Institute of Standards and Technology Gaithersburg, MD 20899-8930, https://nvlpubs.nist.gov/nistpubs/Legacy/SP/nistspecialpublication800-30r1.pdf.

[35]G. Stoneburner, A. Goguen, and A. Feringa. July 2002. "Risk Management Guide for Information Technology Systems—Recommendations of the National Institute of Standards and Technology," NIST Special Publication 800-30, Computer Security Division Information Technology Laboratory National Institute of Standards and Technology Gaithersburg, MD 20899-8930 1Booz Allen Hamilton Inc. 3190 Fairview Park Drive Falls Church, VA 22042. https://www.ucop.edu/information-technology-services/initiatives/resources-and-tools/sp800-30.pdf.

management.[36] The importance and value of engaging the user in the development of the ISMS is highlighted by Spears and Barki.[37]

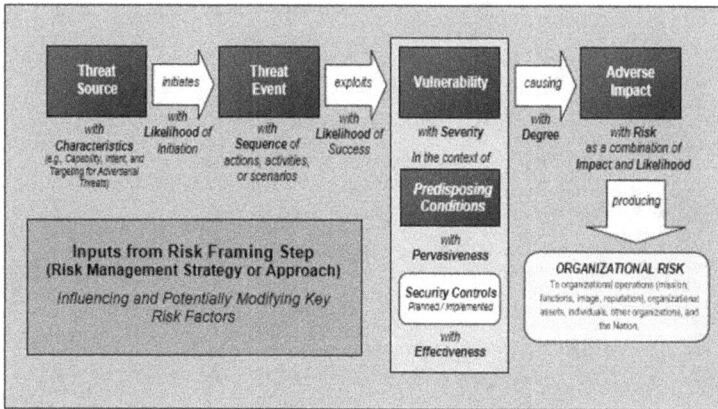

Figure 9.8 Generic risk model with key risk factors[38]

IT System Governance—COBIT

"Control Objectives for Information and related Technology (COBIT) provides good practices across a domain and process framework for adopters to measure IT governance (IT Governance Institute 2007). Within the COBIT framework, these process-oriented domains are as follows: plan and organize (PO), acquire and implement (AI), deliver and support (DS), and monitor and evaluate (ME)."[39] The organization providing and supporting COBIT—ISACA—offers membership, guidance, and certification for IT professionals.[40]

---

[36]See T. Yang, C. Ku, and M. Liu. 2016. "An Integrated System for Information Security Management with the Unified Framework." *Journal of Risk Research* 19, no. 1, pp. 21-41. doi:10.1080/13669877.2014.940593.

[37]See J.L. Spears, and H. Barki. September 2010. "User Participation in Information Systems Security Risk Management," *MIS Quarterly* 34, no. 3, pp. 503-22. https://web.a.ebscohost.com/ehost/pdfviewer/pdfviewer?vid=0&sid=2934acb0-f300-4c03-8e47-634443cc4407%40sdc-v-sessmgr03.

[38]Ibid.

[39]See T. Yang, C. Ku, and M. Liu. 2016. "An Integrated System for Information Security Management with the Unified Framework." *Journal of Risk Research* 19, no. 1, pp. 21-41. doi:10.1080/13669877.2014.940593.

[40]See ISACA. "Introducing COBIT," 1700 E. Golf Road, Suite 400, Schaumburg, IL 60173, USA, Phone: +1.847.253.1545. http://www.isaca.org/cobit/pages/default.aspx.

Input	*Risk Assessment Activities*	*Output*
• Hardware • Software • System interfaces • Data and information • People • System mission	**Step 1.** **System Characterization**	• System Boundary • System Functions • System and Data Criticality • System and Data Sensitivity
• History of system attack • Data from intelligence agencies, NIPC, OIG, FedCIRC, mass media,	**Step 2.** **Threat Identification**	Threat Statement
• Reports from prior risk assessments • Any audit comments • Security requirements • Security test results	**Step 3.** **Vulnerability Identification**	List of Potential Vulnerabilities
• Current controls • Planned controls	**Step 4. Control Analysis**	List of Current and Planned Controls
• Threat-source motivation • Threat capacity • Nature of vulnerability • Current controls	**Step 5.** **Likelihood Determination**	Likelihood Rating
• Mission impact analysis • Asset criticality assessment • Data criticality • Data sensitivity	**Step 6. Impact Analysis** • Loss of Integrity • Loss of Availability • Loss of Confidentiality	Impact Rating
• Likelihood of threat exploitation • Magnitude of impact • Adequacy of planned or current controls	**Step 7. Risk Determination**	Risks and Associated Risk Levels
	Step 8. **Control Recommendations**	Recommended Controls
	Step 9. **Results Documentation**	Risk Assessment Report

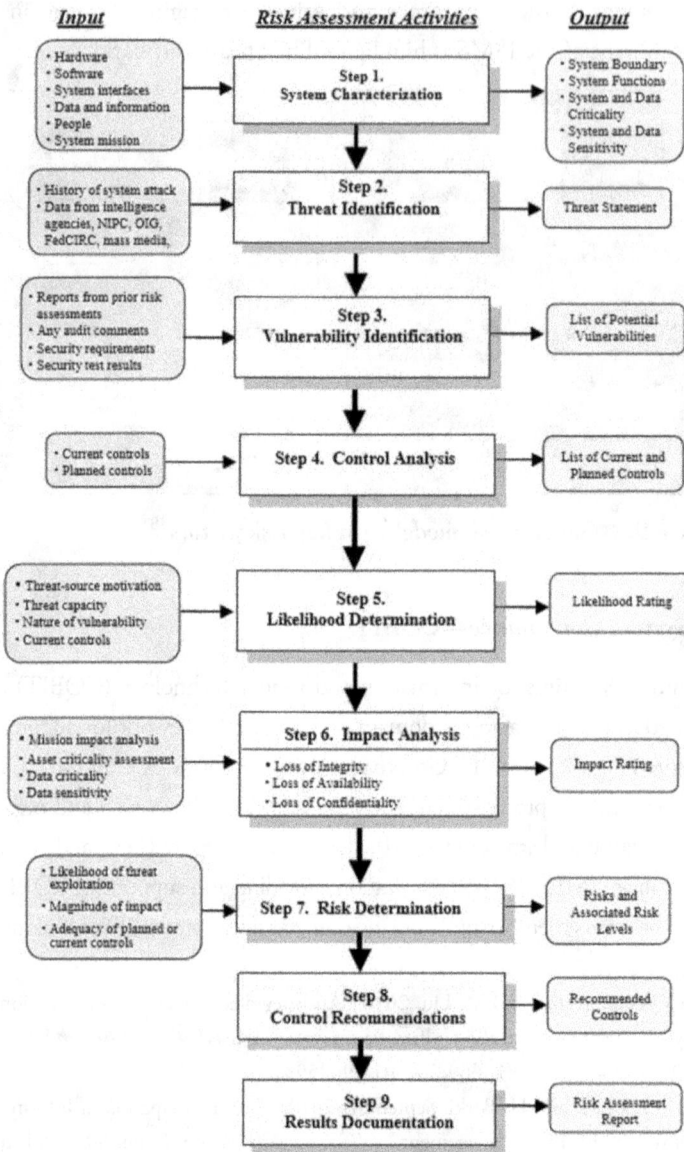

Figure 9.9 Risk assessment methodology flowchart[41]

[41]G. Stoneburner, A. Goguen, and A. Feringa. July 2002. "Risk Management Guide for Information Technology Systems—Recommendations of the National Institute of Standards and Technology," NIST Special Publication 800-30, Computer Security Division Information Technology Laboratory National Institute of Standards and Technology Gaithersburg, MD 20899-8930 1Booz Allen Hamilton Inc. 3190 Fairview Park Drive Falls Church, VA 22042. https://www.ucop.edu/information-technology-services/initiatives/resources-and-tools/sp800-30.pdf.

Traceability and Blockchain

Cryptocurrency is the cool, and somewhat risky, face of the far more important technology for quality—which is blockchain. Blockchain will provide secure traceability for data and associated information integrity.

Nestle is aiming to pilot blockchain technology. "Nestlé consumers will be able to track where their food has come from using a blockchain platform developed by the company to independently verify sustainability and supply chain data. The pilot program will track milk from farms and producers in New Zealand to Nestlé factories and warehouses in the Middle East."[42]

Here is an introduction to blockchain.

"What is blockchain?

Blockchain is "a mathematical structure for storing data in a way that is nearly impossible to fake."[43] Essentially, it's a database that is validated by a larger community rather than by a central authority (that is, banks or governments).

At its very core, a blockchain is like a traditional ledger that keeps records of all the individual transactions made against the product. These transactions can occur in any part of the supply chain.

The transactions could be any movement of money, goods, or secure data related to the product—that is, the purchase of raw materials, the blending of materials to make a new material, purchase orders to buy new material, quality inspection, certificate inspection, invoicing, and bank payment. Each of these transactions is stored digitally as a block within the ledger. Each of the blocks is timestamped and becomes intrinsically linked to one another. The blocks are strung chronologically into a chain—hence the term "blockchain."

To draw an analogy, if each transaction was a picture, stringing them together and looking at them holistically renders a movie—a history of the product—from inception to consumption and to eventual redemption.

---

[42]See Quality World. September 2019. "Nestlé to Pilot Blockchain Technology," Quality World, p. 2. https://members.quality.org/SelfService/My_Professional_Development/Quality_World_Magazine.aspx   https://www.flipsnack.com/5F6FB67EFB5/qw-september-2019/download-pdf.html.

[43]Massachusetts Institute of Technology (MIT) Technology Review editors. April 23, 2018. "Explainer: What Is a Blockchain?" *MIT Technology Review*, www.technologyreview.com/s/610833/explainer-what-is-a-blockchain/.

The most innovative part about blockchain is its verification system and inherent security.

Blockchain technology has the potential to change the way we buy and sell things. The verification and authentication of the product at every step will impart greater traceability, as well as the ability to trust the supply chain. It is virtually impossible to change this data without being detected by other users because no one person owns the entire data set. The other great advantage of blockchain is that every organization or vendor in this supply chain could potentially use a different system, and it does not affect the integrity of the blockchain itself."[44]

"Consider this scenario that's relatable to any industry—with a few big assumptions:

Company B wants to buy product X from vendor A. Product X has many raw materials, including some base metals that vendor A must source from a global metal distributor. Company B issues a purchase order to buy a certain quantity of product X from vendor A.

Because company B is buying this product for the first time from vendor A, company B has instituted a strict receiving quality inspection and certificate inspection as part of its process. After the process and all the raw materials are verified, including material dimensions, the quality team accepts the raw materials into its inventory. Vendor A submits an invoice against the purchase order. Company B processes the invoice and submits it to the bank for payment to complete the transaction.

As shown in Figure 9.10,[45]

"The creation of company B's purchase order is the first block in this process. The block itself could have information pertaining to the quantity of product X, cost, and a need-by date—information gleaned from the purchase order. This block is timestamped and identified using a unique identifier. The blockchain network verifies the veracity of this purchase order and validates it.

Using this purchase order, vendor A sends its own purchase order to the global metal distributor, asking for this certain base material (needed

[44]See N. Rao. October 2018. "The Time Is Now," *Quality Progress*, pp. 19-23. http://asq.org/quality-progress/2018/10/global-quality/the-time-is-now.html.
[45]Ibid.

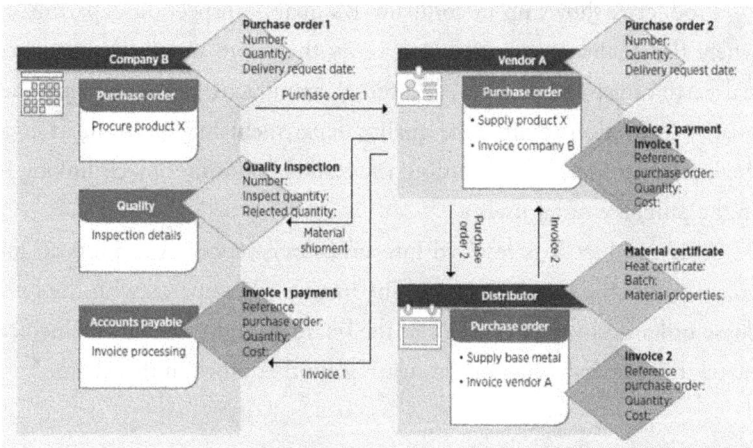

Figure 9.10 Process flow with blockchain

Source: Rao, Nahari, "The Time Is Now", Quality Progress, October 2018, pp 19 - 23, http://asq.
org/quality-progress/2018/10/global-quality/the-time-is-now.html

to make product X). This creates a block inextricably linked to the previous block (see Figure 9.11).

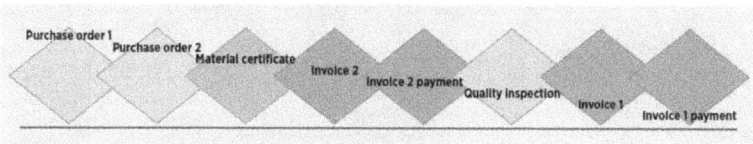

Figure 9.11 Visual representation of a blockchain[46]

Source: Rao, Nahari, "The Time Is Now", Quality Progress, October 2018, pp 19 - 23, http://asq.
org/quality-progress/2018/10/global-quality/the-time-is-now.html

The global metal distributor buys metal from a few foundries around the world. When it makes that shipment of base metal to vendor A, its block includes the sources of the raw material. This information gets tagged to vendor A's purchase order and, consequently, to company B's purchase order as well.

The metal, along with other raw materials, are processed in vendor A's plant, and product X is fabricated. All the routings, machining operations, and internal quality inspections make it to product X's production order, which in turn is tied to company B's purchase order—thus creating a new block.

---

[46]Ibid.

Product X shows up in company B's quality inspection department, where the quality department can verify the entire supply chain, material certificates, and vendor A's internal manufacturing documents and quality inspection results. The quality department may perform its own quality inspection, thus recording the results in another block linking it to the purchase order itself.

After product X is received into inventory, vendor A submits an invoice against the purchase order. The invoice is compared with the purchase order and validates whether the quantity and price on the invoice match the purchase order, thus creating another block in this chain."[47]

---

[47]Ibid.

CHAPTER 10

Tools and Techniques for Quality

Standards and Specifications

The specification is the foundation for knowing what we must achieve for the user—see Chapter 2, The role of specification. The user may be active as a consumer of a product or service, or passive as a patient and under the oversight of a client.

How we successfully deliver the complying product or service using the appropriate tools and processes is a matter of best practice. Best practice is commonly accepted as being defined in national and international standards (of best practice).

Standards and Best Practice

Standards emerge readily during deep and desperate times and war time spurs their emergence and normal commercial use insures their development (see Chapter 22, Quality in history and time of war and Figure 10.1).

A journey through time – ISO 9001

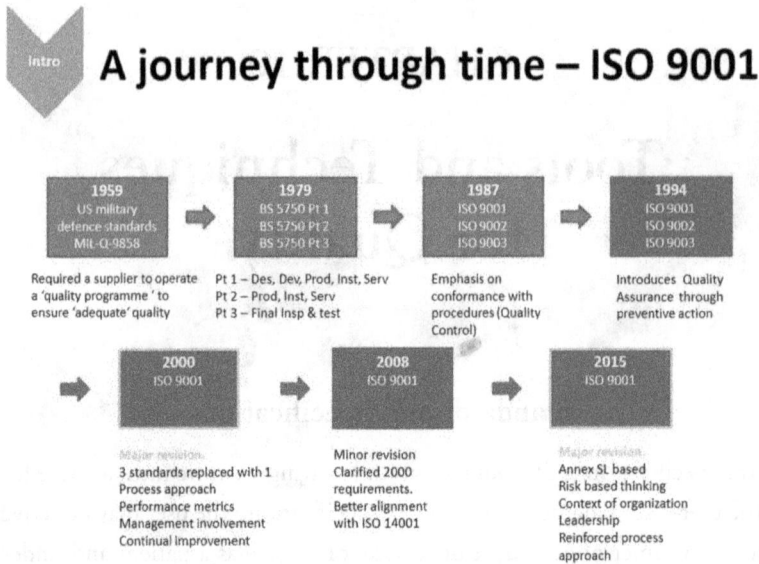

1959	1979	1987	1994
US military defence standards MIL-Q-9858	BS 5750 Pt 1 BS 5750 Pt 2 BS 5750 Pt 3	ISO 9001 ISO 9002 ISO 9003	ISO 9001 ISO 9002 ISO 9003
Required a supplier to operate a 'quality programme' to ensure 'adequate' quality	Pt 1 – Des, Dev, Prod, Inst, Serv Pt 2 – Prod, Inst, Serv Pt 3 – Final Insp & test	Emphasis on conformance with procedures (Quality Control)	Introduces Quality Assurance through preventive action

2000	2008	2015
ISO 9001	ISO 9001	ISO 9001
Major revision. 3 standards replaced with 1 Process approach Performance metrics Management involvement Continual improvement	Minor revision Clarified 2000 requirements. Better alignment with ISO 14001	Major revision. Annex SL based Risk based thinking Context of organization Leadership Reinforced process approach

Figure 10.1 Standards development of the foundation quality management standards[1]

The development and practical application of "how-to" knowledge is clear in many, many standards and examples, from personal experience, include:

- Sampling by attributes (pass/fail) and variables (measurements) in parts per hundred (pph)[2];
- Sampling by attributes (pass/fail) in parts per million (ppm)[3];

---

[1]See R. Green and C. MacNee. 2015. "Implementing ISO 9001:2015–9001:2015 Transition Training," CQI and IRCA, Implementing ISO 9001:2015 Training Course.

[2]See M. Hashim, and M. Khan. June 1990. "Quality Standards—Past, Present, Future," *Quality Progress*, pp. 56-59, ISO 2859-1, "Sampling Procedures for Inspection by Attributes—Part 1: Sampling Schemes Indexed by Acceptance Quality Limit (AQL) for Lot-by-lot Inspection." https://www.iso.org/search.html?q=2859; ISO 3951-1, "Sampling Procedures for Inspection by Variables—Part 1: Specification for Single Sampling Plans Indexed by Acceptance Quality Limit (AQL) for Lot-by-lot Inspection for a Single Quality Characteristic and a Single AQL." https://www.iso.org/search.html?q=3951&hPP=10&idx=all_en&p=0.

[3]See ISO 28597, ISO 28597:2017. "Acceptance Sampling Procedures by Attributes—Specified Quality Levels in Nonconforming Items Per Million," ISO. https://www.iso.org/search.html?q=2859&hPP=10&idx=all_en&p=0.

- Control charts[4];
- Process management methods[5];
- Medical device products—copper-bearing contraceptives[6];
- Critical processes—radiation sterilization.[7]

The perception however is also present that standards are not easy to use and that they could be far more practical in their presentation and that they do not "present a step-by-step program for cost-effective implementation."[8] Communication guidelines for practical implementation are highlighted as issues and the need is acknowledged for "a competent professional who understands the practical aspects of QA/QC and the implication of standards throughout manufacturing and design."[9] There is much in those conclusions and the underlying reason is simply that application will be dependent on the context and vary widely and practical guidelines would be practically impossible at the highest level but more and more feasible as the standard itself gets closer and closer to specific products and processes, and this is exemplified in the standards cited immediately above.

Quality Assurance and Control

The professionals competent in QA/QC are specified as key roles, along with technical management in many standards, in the quality

---

[4]ISO 7870. "ISO 7870-4:2011 Control Charts—Part 4: Cumulative Sum Charts." https://www.iso.org/search.html?q=7870&hPP=10&idx=all_en&p=0.

[5]See ISO 22514, "ISO 22514-1:2014 Statistical Methods in Process Management—Capability and Performance—Part 1: General Principles and Concepts." https://www.iso.org/search.html?q=22514.

[6]See ISO 7439. "ISO 7439:2015 Copper-bearing Contraceptive Intrauterine Devices—Requirements and Tests." https://www.iso.org/search.html?q=7439&hPP=10&idx=all_en&p=0.

[7]See ISO 11737. "ISO 11737—Sterilization of Health Care Products—Radiation—Part 2: Establishing the Sterilization Dose." https://www.iso.org/search.html?q=11737&hPP=10&idx=all_en&p=0.

[8]See "What Quality Standards Lack" in Hashim, Mohammed and Mujeeb Khan, "Quality Standards—Past, Present, Future," *Quality Progress*, June 1990, pp. 56-59.

[9]See M. Hashim and M. Khan. June 1990. "Quality Standards—Past, Present, Future," *Quality Progress*, pp. 56-59.

management standards for many sectors—although there is now a shift on to greater accountability of the whole management team. There are professional bodies of long-standing repute that provide definitions of the bodies of knowledge required, codes of practice, training and qualifications, and wide and deep support networks.

The best practices on the deployment of quality (see Chapter 11) and standards on quality management (see Chapter 12), and the related chapters, expand on how QA and QC are to be put into practice in the service of quality.

There are serious objections to both the foundation quality management standard and the international standards process (see Chapter 12, Quality management) and these should guide how we use and implement best practice in standards.

Audit

The single most important management support for quality is the role of internal audit. Internal audit was only implicit in MIL-Q-9859, the predecessor to ISO 9001 (see Figure 38), as a supplier audit requirement (MIL-Q-9858 was predominantly a supply chain management standard). It isn't until BS 5750 that we see a full-fledged internal audit requirement. Internal audit was the third level of audit:

- Level 1—3rd party—independent external audit
- Level 2—2nd party—dependent, supplier or prequalification body, external audit
- Level 3—1st party—internal audit.

The scope and practice of audit is central to quality management and the achievement of quality objectives (see Chapter 15, Quality and auditing).

Process Management

The single most important principle for the achievement of quality is that of process management which is very closely linked to the Plan–Do–Check–Act (PDCA) cycle (see Chapter 4, Plan–Do–Check–Act above).

Processes take input, add value, and transform these into output deliverables. Usually the output from one process becomes the input to the following process even if that is the use process of the customer or consumer.

Variation is common to all processes, including all life. Understanding the patterns of variation and whether they are normal or abnormal is central[10] and something we introduced in some depth in Chapter 4 Quality, risk, opportunity, and improvement.

A foundational insight that expresses this in a slightly different way comes from an early work from last century by Walter Shewhart and separates the patterns related to "common" or "special" causes:

- Common causes—Those causes that are inherent in a system (process or product) over time, affect everyone working in the system and affect all outcomes of the system.
- Special causes—Those causes that are not always part of a system (process or product) or do not affect everyone but arise because of specific circumstances.[11]

A stable process under control will demonstrate variation but dependent on understanding that variation and that it is within acceptable limits will enable acceptable output.

Design of processes centres along selecting the lowest set of common causes that are as insensitive as possible to the "chaotic" effects of "special" causes and keep change as free of these as well.[12] This leads to establishing

---

[10]See T.W. Nolan and L.P. Provost. May 1990. "Understanding Variation," *Quality Progress*, pp. 70-78; and T.W. Nolan, R.J. Perla, and L.P. Provost. November 2016. "Understanding Variation—26 Years Later—Correctly Assessing Variation is Fundamental to Sound Decisions," *Quality Progress*, pp. 28-37. http://asq.org/quality-progress/2016/11/best-practices/understanding-variation26-years-later.pdf.

[11]See W.A. Shewhart. "The Economic Control of Quality of Manufactured Product," Van Norstrand Co, 1931; reprinted- ASQ Quality Press, 1980, reprinted—Martino Fine Books, April 25, 2015, ISBN-10: 1614278113, ISBN-13: 978-1614278115—Shewhart used "Assignable" and "Chance" and W. Edwards Deming popularized them as "common" and "special"—see T.W. Nolan and L.P. Provost. May 1990. "Understanding Variation," *Quality Progress*, pp. 70-78.

[12]B.K. McGill. November 1990. "Return to Chaos," *Quality Progress*, pp. 55-57.

that the "common cause" variation will result in output that conforms to the process specification related limits.

Establishing that the process is in control on start-up is a primary process management discipline. Another one is monitoring the process to see that it continues in control free from "special causes" that might lead it to drift out of control and compliance. The two great dangers in monitoring and managing processes are (1) reacting to common cause random variation and (2) interfering unnecessarily. The use of a statistical averaging technique to see the underlying trend is necessary and the CUSUM technique already indirectly referenced is one valuable approach.[13]

The controls need applying to the most critical steps most at risk of instability. But the foundations are laid by integrating control throughout the process and applying standards and measurements throughout and is the reason the ancients in Egypt followed by the Greeks, Persians, and Romans created structures of great exactitude that have stood the test of time.[14] These same principles are seen in the principles of scientific management proposed by Frederik W Taylor that came to be known as Taylorism and wrongly blamed for many of the evident ills of industrialized society:

1. Replace working by "rule of thumb," or simple habit and common sense, and instead use the scientific method to study work and determine the most efficient way to perform specific tasks.
2. Rather than simply assign workers to just any job, match workers to their jobs based on capability and motivation, and train them to work at maximum efficiency.
3. Monitor worker performance and provide instructions and supervision to ensure that they're using the most efficient ways of working.
4. Allocate the work between managers and workers so that the managers spend their time planning and training, allowing the workers to perform their tasks efficiently.[15]

---

[13]See ISO 7870. "ISO 7870-4:2011 Control Charts—Part 4: Cumulative Sum Charts." https://www.iso.org/search.html?q=7870&hPP=10&idx=all_en&p=0.

[14]See Q.R. Skrabec Jr. November 1990. "Ancient Process Control and Its Modern Implications," *Quality Progress*, pp. 49-52.

[15]Ibid., F.W. Taylor. June 14, 2014. "The Principles of Scientific Management," CreateSpace Independent Publishing Platform, ISBN-10: 150019090X, ISBN-13: 978-1-5001-9090-3.

Skrabec picks up the stress Taylor laid on the "harmony" of the integrated perspective of production, quality, and safety that he observed in the best-performing producers.[16] This balance is reflected in the modern drive for integrated management systems—see Chapter 8.

We pick up on the unintended consequences of how good ideas can be badly used and result in other damage in Chapter 22, Quality in history and time of war—industrial revolution.

Statistics

We have already shown that understanding and handling variation requires an understanding of how to describe, understand, and measure that variation so that we can assess the likelihood of producing, releasing, or accepting defective product—see Chapter 4, Quality, risk, opportunity, and improvement, and also Appendix, pp. 184–187, Probability distribution functions.

Choice of PDF

We used the properties of the "normal" or "Gaussian" distribution to set criteria for describing and measuring this variation expressed as dispersion around an expected mean value and mentioned that the "normal" distribution is one of a family of many possible underlying probability distribution functions (pdfs)—(see Chapter 4—Quality, risk, opportunity, and improvement).

The normal distribution has been very effectively explained and illustrated by Muelaner.[17]

The choice of the normal distribution was possible because this was a continuous variable—a measurement that we were handling. When it comes to estimating the likelihood of defectives in a lot or batch ready for release, then we have binary—defective/not defective, yes/no, on/off type

---

[16]See Q.R. Skrabec Jr. November 1990. "Ancient Process Control and Its Modern Implications," *Quality Progress*, pp. 49-52.

[17]See J. Muelaner. October 31, 2019. "An Introduction to Statistical Process Control (SPC)—Keeping an Eye on the Big Picture," *Quality Digest*. https://www.quality-digest.com/print/32965 and https://www.qualitydigest.com/inside/management-article/introduction-statistical-process-control-spc-102419.html.

data and the underlying pdf is generally either binomial or Poisson depending on whether we are replacing the sample taken or not. These pdfs are the foundation of the international standards on attribute sampling for estimating lot and process quality[18]. We don't need to understand and handle the underlying pdf if we are using the tables in the standards but if we need to customize the sampling regime to our own requirements, then we do need that competence and cannot avoid a certain mastery of statistics and the necessary knowledge, experience, and their validation.

Goodness of Fit

The data may not perfectly fit the underlying pdf you have chosen. They may, for instance, be skewed and therefore also not symmetrical around the expected value (Figure 10.2).[19]

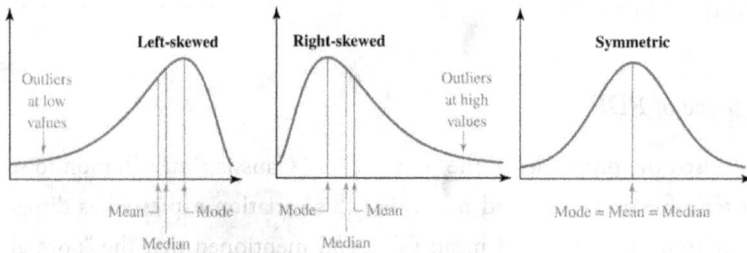

Figure 10.2 Left and right skew and symmetric normal distributions

They may have more than one peak or mode (Figure 10.3), and this probably shows that there is likely more than one underlying distribution.[20]

Or even a time series with cycles based on a given time period or frequency—see Figure 10.4.[21]

---

[18]See ISO 2859-1. "Sampling Procedures for Inspection by Attributes—Part 1: Sampling Schemes Indexed by Acceptance Quality: imit (AQL) for Lot-by-lot Inspection." https://www.iso.org/search.html?q=2859.

[19]See R. DeCook. "4.2 Shapes of Distributions," Iowa University Mathematical Sciences. http://homepage.stat.uiowa.edu/~rdecook/stat1010/notes/Section_4.2_distribution_shapes.pdf.

[20]Ibid.

[21]Ibid.

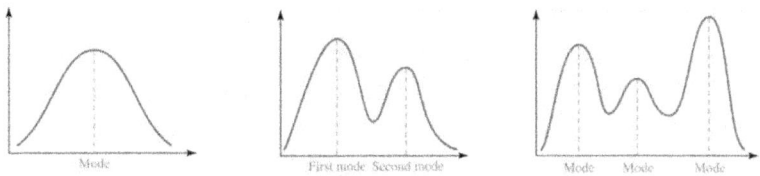

Figure 10.3 One, two, or three peaks

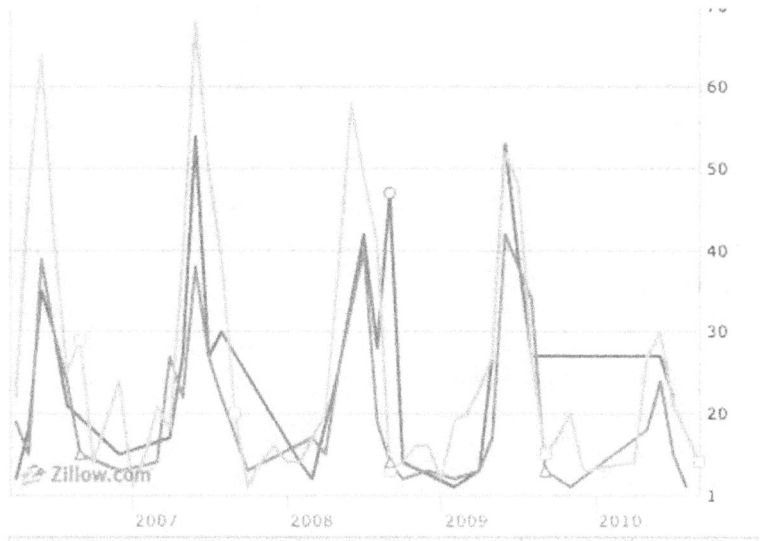

Figure 10.4 Homes sold in a US city by month and zip code

Situations we are handling may, and should if we are thinking statistically, alert us to the possibilities of anomalies that must be handled. "Right skewness is common when a variable is bounded on the left but unbounded on the right. For example, durations (response time, time to failure) typically have right skewness since they cannot take values less than zero; many financial variables (income, wealth, prices) typically have right skewness since body weight has right skewness since most people are closer to the lower limit than to the upper limit of viable body weight. Left skewness is less common in practice, but it can occur when a variable tends to be closer to its maximum than its minimum value. For example, scores on an easy exam are likely to have left skewness, with most scores close to 100 percent and lower scores tailing off to the left. Well-known right-skewed distributions include the Poisson, chi-square, exponential, lognormal, and gamma distributions."[22]

Several initial applications of key statistical techniques presume that the different factors, variables, or contributions to a situation or measurement are independent of each other. Conversely, we may well want to establish the strength of a possible causal relationship between two quantities—though we need to be aware that apparent mathematical relationships are not necessarily proof of causal relationships.[23] What we are looking for is either the absence or presence of correlation—the degree to which the individuals have the same relative positions. This can be seen and most valuably demonstrated with simple graphs—basic descriptive statistics. When correlation is confirmed and variation from one contribution is affecting the variability in another, then this must be allowed for—otherwise you are likely to slip into partial to full double counting and overstating of variability.

The Correlation Coefficient

"A correlation coefficient is a way to put a value to the relationship. Correlation coefficients have a value of between −1 and 1. A '0' means there is no relationship between the variables at all, while −1 or 1 means that there is a perfect negative or positive correlation (negative or positive correlation here refers to the type of graph the relationship will produce)"[24] (Figure 10.5).

These issues will be developed in design of experiments (see Design of experiments in Chapter 17, Quality and design) and in measurement uncertainty (see Measurement uncertainty in Chapter 18, Quality and measurement).

[22]See P.V. Hippel. "Skewness," Entry from M. Lovric (ed.). 2010. *International Encyclopedia of Statistical Science*. New York, NY: Springer.
[23]See W. Reichman. August 30, 1973. "Use and Abuse of Statistics," Penguin; New Impression Edition, ISBN-10: 0140207074, ISBN-13: 978-0-1402-0707-1.
[24]See Statistics How To, "Correlation in Statistics: Correlation Analysis Explained." https://www.statisticshowto.datasciencecentral.com/probability-and-statistics/correlation-analysis/.

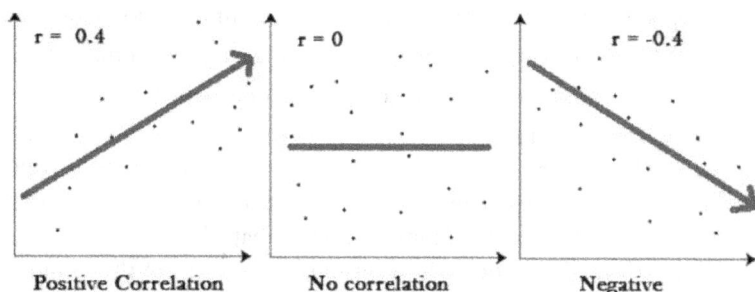

Figure 10.5 *Graphs showing a correlation of 0.4, 1, and −0.4* [25]

Central Limit Theorem

The central limit theorem is of great practical consequence and it is important to be aware of the help and confidence it brings in handling data and to know we have a safety net, of sorts, when making initial assumptions to model the data we want to handle.

"G.2 Central Limit Theorem

G.2.1 If $Y = c_1 X_1 + c_2 X_2 + \ldots + c_N X_N = \sum_{i=1}^{N} c_i X_i$ and all the X_i are characterized by normal distributions, then the resulting convolved distribution of Y will also be normal. However, even if the distributions of the X_i are not normal, the distribution of Y may often be approximated by a normal distribution because of the central limit theorem. This theorem states that the distribution of Y will be approximately normal with expectation $E(Y) = \sum_{i=1}^{N} c_i E(X_i)$ and variance $\sigma^2(Y) = \sum_{i=1}^{N} c_i^2 \sigma^2(X_i)$ where $E(X_i)$ is the expectation of X_i and $\sigma^2(X_i)$ is the variance of X_i, if the X_i are independent and $\sigma^2(Y)$ is much larger than any single component of $c_i^2 \sigma^2(X_i)$ from a non-normally distributed X_i."[26]

---

[25]Ibid.

[26]See G2 page 71 in JCGM. "JCGM 100:2008 GUM 1995 with Minor Corrections—Evaluation of Measurement Data—Guide to the Expression of Uncertainty in Measurement," BIPM, 134 pages. https://www.bipm.org/utils/common/documents/jcgm/JCGM_100_2008_E.pdf.

Independence can be checked from prior technical knowledge and validated by examining plots of one variable against the other. If the known, or assumed, non-normal component does not dominate, then normality may be assumed.

"G.2.2 The Central Limit Theorem is significant because it shows the very important role played by the variances of the probability distributions of the input quantities, compared with that played by the higher moments of the distributions, in determining the form of the resulting convolved distribution of Y. Further, it implies that the convolved distribution converges towards the normal distribution as the number of input quantities contributing to increases; that the convergence will be more rapid the closer the values of are to each other (equivalent in practice to each input estimate contributing a comparable uncertainty to the uncertainty of the estimate y of the measurand Y); and that the closer the distributions of the Xi are to being normal, the fewer are required to yield a normal distribution for Y.

G.2.3 A practical consequence of the Central Limit Theorem is that when it can be established that its requirements are approximately met, in particular, if the combined standard uncertainty (y) is not dominated by a standard uncertainty component obtained from a Type A evaluation based on just a few observations, or by a standard uncertainty component obtained from a Type B evaluation based on an assumed rectangular distribution, a reasonable first approximation to calculating an expanded uncertainty $Up = k_p u_c$ (y) that provides an interval with level of confidence p is to use for a value from the normal distribution. The values most commonly used for this purpose are given in Table G.1."[27]

So if you have a good understanding of the underlying distributions for each uncertainty contribution and that non-normal distributions do not dominate, then you can use k factors that are based on a normal distribution.

This also demonstrates the importance of basic statistical competency in areas to do with measurement.

The Systems Approach

The experience of Motorola in witnessing the effect of an integrated systems approach to one of their previously failing businesses points the need to integrate everything we do in quality within a holistic systems approach:

---

[27]Ibid.

"Quality After Motorola

Motorola's quality evolution shows how the integration of Six Sigma and Baldrige models can be applied in a real-world setting. Motorola's success rests on integrating quality management initiatives with statistical quality control tools and techniques. Influenced by Japanese management practices at one of its previously owned plants, Quasar, Motorola's management learned how to improve the quality of its products. Under Motorola's leadership, the plant was losing market share to foreign competitors that sold better quality products at a lower cost. In 1974, Motorola sold Quasar to a Japanese consumer electronic company, Matsushima. Under Japanese management, the factory made drastic improvements in the quality of its products. For example, the same workforce, technology, and design as Motorola used at the plant was now producing TVs with 1/20th the number of defects. After visiting the factory, Motorola's management realized that such surprising results could be achieved when an organization is focused on processes, people, and quality. Management realized it was the quality system that led the company to produce products of higher quality. To improve the quality of their products, company officials knew they needed to change the focus of their improvement from product attributes to operational procedures. This shift in thinking about quality in Motorola resulted in an emphasis on the systems approach, interactions among processes within the organization and their overall impact on performance. Such a dramatic improvement could not be achieved by just focusing on process management using statistical quality control tools and techniques. The result was improvement in all aspects of the organization, mirroring the seven categories of the Baldrige model. By focusing on management (Baldrige's leadership category), people (human resource management), process (process management), flow of information (information, analysis and knowledge management), voice of customers (customer and market focus), and commitment to higher product quality (strategic planning), Motorola successfully reduced the defect rate in its processes to the Six Sigma level (3.4 defects per million)."[28]

---

[28]See M. Mellat-Parast, E.C. Jones, and S.G. Adam. September 2007. "Six Sigma and Baldrige: A Quality Alliance," *Quality Progress*, pp. 45-51. http://asq.org/quality-progress/2007/09/baldrige-national-quality-program/six-sigma-and-baldrige-a-quality-alliance.pdf.

CHAPTER 11

Deployment for Quality

Early in the 1980s it became clear that Japan had leap-frogged the United States and many other developed countries in providing high-quality products. The videos and the messages that were promoted by the government were quite blunt—Japan was quite happy to share all they had learned—originally from the West, because they didn't believe we would apply it and regain our competitive position in the West.

There were many names and flavours for the best practice in Japan—total quality control (TQC) and company wide quality control (CWQC) but the most important, that now plays a central role worldwide in 6-sigma (see Chapter 16 Six sigma) is quality function deployment (QFD) a technique first developed in Japan.

Quality Function Deployment (QFD)

The benefit of having different cultures view and examine best practice from a radically different perspective is that there is a likelihood of significant innovation. This happened when Japan, which had been a closed society in the 18th century, completed its emergence in World War II and lost. Out of the help that the United States gave Japan came a manufacturing renaissance and among the innovations came the most thoroughgoing application of process to the manufacturing and service industries.

QFD is definitive, clear, and complex. The technique took shape at the Kobe Shipyard of Mitsubishi Heavy Industries Ltd in Japan in the early 1970s and the term "deployment" in Japanese implies an extension or broadening that encompasses the whole of the organization.[1]

---

[1] See N. Karabatsos. June 1988. "Listening to the Voice of the Customer," *Quality Progress*, p. 5.

The enormous strength of QFD is organization and processwide integration of customer requirements down to the detail, of which control points out which processes deliver the characteristics that match the customer requirements. The starting point is the leading matrix—the House of Quality (HOQ) and Voice of the Customer (VOC) where "what" the customer wants is matched to "how" the organization provides (this).

The HOQ structure is shown in Figure 11.1.[2] An example of an HOQ is shown below in Figure 11.2. Notice how the customer needs can be categorized and grouped. This immediately adds power to the technique.

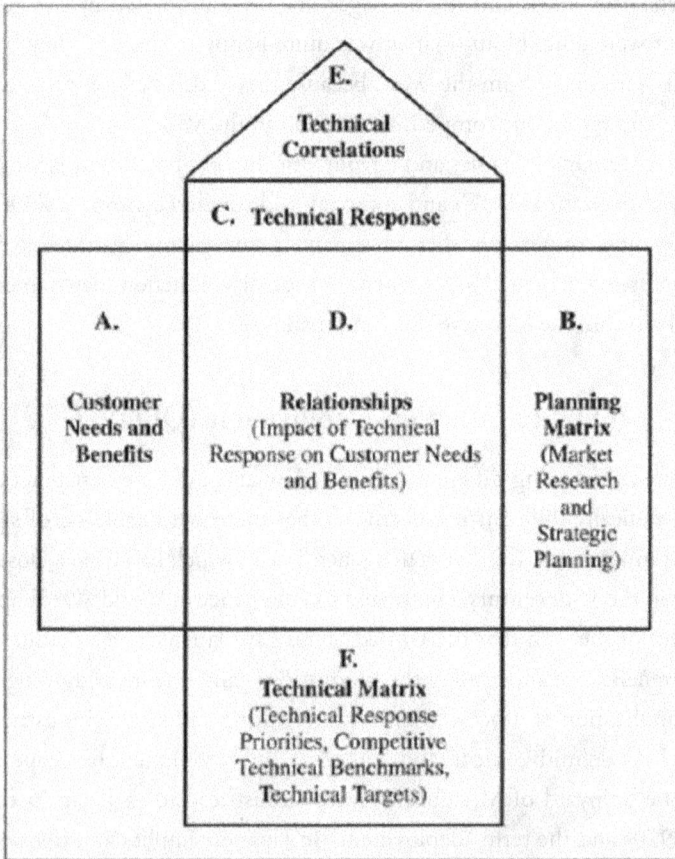

Figure 11.1 The house of quality

---

[2]See L. Cohen. 1995. "Quality Function Deployment—How to Make QFD Work for You," Addison-Wesley, ISBN 0-201-633330-2.

Computer Server Product Planning Matrix

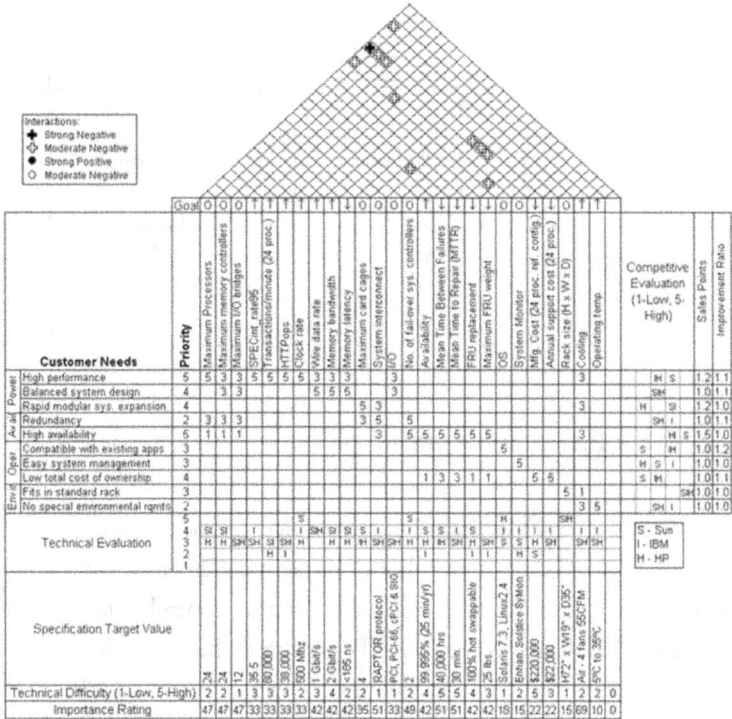

Interactions:
- ✦ Strong Negative
- ◇ Moderate Negative
- ● Strong Positive
- ○ Moderate Negative

Customer Needs (by category):

Power:
- High performance
- Balanced system design
- Rapid modular sys. expansion
- Redundancy
- High availability

Oper:
- Compatible with existing apps
- Easy system management
- Low total cost of ownership

Env:
- Fits in standard rack
- No special environmental rqmts

Competitive Evaluation (1-Low, 5-High)

Sales Points / Improvement Ratio

Technical Evaluation
Specification Target Value
Technical Difficulty (1-Low, 5-High)
Importance Rating

S - Sun
I - IBM
H - HP

Figure 11.2 House of quality (HOQ) QFD example[3]

The HOQ is the first in a series of cascading matrices. We have already pointed out that customer requirements can involve trade-offs—as with quality attributes in software quality engineering. QFD permits inclusion of the trade-offs in the half matrix "top-hat" to the HOQ (Figure 11.3).

The cascade from the HOQ—customer needs downwards enables the integrated deployment of policy and objectives throughout the organization in a way that can help better understand customer needs and the importance and linking of the specification[4] and avoid sub-optimisation by allowing focus on internal objectives decoupled from the voice of the customer.[5]

---

[3]See K. Crow. "Customer-Focused Development with QFD," NPD-Solutions DRM Associates. http://www.npd-solutions.com/qfd.html.

[4]See A.A. Kenny. June 1988. "A New Paradigm for Quality Assurance," *Quality Progress*, pp. 30-32.

[5]See L.P. Sullivan. June 1988. "Policy Management Through Quality Function Deployment," *Quality Progress*, pp. 18-20.

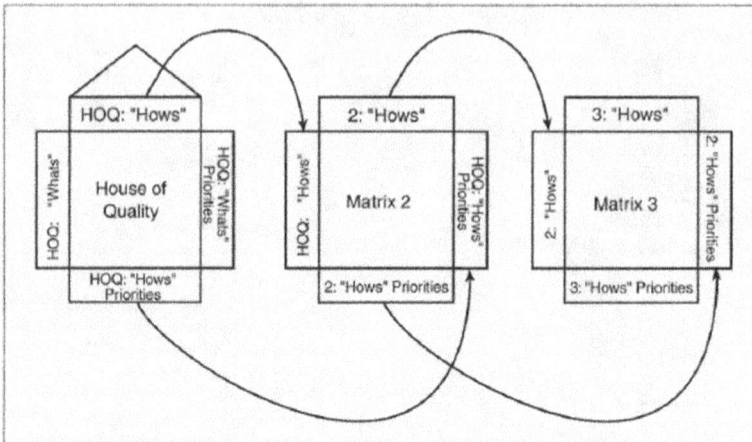

Figure 11.3 Interrelated matrices[6]

Deploying the cascade from the customer onwards radically helps differentiation and categorization of customer requirements,[7] communication with visual documents, helps avoid missing key control issues and other things dropping through the cracks. The benefits to the design-development process are claimed to include reduced changes, shorter cycle times, and lower start-up costs[8] flowing into increased customer satisfaction and market share and reduced warranty claims.[9] QFD is organization wide and allows for integration of many other quality tools and techniques such as Just In Time (JIT) and Total Quality Control (TQC)[10] and Taguchi and

---

[6]See L. Cohen. 1995. "Quality Function Deployment—How to Make QFD Work for You," Addison-Wesley, ISBN 0-201-633330-2.

[7]See B. Graessel and P. Zeidler. November 1993. "Using QFD to Improve Customer Service," *Quality Progress*, pp. 59-63.

[8]See J.R. Hauser and D. Clausing. May to June 1988. "The House of Quality," *Harvard Business Review*. http://blogs.ubc.ca/nvdteamb/files/2013/10/7-The-House-of-Quality.pdf.

[9]See R.M. Fortuna. June 1988. "Beyond Quality: Taking SPC Upstream," *Quality Progress*, pp. 23-28 and A.A. Kenny. June 1988. "A New Paradigm for Quality Assurance," *Quality Progress*, pp. 30-32.

[10]See R.M. Fortuna. June 1988. "Beyond Quality: Taking SPC Upstream," *Quality Progress*, pp. 23-28.

other Design of Experiments improvement tools.[11] It greatly assists internal quality improvement by focusing on answering questions that are central to managing the linked processes and the requirements they have to meet.[12] A case study on an air-conditioning control device is one of many outside the foundation texts[13] in the many helpful articles found in the main monthly magazine of the American Society for Quality (ASQ).[14] Plenty of other sources of information on how to apply QFD are available, including health care.[15]

The QFD technique is now so well founded that there is a whole series of ISO standards covering its use.[16]

Benchmarking

Benchmarking is an illustration of a vital technique for organizations committed to offer the very best irrespective of whether they use QFD or not but[17] which so naturally falls into place as an extension of the Voice

[11]See P.J. Ross. June 1988. "The Role of Taguchi Methods and Design of Experiments in QFD," *Quality Progress*, pp. 41-47.
[12]See K.N. Gopalakrishnan, B.E. McIntyre, and J.C. Sprague. September 1992. "Implementing Internal Quality Improvement With the House of Quality," *Quality Progress*, pp. 57-60.
[13]See L. Cohen. 1995. "Quality Function Deployment—How to Make QFD Work for You," Addison-Wesley, ISBN 0-201-633330-2, and J.P. Ficalora and L. Cohen. July 17, 2009. *Quality Function Deployment and Six Sigma: A QFD Handbook*, 2nd ed. (Prentice, NJ: Prentice Hall), ISBN-10: 0135138353, ISBN-13: 978-0-1351-3835-9.
[14]See D. De Vera, A.A. Kenny, M.A.H. Khan, and M. Mayer. June 1988. "An Automotive Case Study," *Quality Progress*, pp. 35-38.
[15]See B. Dehe and D. Bamford. 2017. "Quality Function Deployment and Operational Design Decisions—A Healthcare Infrastructure Development Case Study," *Production Planning & Control* 28, no. 14, pp. 1177-92. doi:10.1080/09537287.2017.1350767.
[16]See ISO 16355. "ISO 16355-1:2015 Application of Statistical and Related Methods to New Technology and Product Development Process—Part 1: General Principles and Perspectives of Quality Function Deployment (QFD)." https://www.iso.org/search.html?q=16355 and others in the series.
[17]See R.C. Camp. "Benchmarking: The Search for Industry Best Practices That Lead to Superior Performance," ASQC/Quality Press, Dec 89, ISBN-10: 0873890582, ISBN-13: 978-0-8738-9058-8; also Productivity Press (2006) ASIN: B00E7UYBJK.

of the Customer (VOC) and the Voice of the Stakeholder (VOS) requirements dimensions of the House of Quality (HOQ) leading matrix.[18]

Benchmarking can be done within a domain (essentially directed at the
competition) or across domains (looking for process and product-related
best practice wherever it can be found).[19] It is applicable in service sectors
such as education and health care.[20]

The American Society for Quality (ASQ) and the American Productivity & Quality Center (APQC) both provide benchmarking report services and other services.[21]

Maturity Grids

The maturity model first appeared in a seminal work by Phil Crosby and
Table 11.1 shows the stages in quality management maturity, the 14 steps
referred to are specific to his improvement model.

This maturity model has been picked up and applied to Software (and
hardware)[22] and quality management in the foundation ISO guidance
documents for quality management standards.

---

[18]See R. Swanson. December 1993. "Quality Benchmark Deployment," *Quality Progress*, pp. 81-84.

[19]See M. Fargnoli and T. Sakaob. 2017. "Uncovering Differences and Similarities
Among Quality Function Deployment-based Methods in Design for X: Benchmarking in Different Domains." *Quality Engineering* 29, no. 4, pp. 690-712. doi:10.1080
/08982112.2016.1253849.

[20]See J.C. Glassa, G. McCallion, D.G. McKillop, S. Rasaratnama and K.S. Stringer.
2009. "Best-practice Benchmarking in UK Higher Education: New Nonparametric
Approaches Using Financial Ratios and Profit Efficiency Methodologies." *Applied
Economics* 41, pp. 249-67, ISSN 0003–6846 print/ISSN 1466–4283, http://www
.informaworld.com, doi:10.1080/00036840600994278; and B. Dehe and D. Bamford. 2017. "Quality Function Deployment and Operational Design Decisions—A
Healthcare Infrastructure Development Case Study." *Production Planning & Control*
28, no. 14, pp. 1177-92. doi:10.1080/09537287.2017.1350767.

[21]See American Society for Quality—ASQ. "Benchmarking Studies." https://asq.org/
quality-resources/benchmarking-reports; and American Productivity & Quality Center (APQC). "Benchmarks on Demand." https://www.apqc.org/what-we-do/bench-
marking/benchmarks-on-demand; and https://videos.asq.org/benchmarking.

[22]See M.C. Paulk. 2009. "A History of the Capability Maturity Model for Software."
SQP 12, no. 1, ASQ. http://citeseerx.ist.psu.edu/viewdoc/download?rep=rep1&type
=pdf&doi=10.1.1.216.199.

Table 11.1 *Quality management maturity grid*[23]

Measurement categories	Stage 1: Uncertainty	Stage 2: Awakening	Stage 3: Enlightenment	Stage 4: Wisdom	Stage 5: Certainty
Management under-standing and attitude	No comprehension of quality as a management tool. Tend to blame qual-ity department for "qual-ity problems"	Recognizing that quality management may be of value but not willing to provide money or time to make it all happen.	While going through quality improvement programme, learning more about quality Manage-ment; becoming support-ive and helpful	Participating under-standing absolutes of quality management. Recognize their per-sonal role in continu-ing emphasis.	Consider quality management an essen-tial part of company system
Quality organization status	Quality is hidden in man-ufacturing or engineering departments. Inspection is probably not part of the organization. Emphasis on appraisal and sorting.	A stronger quality leader is appointed but main emphasis is still on appraisal and getting product out of the door. Still part of manufactur-ing or other function.	Quality department re-ports to top management, all appraisal is incorpo-rated and quality manager has role in management of company.	Quality manager is an officer of the company; effective status report-ing and preventative action. Involved with consumer affairs and special assignments.	Quality manager on board of directors. Pre-vention is main con-cern. Quality manager is a thought leader.

(*continued*)

[23]See P.B. Crosby. October 22, 1987. *Quality is Free*, New edition (Penguin), pp. 32, 33, ISBN-10: 0451621298, ISBN-13: 978-0451621290. http://businessprocesstangles.com/philip-crosby-5-original-quality-maturity-grid/ or https://www.qualityandproducts.com/2012/07/09/crosbys-quality-management-maturity-grid/.

Table 11.1 *Quality management maturity grid*

Measurement categories	Stage 1: Uncertainty	Stage 2: Awakening	Stage 3: Enlightenment	Stage 4: Wisdom	Stage 5: Certainty
Problem handing	Problems are fought as they occur; no resolution; inadequate definition; lots of yelling and accusations.	Teams are set up to attack major problems. Long-range solutions are not solicited. Fire fighting.	Corrective action communication established. Problems are faced openly and resolved in an orderly way.	Problems identified early in their development. All functions are open to suggestion and improvement.	Except in the most unusual cases, problems are prevented.
Cost of quality as % of sales	Reported: Unknown. Actual: 20 %	Reported: 3% Actual: 18%	Reported:8% Actual: 12%	Reported: 6.5% Actual: 8%	Reported: 2.5% Actual: 2.5%
Quality improvement actions	No organised activities. No understanding of such activities.	Trying obvious "motivational" short range efforts	Implementation of the 14 Step Programme with thorough understanding and establishment of each step	Continuing the 14 Step Programme and starting to make certain	Quality improvement is a normal and continued activity.
Summation of company quality posture	"We don't know why we have problems with quality."	"Is it absolutely necessary to always have problems with quality?"	"Through management commitment and quality improvements we are identifying and resolving out problems"	"Defect prevention is a routine part of our operation"	"We know why we do not have problems with quality."

The application to quality management in ISO 9004 is described as follows:

"Maturity model

A mature organization performs effectively and efficiently and achieves sustained success by:

A) understanding and satisfying the needs and expectations of interested parties;

B) monitoring changes in the context of the organization;

C) identifying possible areas for improvement, learning, and innovation;

D) defining and deploying policies, strategy and objectives;

E) managing its processes and resources;

F) demonstrating confidence in its people, leading to increased engagement;

G) establishing beneficial relationships with interested parties, such as external providers, and other partners.

This self-assessment tool uses five maturity levels, which can be extended to include additional levels or otherwise customized as needed.

Table A.1 gives a generic framework for setting out how performance criteria can be related to the levels of maturity in a tabular format. The organization should review its performance against the specified criteria, identify its current maturity levels, and determine its strengths and weaknesses and the related risks and opportunities for improvement.

Table 11.2 (Table A.1) Generic model for self-assessment elements and criteria related to maturity levels[24]

Maturity level toward sustained success					
Key element	Level 1	Level 2	Level 3	Level 4	Level 5
Element 1	Criteria 1 Base level				Criteria 1 Best practice
Element 2	Criteria 2 Base level				Criteria 2 Best practice
Element 3	Criteria 3 Base level				Criteria 3 Best practice

---

[24]See ISO 9004. "ISO 9004: 2018—Quality Management—Quality of an Organization—Guidance to Achieve Sustained Success."

The criteria given for the higher levels can help the organization understand the issues it needs to consider and to determine the improvements needed to reach higher levels of maturity. Tables A.2 to A.32 give self-assessment criteria based on this document."

An example using Table A.2 shows the usability of the approach:

The software development application describes the foundation like this: "Capability maturity model (CMM) broadly refers to a process improvement approach that is based on a process model. CMM also refers specifically to the first such model, developed by the Software Engineering Institute (SEI) in the mid-1980s, as well as the family of process models that followed. A process model is a structured collection of practices that describe the characteristics of effective processes; the practices included are those proven by experience to be effective.

CMM can be used to assess an organization against a scale of five process maturity levels. Each level ranks the organization according to its standardization of processes in the subject area being assessed. The subject areas can be as diverse as software engineering, systems engineering, project management, risk management, system acquisition, information technology (IT) services, and personnel management.

CMM was developed by the SEI at Carnegie Mellon University in Pittsburgh. It has been used extensively for avionics software and government projects, in North America, Europe, Asia, Australia, South America, and Africa. Currently, some government departments require software development contract organizations to achieve and operate at a level 3 standard."[25]

The CMM model has been superseded by the Capability Maturity Model Integration—"The CMMI is the successor of CMM. The goal of the CMMI project is to improve usability of maturity models for software engineering and other disciplines, by integrating many different models into one framework. It was created by members of industry, government, and the SEI."[26]

---

[25]See Select Business Solutions, Inc. "What is the Capability Maturity Model? (CMM)." http://www.selectbs.com/process-maturity/what-is-the-capability-maturity-model.
[26]See Select Business Solutions, Inc. "What is Capability Maturity Model Integration? (CMMI)." http://www.selectbs.com/process-maturity/what-is-capability-maturity-model-integration.

Table 11.3 (Table A.2) Self-assessment of the detailed elements of 5.2[27]

Subclause	Maturity level Level	Maturity level Item[a]	Conclusion YES	Conclusion Results/comment[b]
5.2 Relevant interested parties	1	The interested parties are determined, including their needs and expectations and whether the associated risks and opportunities are informal or ad hoc.		
	2	Processes to meet the needs of some interested parties are established.		
		Ongoing relationships with interested parties are established as informal or ad hoc.		
	3	Processes for determining which interested parties are relevant are in place.		
		Processes for determining the relevance of interested parties include consideration of those that are a risk to sustained success if their needs and expectations are not met and those that can provide opportunities to enhance sustained success.		
		The needs and expectations of the relevant interested parties are identified.		
		Processes to fulfil the needs and expectations of the interested parties are established.		
	4	Processes for assessing the relevance of the needs and expectations for relevant interested parties are in place and are used to determine which ones need to be addressed.		
		The needs and expectations of key interested parties are addressed and reviewed such that improved performance, common understanding of objectives and values, and enhanced stability have been realized in some of these ongoing relationships.		
	5	Processes and relationships with relevant interested parties are fulfilled according to the relevant needs and expectations determined. This has been done as part of understanding the benefits, risks, and opportunities of ongoing relationships.		
		The needs and expectations of all relevant interested parties are addressed, analysed, evaluated, and reviewed, such that there is improved and sustained performance, common understanding of objectives and values, and enhanced stability, including recognition of the benefits derived from these ongoing relationships.		

a. Items outlined in levels 3–5 are intended to be a progression of thought that is based on the guidance provided in the applicable subclause.
b. This may include recognition of aspects where the organization is partially meeting a maturity level.

[27]Ibid.

145

There are three models available:

- CMMI® for Acquisition, Version 1.3[28]
- CMMI® for Development, Version 1.2[29]
- CMMI® for Services, Version 1.3[30]

These provide a complete, yet flexible, model and methodology for establishing and growing integrated management systems through the maturity levels of the model.

The model is focused on the management of people and assets (Figure 11.4):

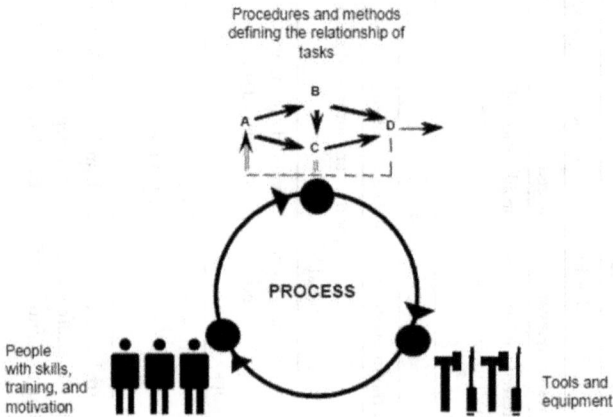

Figure 11.4 SEI CMMI—the three critical dimensions[31]

[28]See Carnegie-Mellon University SEI, "CMMI® for Acquisition, Version 1.3 CMMI-ACQ, V1.3," CMMI Product Team, Carnegie Mellon, Software Engineering Institute, Pittsburgh, PA 15213-3890. https://resources.sei.cmu.edu/asset_files/TechnicalReport/2010_005_001_15284.pdf.

[29]See Carnegie-Mellon University SEI, "CMMI® for Development, Version 1.2, CMMI-DEV, V1.2, CMU/SEI-2006-TR-008 ESC-TR-2006-008," CMMI Product Team, Carnegie Mellon, Software Engineering Institute, Pittsburgh, PA 15213-3890. https://resources.sei.cmu.edu/asset_files/TechnicalReport/2006_005_001_14771.pdf.

[30]See Carnegie-Mellon University SEI, "CMMI® for Services, Version 1.3 CMMI-SVC, V1.3," CMMI Product Team, Carnegie Mellon, Software Engineering Institute, Pittsburgh, PA 15213-3890. https://resources.sei.cmu.edu/asset_files/TechnicalReport/2010_005_001_15290.pdf.

[31]See Figure 1.1, p. 16, Carnegie-Mellon University SEI, "CMMI® for Development, Version 1.2, CMMI-DEV, V1.2, CMU/SEI-2006-TR-008 ESC-TR-2006-008," CMMI Product Team, Carnegie Mellon, Software Engineering Institute, Pittsburgh, PA 15213-3890. https://resources.sei.cmu.edu/asset_files/TechnicalReport/2006_005_001_14771.pdf.

The definition, establishment, and sharing of the processes is what the SEI in the CMMI concludes holds everything together—"But what holds everything together? It is the processes used in your organization. Processes allow you to align the way you do business. They allow you to address scalability and provide a way to incorporate knowledge of how to do things better. Processes allow you to leverage your resources and to examine business trends."[32]

Process management is at the heart of quality management systems and what they are all about (Figure 11.5).

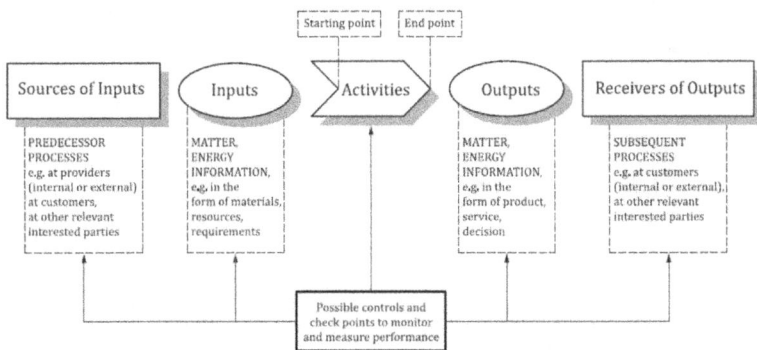

Figure 11.5 Schematic representation of the elements of a single process[33]

Management Systems

The term "management system" and "quality management system" are synonymous and in terms of set theory and Venn Diagrams they are contiguous—usage in the ISO 9000 series of documents confirms this.[34] There need be no distinction or separation. The quality management

---

[32]See p. 16, Carnegie-Mellon University SEI, "CMMI® for Development, Version 1.2, CMMI-DEV, V1.2, CMU/SEI-2006-TR-008 ESC-TR-2006-008", CMMI Product Team, Carnegie Mellon, Software Engineering Institute, Pittsburgh, PA 15213-3890. https://resources.sei.cmu.edu/asset_files/TechnicalReport/2006_005_001_14771.pdf.
[33]See Figure 1, p. viii, in ISO 9001:2015, "Quality Management Systems— Requirements."
[34]See clause 5.1.1 c) in ISO 9001:2015, "Quality Management Systems — Requirements."

standards are about business management of the core processes, and all the ancillary support processes, and the elements that make them up—see Figure 11.6. The free open source standard MSS 1000 is particularly clear, open, and explicit on this.[35]

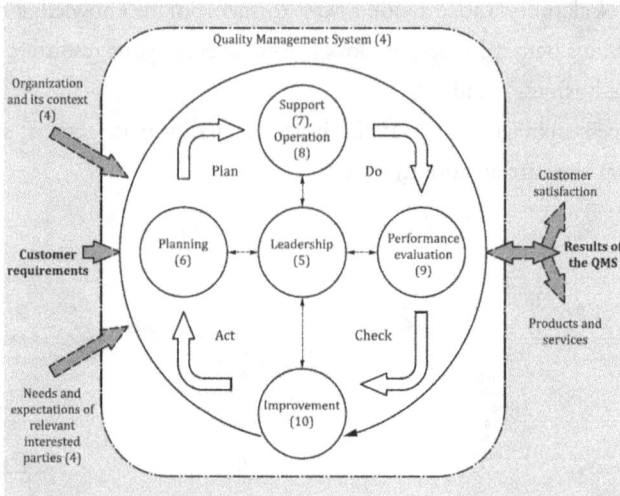

Figure 11.6 Representation of the structure of ISO 9001 in the PDCA cycle[36]

The standard can fit into one PDCA cycle—the numbers in Figure 11.7 refer to the clauses of the standard.

There is the basis of a continuous improvement cycle to the whole management system standard and the integration of the other elements of quality that we have already touched on will provide the necessary resources for this (see Figure 11.7).

This PDCA cycle view is complementary to the process flow view of the core business given in a valuable free document available from the ISO Technical Committee responsible for ISO 9001.[37]

---

[35]See C3 commerce, p. 56 in "Management System Specification and Guidance MSS 1000:2014," CQI Integrated Management SIG. https://www.integratedmanagement .info/mss-1000.

[36]See Figure 2, p. viii, in ISO 9001:2015, "Quality Management Systems—Requirements."

[37]See ISO/TC 176/SC 2/, "ISO 9000 Introduction and Support Package: Guidance on the Concept and Use of the Process Approach for management systems." https:// www.iso.org/files/live/sites/isoorg/files/archive/pdf/en/04_concept_and_use_of_the_ process_approach_for_management_systems.pdf.

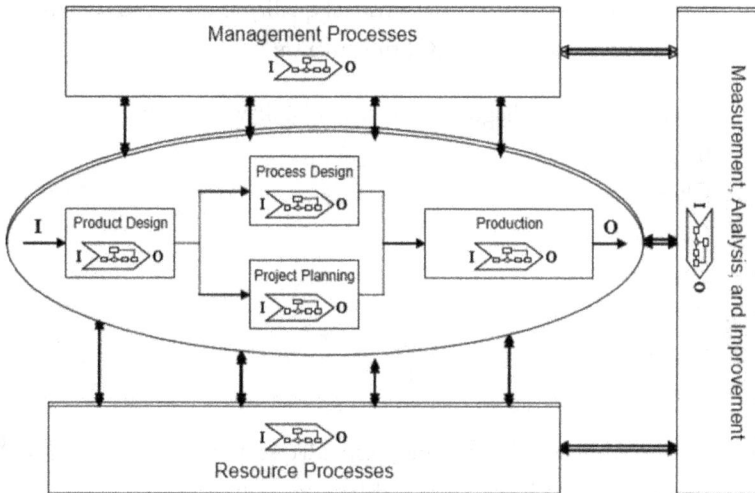

Figure 11.7 Example of a process sequence and its interactions[38]

We develop this further below in Chapter 13 Quality management and look at the promoted and perceived benefits, and risks, of how standards are used in quality management systems.

Statistical Quality and Process Control

The control of the processes in an organization is central to its success and, as we have already addressed from the outset, variation is the potential enemy of consistent quality and so Statistical Quality and Process Control (SPC and SQC) are vital tools to be deployed in the achievement of quality.

We have already mentioned the use of attributes and variable sampling schemes (see Chapter 3, The central role of specification) in the application of statistics to product acceptance. This is statistical quality control—statistics applied to process output—but the terms are often used interchangeably.[39] Our discussion there centered on operating curves and sampling errors.

---

[38]See Figure 4, p. 7 in ISO/TC 176/SC 2/, "ISO 9000 Introduction and Support Package: Guidance on the Concept and Use of the Process Approach for management systems." https://www.iso.org/files/live/sites/isoorg/files/archive/pdf/en/04_concept_and_use_of_the_process_approach_for_management_systems.pdf.

[39]See American Society for Quality—ASQ, "What is Statistical Process Control." https://asq.org/quality-resources/statistical-process-control.

The key core components of statistical quality and process control are the seven tools defined by Dr. Kaoru Ishikawa:[40]

1. Cause-and-effect diagram (also called Ishikawa diagram or fishbone diagram)
2. Check sheet
3. Control chart
4. Histogram
5. Pareto chart
6. Scatter diagram
7. Stratification

ASQ provides a set of useful templates, with case studies, for each of these.[41]

The control chart is the most well-known application and figures centrally in the NHS improvement approach.[42] A minimum run length is necessary to establish the base line, and this can be a problem in short run lengths and alternative approaches are necessary.[43] The golden rule again is "to select process control items to chart, not as a substitute for inspection or testing, but that provide the maximum amount of information on the state of the process at a minimum cost."[44] The Cusum or moving average charts are useful charts.[45] ISO also offers SPC/SQC best practice guidelines.[46]

---

[40]K. Ishikawa. "Guide to Quality Control," Asian Productivity Organization; Highlighting edition (1991), ASIN: B004W5A0CC.

[41]See American Society for Quality—ASQ. "The 7 Basic Quality Tools for Process Improvement." https://asq.org/quality-resources/seven-basic-quality-tools.

[42]See NHS Improvement. October 2011. "An Overview of Statistical Process Control (SPC)." https://www.england.nhs.uk/improvement-hub/wp-content/uploads/sites/44/2017/11/An-Overview-of-Statistical-Process-Control-SPC.pdf and NHS Improvement. "Statistical Process Control." https://improvement.nhs.uk/documents/2171/statistical-process-control.pdf.

[43]See T. Pyzdek. April 1993. "Process Control for Short and Small Runs," *Quality Progress*, pp. 51-60.

[44]See T. Pyzdek. April 1993. "Process Control for Short and Small Runs," *Quality Progress*, pp. 51-60.

[45]See ISO 7870, "ISO 7870-4:2011 Control Charts—Part 4: Cumulative Sum Charts." https://www.iso.org/search.html?q=7870&hPP=10&idx=all_en&p=0.

[46]See ISO 11462, "ISO 11462-1:2001(en) Guidelines for Implementation of Statistical Process Control (SPC)—Part 1: Elements of SPC." https://www.iso.org/obp/ui/#iso:std:33381:en.

The focus should be on variation reduction because the manufacturing specification for the product can never be tighter than the capability of the process responsible for its manufacture.[47] The variation is not always expressed just as common and special cause. Hare adds a further category to common—structural (Figure 11.8):

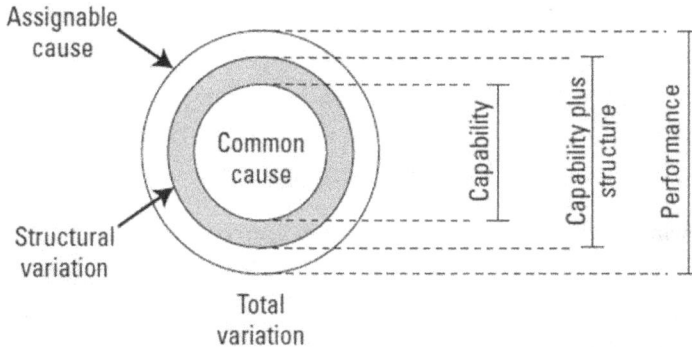

Figure 11.8 is labeled with: Assignable cause, Common cause, Structural variation, Total variation, Capability, Capability plus structure, Performance

Figure 11.8 Understanding sources of variation[48]
Source: Hare, Lynne B. "Chicken Soup for Processes—Understanding process variation is a prerequisite to using SPC." Quality Progress, August 2001, pp.76–79, http://asq.org/pub/qualityprogress/past/0801/qp0801stats.pdf

Reprinted with permission from *Quality Progress* © 2001 ASQ, www.asq.org
All rights reserved. No further distribution allowed without permission.

Structural variation she assigns to differences between, for example, filler heads—another example would be mold cavities in a die. The capability element is the repeatability under identical conditions, and the capability plus structure is analogous to the addition of a reproducibility contribution. We will see this kind of assignment later in measurement uncertainty (see Chapter 19).

The aim of control is to know that it will be possible to operate the process such that output is consistent within the control limits that can be established from assessing the variability encompassing plain repeatability and other structural elements such as multiple cavities and dies.[49]

---

[47]See L.B. Hare. August 2001. "Chicken Soup for Processes—Understanding Process Variation is a Prerequisite to using SPC," *Quality Progress*, pp. 76-79. http://asq.org/pub/qualityprogress/past/0801/qp0801stats.pdf and W.H. Woodhall. October 2000. "Controversies and Contradictions in Statistical Process Control." *Journal of Quality Technology* 32, no. 4. http://asq.org/pub/jqt/past/vol32_issue4/qtec-341.pdf.
[48]See Figure 1 in L.B. Hare. August 2001. "Chicken Soup for Processes—Understanding Process Variation is a Prerequisite to Using SPC," *Quality Progress*, pp. 76-79. http://asq.org/pub/qualityprogress/past/0801/qp0801stats.pdf.
[49]See L. Hare. July 2003. "SPC: From Chaos to Wiping the Floor," *Quality Progress*, pp. 58-63. http://asq.org/pub/qualityprogress/past/0703/qp0703hare.pdf.

The process may comprise several steps and different technical operations and these will all have their contribution to the final product and service quality.[50]

Statistical Process Control addressing the acceptable minimal variation in the product across all critical fabrication processes is the aim and automatic process monitoring and control provide the foundation for computer integrated manufacturing that lead to control to specification and minimal waste.[51]

Process Management

Knowing where to apply controls requires us to understand our processes and how they work. This extends to showing how they link together.

Processes are at the heart of an organization's management system and the following are the best practice requirements now recognized in the international standard:

"The organization shall determine the processes needed for the quality management system and their application throughout the organization, and shall:

A) determine the inputs required and the outputs expected from these processes;
B) determine the sequence and interaction of these processes;
C) determine and apply the criteria and methods (including monitoring, measurements, and related performance indicators) needed to ensure the effective operation and control of these processes;

[50]See J. Oakland and R.J. Oakland. October 22, 2018. *Statistical Process Control*, 7th ed. (New York, NY: Routledge), ISBN-10: 1138064262, ISBN-13: 978-1138064263 and D.C. *Montgomery. Statistical Quality Control: A Modern Introduction*, 7th ed. (New York, NY: John Wiley & Sons); International Student Version edition (August 7, 2012), ISBN-10: 1118322576, ISBN-13: 978-1118322574.
[51]See L.H. Andersen. August 1990. "Controlling Variation is Key to Manufacturing Success," *Quality Progress*, pp. 91-93; J. Muelaner. October 31, 2019. "An Introduction to Statistical Process Control (SPC)—Keeping an Eye on the Big Picture." *Quality Digest*. https://www.qualitydigest.com/print/32965 and https://www.qualitydigest.com/inside/management-article/introduction-statistical-process-control-spc-102419.html.

D) determine the resources needed for these processes and ensure their availability;

E) assign the responsibilities and authorities for these processes;

F) address the risks and opportunities as determined in accordance with the requirements of (clause) 6.1 (of the standard);

G) evaluate these processes and implement any changes needed to ensure that these processes achieve their intended results;

H) improve the processes and the quality management system."[52]

Mapping Processes

There is a vast range of mapping techniques and many of them come from information system design and development and many, but by no means all, deal only with the information flows about the inputs and outputs without explicitly describing and defining these as well.

There are many useful works[53]. All show the importance of simplifying the process flow with cross functional flow diagrams—or something very close to them. The vital lesson is that everyone must understand, agree, and use the same modelling/descriptive tools in the same way if they are going to succeed in establishing a process model that everyone can share and use.

The methods most widely used are based on the Unified Modelling Language (UML) and the use case diagram, alongside cross-functional flow charts to show linking of atomic processes, is the most popular diagram. All of these have utility and value in describing process flows and the information about inputs and outputs.

---

[52]See clause 4.4.1 in ISO 9001:2015, "Quality Management Systems—Requirements."

[53]See M. Havey. 2005. *Essential Business Process Modelling* (Newton, MA: O'Reilly Media Inc), ISBN-10: 9780596008437, ISBN-13: 978-0596008437, ASIN: 0596008430; J. Holt. 2005. *A Pragmatic Guide to Business Process Modelling* (London: The British Computer Society), ISBN 1-902505-66-2; R. Darmelio. May 17, 2011. *The Basics of Process Mapping*, 2nd ed. (New York, NY: Routledge), ISBN-10: 9781563273766, ISBN-13: 978-1563273766, ASIN: 1563273764; D. Paul, J. Cadle, and D. Yeates (eds.), 2014. "Business Analysis," BCS Learning and Development First Floor, Block D, North Star House, North Star Avenue, Swindon, SN2 1FA, UK, ISBN 978-1-78017-277-4.

When object orientation is aligned with Use Case diagrams then real-world objects and the information they contain and the behaviors that are inherent become more visible—but the emphasis is still, quite properly for the aims and objectives involved, on information flows.[54] Built into Object Technology is the idea of grouping into classes and defining properties at a class level and allowing these to be inherited by instances of the object. There is an obvious, immediate, and important linking to specifications and the characteristics and measurement and monitoring criteria of product and service items that are manufactured or provided in accordance with specifications.

A front page to the management system can be followed with linked cross functional flowcharts (Figure 11.9).

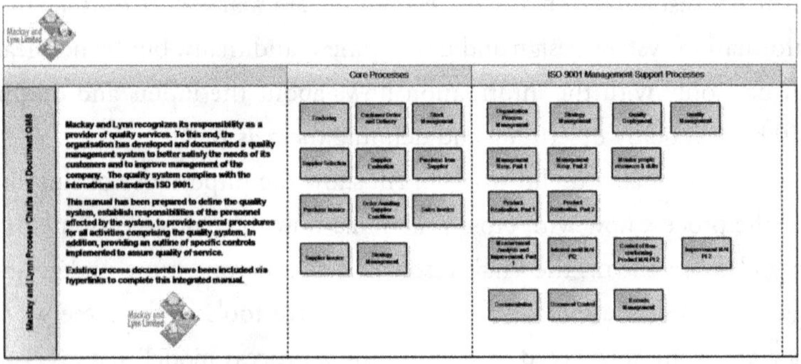

Figure 11.9 Management system front page

Linked cross functional flowcharts example (Figure 11.10):

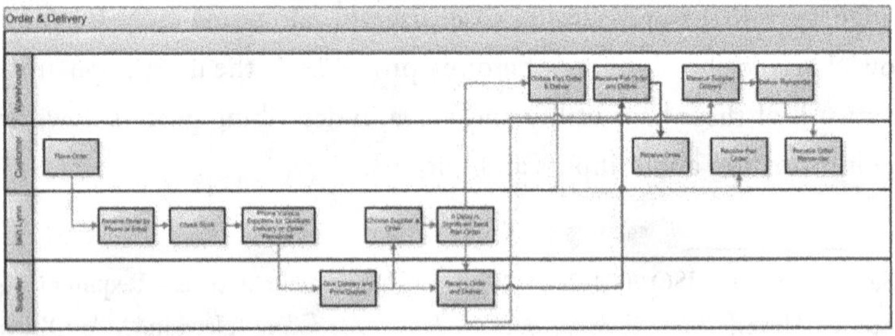

Figure 11.10 Order and delivery flowchart

---

[54]See I. Jacobson, M. Ericsson, and A. Jacobson. September 28, 1994. *The Object Advantage—Business Process Reengineering with Object Technology* (Boston, MA: Addison Wesley), ISBN-10: 0201422891, ISBN-13: 978-0201422894; I. Jacobson, M. Christerson, P. Jonsson, and G. Overgaard. June 30, 1992. *Object-Oriented Software Engineering—A Use Case Driven Approach*, 1st ed. (Boston, MA: Addison-Wesley Professional), ISBN-10: 0201544350, ISBN-13: 978-0201544350.

The detail of what is delivered and by whowould make the chart too complex and fussy and render it almost valueless and for that we need the kind of chart shown in below in 'Inputs, Outputs, and Accountability', in fig 11.11, and in the Appendix – see Example Process Flowchart.

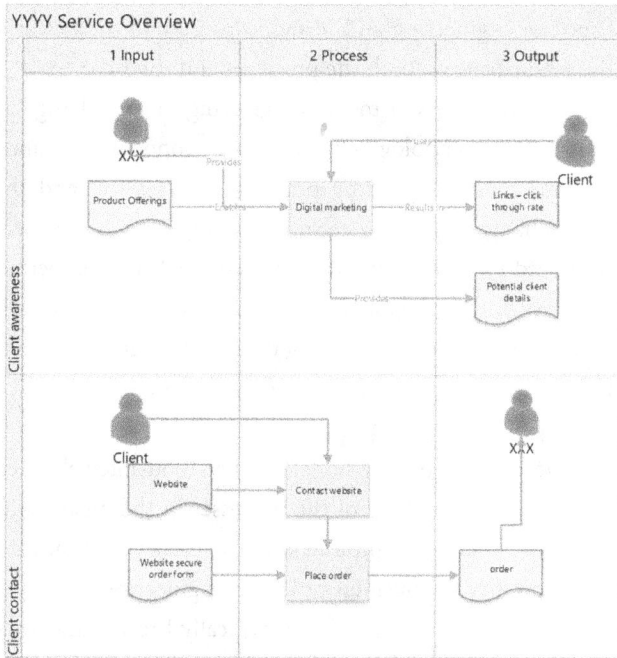

Figure 11.11 Input—process—output cross-functional flowchart–vertical

Inputs, Outputs, and Accountability

Greater detail can easily be added with a simple three-column input, process, and output flowchart that is a simplified cross-functional chart, analogous to the USE CASE chart 3 column-type approach and that also shows material and information inputs and outputs and personal involvement and responsibility as well. This is also a form of what is known as a supplier, input, process, output, and customer (SIPOC) chart (Figure 11.11).[55]

---

[55]See C.B. Montano, and G.H. Utter. August 1999. "Total Quality Management In Higher Education—An Application of Quality Improvement in a Iniversity," *Quality Progress*, pp. 52-59. http://asq.org/data/subscriptions/qp/1999/0899/qp0899montano.pdf; K. Simon. "SIPOC Diagram," *ISixSigma*. https://www.isixsigma.com/tools-templates/sipoc-copis/sipoc-diagram/.

See Appendix pp. 190–193, Example process flowchart for a fuller example that shows material as well as information inputs and outputs.

Business Process Engineering and Reengineering

Business process engineering and reengineering build on a clear knowledge of the whole process, both the processes and their context.

The drivers are perceived to be the growing rate of change and development of new technologies which open opportunities and needs for fresh approaches to providing products and services and the need for structural change in core processes and competencies in order to use these.[56] The need to respond to external pressures from competition and societal demands and the opportunities identified by the organization can easily combine to provide a compelling case for radical change.

The four major components have been identified as:

1. A greater focus on the organization's customers (both internal and external)
2. A fundamental rethinking of the processes in the organization that lead to improvements in productivity and cycle time (known as process improvement or business process reengineering)
3. A structural reorganization, which typically breaks functional hierarchies into cross-functional teams, such as those engaged in team building and organizational development activity.
4. New information and measurement systems, which use the latest technology to drive improved data distribution and decision-making, such as quality and information technology.

The routes to achieving these changes in an effective and integrated manner is highly challenging and the most quoted authority in this area—Michael Hammer estimates that as many as 50–70% of the organizations that attempt reengineering do not achieve the results they aimed for.[57]

---

[56]See J.N. Lowenthal. January 1994. "Reengineering the Organization: A Step-by-Step Approach to Corporate Revitilization—Part 1," *Quality Progress*, pp. 93-95.

[57]See Chapter 13, p. 221 in M. Hammer and J. Champy. August 23, 2001. *Reengineering the Corporation: A Manifesto for Business Revolution*, 3rd ed. (Nicholas Brealey Publishing), 272 pages, ISBN-10: 1857880978, ISBN-13: 978-1857880977.

The working definition proposed by Lowenthal focuses on the radical and dramatic change aims:

"The fundamental rethinking and redesign of operating processes and organizational structures, focused on the organization's core competencies, to achieve dramatic improvements in organizational performance."[58]

Redesigning the way work flows can, and often does, lead to system and infrastructure changes and throws a focus on core competencies. "Core competencies are its collective knowledge, including the processes by which it coordinates and integrates diverse production skills and multiple streams of technology."[59] The changes in work flows, waste reduction, combining process steps, and eliminating repetitive tasks all lead to a level of change that challenge and require change in the corporate culture (see also Chapter 23 Quality and management consultancy and Chapter 24 Quality, faith and transcendent values).

Business Process Reengineering (BPR)—the reengineering process for the organization that Lowenthal describes must have a sound strategic external context and requires careful preparation and planning, followed by design of the change before execution and evaluation.[60]

Both Lowenthal[61] and Hammer[62] provide a wealth of case studies which illustrate the problems, pitfalls, challenges, and ingredients for success. Hammer summarizes his lessons in the final chapter "Succeeding in reengineering" in approaches to avoid[63]:

---

[58]See J.N. Lowenthal. February 1994. "Reengineering the Organization: A Step-by-Step Approach to Corporate Revitilization—Part 2," *Quality Progress*, pp. 61-63; J.N. Lowenthal. January 1, 1994. "Re-engineering the Organization: A Step-By-Step Approach to Corporate Revitalization," Brown (William C.) Co, U.S., 185 pages, ISBN-10: 0873892585, ISBN-13: 978-0873892582.

[59]Ibid.

[60]Ibid.

[61]See J.N. Lowenthal. January 1, 1994. "Re-engineering the Organization: A Step-by-Step Approach to Corporate Revitalization," Brown (William C.) Co, U.S., 185 pages, ISBN-10: 0873892585, ISBN-13: 978-0873892582.

[62]See M. Hammer and J. Champy. August 23, 2001. *Reengineering the Corporation: A Manifesto for Business Revolution*, 3rd ed., (Nicholas Brealey Publishing), 272 pages, ISBN-10: 1857880978, ISBN-13: 978-1857880977.

[63]See Ibid., Chapter 13, page 220.

- Try to fix the process instead of changing it;
- Don't focus on the business processes;
- Ignore everything except process redesign;
- Neglect people's values and beliefs;
- Be willing to settle for minor result;
- Quit too early;
- Place prior constraints on the definition of the problem and the scope of the reengineering effort;
- Allow existing corporate cultures and management attitudes to prevent reengineering from getting started;
- Try to make reengineering work from the bottom up;
- Assign someone who doesn't understand reengineering to lead the effort;
- Skimp on the resources devoted to reengineering;
- Bury engineering in the middle of the corporate agenda;
- Dissipate energy across a great many reengineering projects;
- Attempt to reengineer when the CEO is two years away from retirement;
- Fail to distinguish reengineering from other business improvement programmes;
- Concentrate exclusively on design;
- Try to make reengineering happen without making anyone unhappy;
- Pull back when people resist making reengineering's changes;
- Drag the effort out.

From which it is easy to see the positive statements.

A starting knowledge in depth of the whole process and the major rate-limiting steps will reveal whether there are any inherent rate-limiting steps that are so closely defined and externally regulated that set clear limits to the scale of reengineering that is possible. Knowledge of these steps and careful research into possible safe, acceptable, and effective change may open the timetable to stunning change.

CHAPTER 12

Quality Management

Responsibility

Until the latest version of the foundation international standard for quality management systems requirements,[1] there was a requirement to have a management representative role[2]—a focus for the responsibility.

The CQI draws out the issues on responsibility as they look behind the changes:

"Top management is required to demonstrate that they engage in key quality management system activities as opposed to simply ensuring that these activities occur. This means that there is a need for top management to be actively involved in the operation of their quality management system. The removal of all references to the role of "management representative" reinforces the requirement to see quality management systems embedded into routine business operations, rather than operating as an independent system in its own right with its own specialist management structure and processes."[3]

And the changes that need to be made resulting from that: "While there is no requirement in ISO 9001:2015 for a management representative, this does not prevent the organization from choosing to retain this role if they so wish. Be aware, however, that some of the duties (responsibilities) traditionally assigned to the management representative by top

---

[1] See ISO 9001:2015, "Quality Management Systems—Requirements."
[2] See clause 5.5.2 in ISO 9001:2008, "Quality Management Systems—Requirements."
[3] See CQI. "CQI ISO 9001:2015—Understanding the International Standard," p. 16. https://www.amazon.co.uk/ISO-9001-Understanding-International-Standard-ebook/dp/B07B8T9Y78/ref=sr_1_1?dchild=1&qid=1586165356&refinements=p_2 7%3AThe+Chartered+Quality+Institute&s=books&sr=1-1&text=The+Chartered+Q uality+Institute.

management will, in future, need to be undertaken directly by top management themselves."[4]

This will have ramifications for top management who were not directly taking responsibility: "For those where the most senior members of the organization currently play an active role in driving its quality management system forward, the changes will simply be a formalization of what is happening now. However, for those organizations where top management have effectively devolved responsibility for their quality management system to their management representative, the ramifications of the ISO 9001:2015 changes will be significantly greater.

ISO 9001:2015 requires top management to be much more "hands on" with respect to their quality management systems than ISO 9001:2008 does. Where the word "ensuring" is used in subclause 5.1.1, top management may still assign this task to others for completion, i.e. delegation plus confirmation. Where the words "promoting," "taking," "engaging," or "supporting" appear, these activities cannot be assigned and must be undertaken by top management themselves.

Implementers will need to make top management aware of the new requirements, and the fact that they will now be audited as a matter of routine.

Note: when ISO 9001:2015 uses the term "top management," it is referring to a person or a group of people at the highest level within an organization, i.e. the people who coordinate, direct, and control the organization."[5]

This is a major shift in emphasis in this increasingly business-centric emphasis standard.

Accountability, Transparency

There is a shift in accountability as a result. "This starts with their taking accountability for the effectiveness of their organization's quality management system. They must ensure that their organization's quality policy and quality objectives are consistent with the organization's overall

---

[4]Ibid., p. 17.
[5]Ibid., p. 17.

strategic direction and the context in which the organization is operating. They must also work alongside their people in order to ensure that the quality objectives are achieved. In addition, top management must ensure that the quality policy is communicated, understood, and applied across the organization.

Top management must also ensure that quality management system requirements are integral to the organization's business processes—that is, the quality management system must not be just a "bolt on". They must promote awareness and the adoption of the use of both the "process approach" and "risk-based thinking" and must make sure that the resources required for the effective operation of the quality management system are made available.

Top management must stress the importance of effective quality management and of conforming to the requirements of the quality management system. They must make sure that the quality management system is achieving the results intended and must lead people to contribute to the effective operation of the system. They must drive continual improvement and develop leadership in their managers."[6]

A conclusion of the same report is that activities such as identifying stake holders (referred to as "interested parties") may have to be demonstrable and transparent so there is overall a move also to greater transparency.

Triple Bottom Line, Internal Values, and Management of Behavior, Corruption

The originator of the term "triple bottom line" (TBL) acknowledges that it has been adopted without real reflection on its aims: "A decade ago, *The Economist* was already signaling that the term had become part of the business lexicon. As the magazine explained, the (TBL) approach, "aims to measure the financial, social, and environmental performance of the corporation over a period of time. Only a company that produces a TBL is taking account of the full cost involved in doing business."

---

[6]Ibid., p. 16.

Well yes... but the original idea was wider still, encouraging businesses to track and manage economic (not just financial), social, and environmental value added—or destroyed. This idea infused platforms like the Global Reporting Initiative (GRI) and Dow Jones Sustainability Indexes (DJSI), influencing corporate accounting, stakeholder engagement, and, increasingly, strategy. But the TBL wasn't designed to be just an accounting tool. It was supposed to provoke deeper thinking about capitalism and its future, but many early adopters understood the concept as a balancing act, adopting a trade-off mentality."[7] The tendency to apply and use without real or full understanding is something we shall reflect on as part of a wider tendency to misuse standards.

The originator of the "triple bottom line" wanted "to provoke deeper thinking about capitalism and its future" and this at the heart of a central debate about internal values and management behaviour and related issues such as corruption.

There is no shortage of examples of questionable internal values and management behavior. "Enron Corp., Adelphia Communications Corp., Arthur Andersen, Tyco International and WorldCom Inc. are but some of the many scandals that have cast a chilling pall over the way business is conducted. These companies have given people the perception that corporations are amoral, corrupt, and lack both ethical leadership and a sense of social responsibility."[8] By way of contrast "... there are companies, such as SAS Institute, Google, Shell Oil Co., NEC Corp., and Procter & Gamble Co., that have committed themselves to a course of developing business models that accentuate ethical leadership, employee well-being, sustainability, and social responsibility. These companies believe this can be done without sacrificing profitability, revenue growth, and other areas of financial and performance excellence."[9]

---

[7] See J. Elkington. "25 Years Ago I Coined the Phrase 'Triple Bottom Line.' Here's Why It's Time to Rethink It." https://hbr.org/2018/06/25-years-ago-i-coined-the-phrase-triple-bottom-line-heres-why-im-giving-up-on-it.

[8] See L.W. Fry and J.W. Slocum Jr. 2008. "Maximizing the Triple Bottom Line through Spiritual Leadership," *Organizational Dynamics* 37, no. 1, pp. 86-96, ISSN: 0090-2616, doi:10.1016/j.orgd yn.2007.11.004. https://www.researchgate.net/publication/228618000_Maximizing_the_Triple_Bottom_Line_through_Spiritual_Leadership.

[9] Ibid.

The very models of business that are being implicitly challenged we consider further in Chapter 21 Quality—Unifying.

The issue of morals, ethics, and behavior flow into the culture of the organization. "People bring to work values and attitudes that drive their behavior. Core values reflect the moral principles that an individual considers to be important and act as guidelines for his or her decisions. These core values greatly determine what a person considers to be good or bad. In turn, they make up the foundation for moral principles that collectively form an organization's ethical system. Corporate culture stems from fundamental ethical values of top managers that affect employees' behaviors. World renowned organizational psychologist Edgar Schein defines corporate culture as the learned pattern of shared basic assumptions that employees and groups hold. Organizational culture significantly influences the way things are done. It influences the range of behaviors that members view as appropriate and provides them with a framework that influences their thinking and behavior. Cultures that are based on values of dishonesty, deceit, favoritism, and greed (e.g., Enron, WorldCom and Tyco International) can lead top managers to make choices that are injurious to key stakeholders. When altruistic values of respect, fairness, honesty, care, compassion, and the like are integral parts of an organization's culture, a culture of trust emerges."[10]

Although not raised in the foreword to standards, these considerations are foundational to effective use of standards and I believe that they lie at the root of the many failures in the use of standards.

Role and Effect of Standards

Plus and Minus

The largest determinant of whether any standard will play the role and have the effect of really embedding best practice and enabling serious improvement and creation of really effective organizations is the mindset at adoption, and if the reason for adoption is compulsion, and around 80 percent of organizations are required to adopt it by their customers, then the mindset is likely not to be optimal.

---

[10]Ibid.

Results from the wrong mindset are listed by Seddon[11] as the following:

1. ISO 9000 encourages organizations to act in ways which make things worse for their customers—doing things "right" as perceived in the standard, not the "right things for customers in the right way for them".
2. Quality by inspection is not quality—the quality is fixed by the time you get to inspection, all you can do is partition the poor quality as waste and, marginally, minimize the defects the customer will see.
3. ISO 9000 starts from the flawed presumption that work is best controlled by specifying and controlling procedures—"having documentation, that was often irrelevant and over specified and missing important features, for the sake of it";
4. The typical method of implementation is bound to cause suboptimization of performance—because it doesn't start with performance;
5. The standard relies too much on people's and, in particular, assessor's interpretation of quality—all too often the assessor has little or no relevant experience to draw on;
6. When people are subject to external controls, they will be inclined to pay attention only to those things which are affected by the controls—keeping the assessor happy can take over and displace keeping the customer happy;
7. ISO 9000 has discouraged managers from learning about the theory of a system and the theory of variation—there is understanding and there are concepts that are vital to underpinning a system;
8. ISO 9000 has failed to foster good customer-supplier relations—seeing the supplier relationship as primarily contractual and not part of your supply chain and in "your family" is the issue here.
9. Coercion does not foster learning—having to do it and using others to put it in place and others to assess is hardly conducive to learning.
10. As an intervention, ISO 90000 has not encouraged managers to think differently—division of roles and a system that was placed on people is not conducive to good management.

---

[11]See J. Seddon. September 15, 2000. *The Case Against ISO 9000*, 2nd ed. (Oak Tree Press), ISBN-10: 1860761736, ISBN-13: 978-1-8607-6173-7.

These were written for ISO 9001: 1994 but little changed until ISO 9001: 2015 and although there are significant changes, there is still too much potential in the wrong approach, not the standard itself, for real damage.

The arguments in defense of the standard from the same author lead us into the heart of the argument—the organization is a system and you need systems thinking, that especially include the people embedded in the system, and Seddon describes that as follows (Table 12.1) for each of the main system elements:

Table 12.1 Command and control vs system thinking[12]

	Command and control thinking	**Systems thinking**
Perspective	Top-down hierarchy, functional procedures.	Outside—in, process and "flow"
Attitude to customers	Contractual	What matters
Decision making	Separated from work	Integrated with work
Measurement	Outputs, targets, standards: related to budget	Co-operative
Attitude to suppliers	Contractual	Cooperative
Ethos	Control	Learning

These are attitudes of management and only to the extent that they appear to find succour in the standard, have they anything to do with the standard per se.

Seddon extended his table to this (Table 12.2) to show how 'Command and control thinking' compares to 'Systems thinking' for 'Perspective', 'Design' and each of the main system elements:

Seddon provides an introduction to variation and "common" and "special" causes, as a counter to just be manufacturing to specification limits, that we have already covered.

West and Cianfrani provide a review of the key clauses of ISO 9001:2015 and then stress that you have to go "above and beyond the requirements":—"Quality professionals must be concerned about complying with the requirements of ISO 9001:2015, but the job does not stop there.

To be successful, you need a sharp focus on developing and deploying processes that add value.

---

[12]Ibid.

Table 12.2 Command and control vs system thinking[13]

Command and control thinking		Systems thinking
Top down hierarchy, functional procedures.	**Perspective**	Outside—in, process and "flow"
Functional	**Design**	Demand, value, and flow
Separated from work	**Decision making**	Integrated with work
Outputs, targets, standards: related to budget	**Measurement**	Co-operative
Contractual	**Attitude to customers**	What matters?
Contractual	**Attitude to suppliers**	Cooperative
Manage people and budgets	**Role of management**	Act on the system
Control	**Ethos**	Learning
Reactive, projects	**Change**	Adaptive, integral
Extrinsic	**Motivation**	Intrinsic

These processes must be aligned with the mission, vision, and objectives of the organization to ensure its sustainability."[14]

ISO 9001 and its plusses and minuses evoke strong feelings say Castka and Corbett introducing a "review of more than 2,000 scientific studies on management systems standards whose findings have been published in a research monograph"[15]. They describe these feelings with: "You might think that ISO standards for management systems are too dry to

---

[13]See J. Seddon. October 1, 2003. "Freedom from Command & Control: A Better Way to Make the Work Work," Vanguard Consulting Ltd, ISBN-10: 0954618300, ISBN-13: 978-0954618308.

[14]See J.E. "Jack" West and C.A. Cianfrani. April 2017. "Standard Issues—Beyond the Requirements—ISO 9001 Compliance Alone Isn't Sufficient to Sustain an Organization," *Quality Progress*. http://asq.org/quality-progress/2017/04/standard-issues/ beyond-the-requirements.html.

[15]See P. Castka and C.J. Corbett. 2015. "Management Systems Standards: Diffusion, Impact and Governance of ISO 9000, ISO 14000, and Other Management Systems Standards." *Foundations and Trends in Technology and Operations Management* 7, no. 3-4, also Now Publishers Inc, 8 May 2015, ISBN-10: 1601988842, ISBN-13: 978-1-6019-8884-3.

evoke much passion. But the many derogatory Dilbert cartoons and other jokes—as well as heated discussions on LinkedIn groups and elsewhere—prove otherwise.

To what extent is this unflattering attention deserved? What do we actually know about these standards?"[16]
Sadly they summarize their findings with:

"More questions to answer

From this summary of the literature, we conclude there is enough ambiguity surrounding management systems standards that the cartoons, jokes, and discussions referred to earlier do reflect the state of the research.

Although there is reason for some cautious optimism about the over-all average effect of standards on organizational performance, there is also reason for some concern about the lack of consistency—among organizations and auditors."[17]

So when we come to the extremes expressed by Christopher Paris[18] we can be prepared for the truth behind the extreme characterization of situation, motive, and behaviour – which looks all too sadly all too often to be based on some very questionable organizational and regulatory behavior.

He also highlights many positive aspects of the latest version of the standard amid some very practical guidance on avoiding the worst of the pitfalls.

The introduction to the standard at the start of the requirements covers the Context Of The Organization (COTO as Paris labels it) and he concludes "The goal of the COTO clauses isn't clear at the outset, and many assume it is just so the organization gets a better sense of itself. This isn't quite true; in fact, there's another goal entirely, and I'll cast aside all professional business book-writing etiquette and jump to the spoiler:

---

[16]P. Castka and C.J. Corbett. January 2018. "Standards—No Joking Matter—Research Analyzes Management Systems Standards and the Implications for Managers and Auditing Bodies," *Quality Progress*, pp. 32-37. http://asq.org/quality-progress/2018/01/standards/no-joking-matter.html.

[17]Ibid.

[18]See C. Paris. April 12, 2019. "Surviving ISO 9001: 2015," Oxebridge Quality Resources International; 2nd edition, ASIN: B07QLFPGSK.

COTO isn't about the middle steps, even if those take the most effort. The goal is the development of a strategic direction for the organization… remember, all of them are intended to inform top management of its strategic direction."

Here, Figure 12.1, is one of the "middle" steps listing internal and external stakeholder with a justification providing further description and then providing for listing their concerns.

Stakeholder	Internal / External	Reason for inclusion	Issues of Concern
Employees	Internal	Directly responsible for manufacture of products	1. Expect to be paid 2. Expect not to die at work 3. Expect to be trained 4. Need proper equipment
Suppliers	External	Responsible for providing critical raw materials and services	1. Expect to be paid, too 2. Need us to specify clearly what we want 3. Need adequate time to fulfill orders
Dept. of Health	External	Enforces regulations regarding safety of our products	1. State law says we can't poison people, apparently 2. We must pass DOH audits every year

Figure 12.1 Stakeholders or interested parties and issues or requirements[19]

The linking of processes to the standard, shown for a small machine shop, is helpful and there is a hotel/catering example as well.[20] The mapping between the core business and the best practice in the standard enables a business-centric approach to management system design (Table 12.3).

There are risks, severe and serious very often, arising from misunderstanding and misapplication of standards which are necessarily couched in language that is generalized for application to specific situations.

---

[19]Ibid.
[20]Ibid.

Table 12.3 Linking of processes to the standard[21]

Process	Applicable ISO 9001:2015 clause(s)
QMS administration	4.0 Context of the Organization 5.0 Leadership 6.0 Planning 7.0 Support 9.3 Management review
Improvement	9.1 Monitoring, measurement, analysis and evaluation 10.0 Improvement
Internal auditing	9.2 Internal audit
Sales, quoting, and order entry	8.1 Operational planning and control 8.2 Requirements for products and services 8.3 Design and development of products and services
Purchasing	8.4 Control of externally provided processes, products, and services
Receiving	8.4 Control of externally provided processes, products, and services 8.5.2 Identification and traceability 8.5.4 Preservation 8.7 Control of nonconforming outputs
Manufacturing	8.5 Production and service provision (all)
Shipping	8.5.2 Identification and traceability 8.5.4 Preservation 8.6 Release of products and services 8.7 Control of nonconforming outputs

Like Pilgrim we need to be aware of the pitfalls and dangers and the damage that is possible through less than the very best of understanding, motivation, and commitment.

Given all that however, as the critics and skeptics acknowledge, there are gems for the taking to enrich and adorn the organization and genuinely enable effective goal management and continuous improvement.

Codifying Best Practice

Context of the Organization—Clause 4

We have the witness of a very prominent critic that the strategic management dimension of clause 4 is of real value.

---

[21]Ibid.

Leadership—Clause 5

We have already pointed out that anyone exercising influence is in a position of leadership irrespective of whether this is reflected in the wording of the job role—which it ought to be—see Chapter 5, Leadership and the individual, and introduced this chapter with the emphasis on the leadership responsibilities of top management.

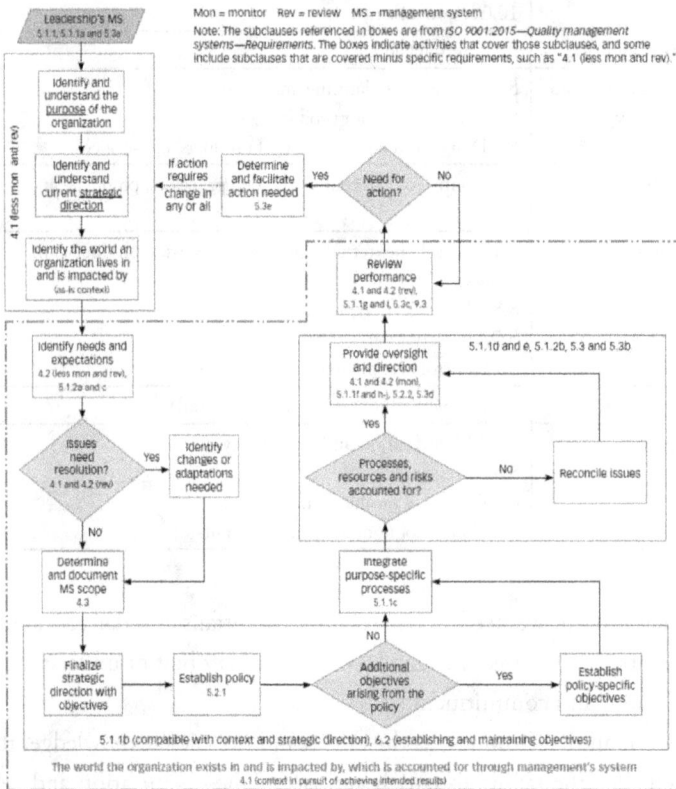

Figure 12.2 Leadership seen through ISO 9001:2015[22]
Source: Freeman, Robert and Jennifer Drown. "Leading the Way Determining leadership's role in ISO 9001:2015." Quality Progress, October 2016, pp. 16–20, http://asq.org/quality-progress/2016/10/auditing/leading-the-way.html

This flowchart (see Figure 12.2, Leadership seen through ISO 9001:2015) shows the dimensions of leadership in the standard, that it

---

[22]See R. Freeman and J. Drown. October 2016. "Leading the Way Determining Leadership's Role in ISO 9001:2015," Quality Progress, pp. 16-20. http://asq.org/quality-progress/2016/10/auditing/leading-the-way.html.

is a cycle with feedback to management review and strategic direction. Objectives and policy are established as a basis for processes and before oversight and review of performance—as you would expect in the whole PDCA sequence.

In safety situations a particular model of leadership is required (Figure 12.3):

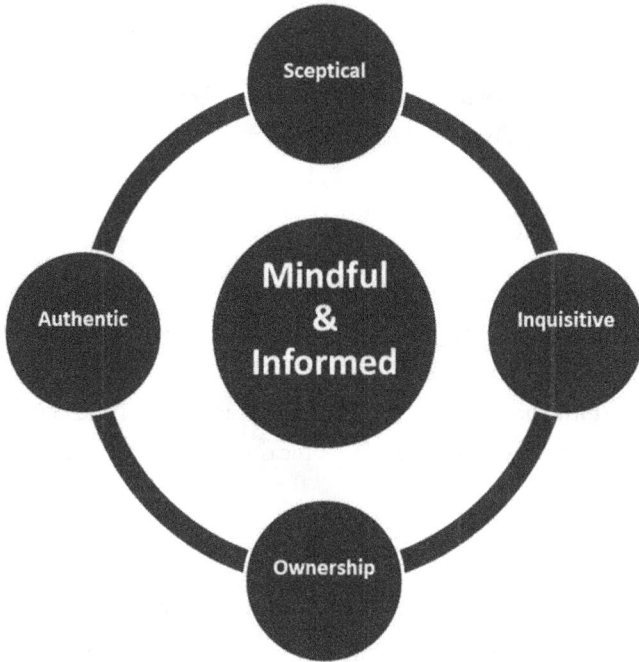

Figure 12.3 Informed mindful safety leadership[23]

A committed and thoughtful approach can make for positive outcomes as shown in the relative success of the safety approach in the 2012 Olympics—see Chapter 8, Quality, safety and environment go together above.

Policy Management—Clause 5.2

Expresses strategic direction and values as well as the foundation of process and procedure they have.

---

[23]See T. Ingram. "Project Risk Management." http://www.strategic-safety-consultants.com.

Communication—Clause 5.2.2 and 7.4

There is a clearer emphasis on communication in the current standard. "The new clause is more prescriptive in respect of the mechanics of the communication; ISO 9001:2008 sub-clause 5.5.3 refers to the need for "communication to take place" whereas ISO 9001:2015 clause 7.4 requires the organization to determine on what it will communicate, when it will communicate, with whom it will communicate, how it will communicate, and who communicates."[24]

There is a process which in all channels—speech and body language, needs to include feedback and listening.[25]

Objectives—Clause 6.2

Objectives are the expression of what we are aiming for and, as the standard makes clear, need deploying "at relevant functions, levels, and processes"[26] in the organization[27].

The performance must be measurable and monitored and one of the worldwide authorities on performance measurement is Stacey Barr.[28]

Knowledge

"This is a new requirement aimed at ensuring that an organization takes steps to capture and preserve knowledge, which is necessary for the effective operation of their processes and for ensuring the conformity of their products and services."[29]

I can certainly remember many occasions in my career when I wondered how an organization was going to cope with the loss of so many experienced people with little or no effort to capture and preserve their

---

[24]See CQI. "CQI ISO 9001:2015—Understanding the International Standard," p. 31.
[25]See D.L. Hopen. June 1991. "The Process of Communication," *Quality Progress*, pp. 48-50.
[26]See clause 6.2.1 in ISO 9001:2015, "Quality Management Systems—Requirements."
[27]See also B. Stein. July 1991. "Management by Quality Objectives," *Quality Progress*, pp. 78-80.
[28]https://www.staceybarr.com/.
[29]See CQI. "CQI ISO 9001:2015—Understanding the International Standard," p. 28.

experience and knowledge. These persons are often the subject matter experts and internal trainers and with their loss goes the essential knowledge for the organization that resided in them.[30] And, more recently, pointing out how exposed a single management person organization was to the possible loss of the knowledge residing in that person.

"The organization must re-assess the extent of its organizational knowledge if it is considering making changes to its quality management systems in response to changing needs or trends in its operational environment. The organization needs to keep organizational knowledge current and if it is deemed insufficient then the organization must take steps to enhance it. This is an attempt to ensure that organizations make informed decisions in respect of updates to their quality management systems.

Note 1 identifies types of organizational knowledge while Note 2 identifies potential sources of organizational knowledge."[31]

Continuous professional development clearly links in with this management topic.

There is a definition of profound knowledge that was put forward by Deming and which offers a base line for organizational knowledge—see Table 12.4.

Accreditation and certification

This causes confusion and the terms are often used interchangeably, but they are not the same at all, and not interchangeable.

The UK national competent authority for product and service accreditation and certification describes it by reference to an article by its marketing manager:

"The terms accreditation and certification are often used interchangeably and occasionally together. Despite the obvious confusion this can cause, the difference between the two distinct quality management processes can be easily explained. Certification represents a written assurance by a third party of the conformity of a product, process, or service to

---

[30]See P.E. Boyers. May 2017. "Back to Basics—Maintaining Knowledge—How ISO 9001:2015 is Helping Organizations Remember Their Future," *Quality Progress*, p. 64. http://asq.org/quality-progress/2017/05/back-to-basics/maintaining-knowledge.html.
[31]See CQI. "CQI ISO 9001:2015—Understanding the International Standard," p. 28.

Table 12.4 Components of the system of profound knowledge[32]

Knowledge about variation	Psychology (psychology of individuals, groups, society, and change)
• Awareness that there will always be variation. • Appreciation of a stable system and capability. • Some understanding of special causes and common causes of variation. • Some understanding of the costly mistake of tampering. • Use of data requires knowledge about the different sources of uncertainty. • Use of data requires understanding of the distinction between enumerative studies (information about the framework) and analytic problems (results of a test or experiment must be inferred to the future—prediction).	• Psychology helps the understanding of people and interactions between people. • People are different from one another. • People are born with a natural inclination to learn. • People learn in different ways and at different speeds. • People are born with a need for relationships with other people and a need for love and esteem from others. • There are intrinsic and extrinsic sources of motivation. • Total submission to extrinsic motivation leads to destruction of the individual. • All people are motivated to a different degree extrinsically and intrinsically.
Theory of knowledge	**Appreciation for a system**
• Management is prediction. • Knowledge is built on theory. • Information is not knowledge. • Rational prediction requires theory. • Interpretation of data from a test or experiment is prediction. • There is a need for operational definitions. • Enlargement of a committee is not a reliable way to acquire knowledge.	• A system must have an aim. • A system includes the future and competitors. • The aim is a value judgment. • A system must be managed—it will not manage itself. • Left to themselves in the Western world, the components become selfish, competitive, and thus destroy the system. • The bigger the system, the more difficult to manage. What are the boundaries of the system? • A system cannot understand itself and needs guidance from outside. • The greater the interdependence between components, the greater the need for cooperation among them. • Management must manage the interdependence between components toward the aim of the system.

---

[32]See R.D. Moen and C.L. Norman. June 2016. "Quality History—Always Applicable Deming's System of Profound Knowledge Remains Relevant for Management and Quality Professionals Today," *Quality Progress*, pp. 46-53. http://asq.org/quality-progress/2016/06/basic-quality/always-applicable.pdf.

specified requirements. Accreditation, on the other hand, is the formal recognition by an authoritative body of competencies to work to specified standards. All accreditation standards include the principles of quality management systems, such as those found in the well-recognized ISO 9001 QMS standard. It is the ability to demonstrate technical competence that puts accredited certification on a level above non-accredited certification.

In effect, certification is the third-party endorsement of an organization's systems or products, while accreditation is an independent third-party endorsement of the certification. The United Kingdom Accreditation Service (UKAS) is the national accreditation body for the UK. Its role is to assess organizations that are providing testing, inspection, calibration, and certification services (collectively known as conformity assessment bodies) against internationally recognized standards. In the UK, if conformity assessment bodies are the watchmen, then UKAS watches the watchmen.

Another crucial difference between accreditation and certification relates to the activities it covers. Organizations receive accreditation for specific activities whereas certification relates to the company as a whole. For example, if you are looking to test air leakage of a building, it would be best to choose an organization that has been accredited against the testing standard ISO 17025 rather than one that has a general quality certification of ISO 9001. Further, the ISO 17025 testing activities themselves are tightly defined, so it is advisable to check the organization's schedule of accreditation closely; one that holds ISO 17025 accreditation for sound-proof testing would not necessarily hold ISO 17025 accreditation for air leakage."[33]

This very useful reference needs one important qualification in respect of certification—it is also important to check the scope of the

---

[33] See J. Murthy. "What is the Difference between Accreditation and Certification?" Planning and Building Control Today, Adjacent Digital Politics Ltd, 1st Floor, Datum House, Electra Way, Crewe Business Park, Crewe, Cheshire, CW1 6ZF, Andy Jowett, ajowett@pbctoday.co.uk, , 1270 502876. https://www.pbctoday.co.uk/news/planning-construction-news/accreditation-and-certification-difference/32133/ and https://www.ukas.com/download/case-studies/pr/Plannin-and-Building-Control-Today-April-issue-2017.pdf.

certification—the boundaries of the organization being certified and any justified "requirements determined as not being applicable" (previously called exclusions).

Another point in respect of accreditations is that alongside any reference to the standard, such as ISO 17025, there is also the specific test or other competence being claimed.

Total Quality Management, Companywide Quality Control

What marks the difference between Total Quality Management (TQM) and Companywide Quality Control (CWQC) and quality management in general is a commitment to excellence—and we shall see that brought out in Chapter 16 Quality awards.

The opportunity dimension, alongside risk, provides a potential link to excellence and excellence awards in the development of a more business-centric approach in 9001: 2015.

A starting point is recognizing that the foundation quality management standard[34] is just that—a foundation, and it is necessary to build on it and journey on from it.[35] Success through total quality commitment meant to Conner Peripherals finding out customer's needs before selecting what to design in their sector and then building on the ISO 9001 foundation to offer excellence.[36]How to define what total quality means in your organization and where it stands on progress is a central issue. Alcatel made use of a total quality appraisal survey based on the maturity grid and their own learnings.[37]

---

[34]See ISO 9001:2015, "Quality Management Systems—Requirements."

[35]See J.E. "Jack" West and C.A. Cianfrani. April 2017. "Standard Issues—Beyond the Requirements—ISO 9001 Compliance Alone Isn't Sufficient to Sustain an Organization," *Quality Progress*. http://asq.org/quality-progress/2017/04/standard-issues/beyond-the-requirements.html.

[36]See M. Desai. November 1993. "Success Through Total Quality Commitment," *Quality Progress*, pp. 65-67.

[37]See M.M. Rollefson. November 1991. "The Total Quality Appraisal Survey: Where Do You Stand?" *Quality Progress*, pp. 54-57.

The process of implementing TQM/CWQC has common elements across linked models[38]:

1. TQM starts at the top;
2. TQM requires total involvement;
3. TQM focuses on the customer;
4. TQM uses teams;
5. TQM requires training for everybody;
6. TQM uses tools to measure and follow progress.

The team aspects of TQM can find expression in quality circle[39]

Table 12.5 Alexander the Great 356 BC, logistics and supply chain

If Alexander were a CEO today, he would
• Include logistics in strategic planning
• Consistently make changes in his organization that were demonstrated to provide specific benefits
• Develop a working knowledge and detailed understanding of his customers and their products, competition, industry, logistics requirements, and technologies and utilize this knowledge, along with other assets, to develop competitive advantages, market share, and profit
• Appoint a single person to lead all logistics functions and participate in strategic-planning sessions
• Develop alliances with key suppliers and service providers, accessing their infrastructure by allowing them to entrench themselves in his own company
• Utilize technology and other business tools only to the extent that they further the goals of profitability and competitive advantage
In fact, if Alexander the Great were a CEO today, he would strike fear into the hearts of his competition.

Quality in the Supply Chain

Excellence in logistics and supply chain management was key to the great achievements of antiquity.

---

[38]J. T. Burr. March 1993. "A New Name for a Not-So-New Concept," *Quality Progress*, pp. 87-88.

[39]See I. Nonaka. September 1993. "The History of the Quality Circle," *Quality Progress*, pp. 81-83.

"Alexander's (Alexander the Great 356–323 BC) 35,000-man army could carry no more than a 10-day supply of food when remote from sea transport.[40] Yet, he and his troops marched over thousands of miles at a rate of 19.5 miles in any one day without any problem. In the process, Alexander conquered every nation and city on which he set his sights. At the most basic level, he was able to perform his legendary feats because he included logistics and supply-chain management into his strategic plans, just as any modern-day corporation should do to maintain a competitive edge (see Table 12.5)."[41]

Clearly a strong element of 'Just In Time' was present in this Logistics excellence.

The most important lesson of all in this list is that Alexander saw his supply chain as an extension of his army, part of his family. This is the consistent message we are seeing emerge. It all begins with people and relationships. Having said that you need the competence and resources— but you may have to work with the supply chain to help develop that.

"Externally provided processes, products and services" is how the QMS standard[42] describes the input logistics and supply chain, while the standard's guidance document describes it more generically as "Externally provided resources".[43] The guidance document makes this vital point— "The organization and its external providers or partners are interdependent. The organization should seek to establish relationships that enhance the capabilities of itself and its providers or partners to create value in a manner that is mutually beneficial to all involved."

Scientifically selecting suppliers based on as much knowledge as one can garner about their specifications, capabilities, and performance in all area is vital[44] but not the whole story. The emerging picture with Industry 4.0 is of much greater integration with every aspect of supply and logistics (Table 12.6).

---

[40]See D.E. Engels. 1978. *Alexander the Great and the Logistics of the Macedonian Army.* Berkeley, CA: University of California Press.

[41]See T. Van Mieghem. January 1998. "Lessons Learned From Alexander the Great," *Quality Progress,* pp. 41-46. http://asq.org/data/subscriptions/qp/1998/0198/qp0198vanmieghem.pdf.

[42]See ISO 9001:2015, "Quality Management Systems—Requirements."

[43]See ISO 9004, "ISO 9004: 2018—Quality Management—Quality of an Organization—Guidance to Achieve Sustained Success."

[44]See V.K. Pang. February 1992. "Scientifically Selecting Suppliers," *Quality Progress,* pp. 43-45.

Table 12.6 Digital age evolution[45]

	Industry age	Logistics age	SCM age
2020	Industry 4.0	Logistics 4.0	SCM 4.0
2010	Strong products individualization under production conditions with great flexibility (current...)	Intelligent Transportation Systems (ITS), Real Time Locating Systems (RTLS) (current...)	Total network integration (current)
2000	Industry 3.0	Logistics 3.0	SCM 3.0
1990	Micro-processors. First programmable logic controller (PLC). Use of electronics and Information Technology (1969 to 2000s)	System of Logistics Management (from the 1980s)	Integration between two channels (beginning of the 1980s)
1980			
1970	Industry 2.0	Logistics 2.0 Automation of handling system (from the 1960s)	There is no SCM concept in this period
1960	Mass production using electrical energy (1870–1969)		
1880		Logistics 1.0 Mechanization of transport (late 19th century and early 20th century)	
1870			
1860	Industry 1.0		
1850	Mechanical weaving loom, water, steam power (1784–1870)		
1800			
1790			
1780			

In the present Supply Chain Management (SCM) 3.0 situation individual elements such as use of barcodes for identifying products and monitoring the inventory, electronic data interchange, zero inventory to continuously reducing costs, Enterprise Requirements Planning (ERP) materials management integration, Warehouse Management System (WMS) real-time systems to maximize warehouse space and transport management systems for routing and logistics provide the base for SCM 4.0.

SCM 4.0 seeks to add "four attributes: connectivity, visualization, optimization, and autonomy. While connectivity would link production

---

[45]See E.M. Frazzon, C.M.T. Rodriguez, M.M. Pereira, M.C. Pires and I. Uhlmann. 2019. "Towards Supply Chain Management 4.0," *Brazilian Journal of Operations & Production Management* 16, no. 2, pp. 180-91. https://bjopm.emnuvens.com.br/bjopm/article/view/539/823.

and the supply chain in the same network, visualization would help to overview supply chain's performance and status. Meanwhile, optimization would increase the performance at a supply chain level and autonomy would represent the capability of the operations to handle themselves. This can lead to an adaptive and intelligent supply chain and can be especially interesting in a competitive environment."[46]

The integration of supplier process control performance and data in IBM Greenock I witnessed here in Scotland in the late 1980s is an early example of very effective supply chain management.

---

[46]See A. Jayaram. 2016. "Lean Six Sigma Approach for Global Supply Chain Management using Industry 4.0 and IIoT," 2nd International Conference on Contemporary Computing and Informatics (IC3I), Noida, India, December 14–17, 2016. doi:10.1109/IC3I.2016.7917940 cited in E.M. Frazzon, C.M.T. Rodriguez, M.M. Pereira, M.C. Pires and I. Uhlmann. 2019. "Towards Supply Chain Management 4.0," *Brazilian Journal of Operations & Production Management* 16, no. 2, pp. 180-191. https://bjopm.emnuvens.com.br/bjopm/article/view/539.

APPENDIX 1

Abbreviations

Abbreviation	Meaning
AI	Appreciative Inquiry
AQL	Acceptable Quality Level
ASQ	American Society for Quality—USA
CEO	Chief Executive Officer
CMM	Capability Maturity Model
COPQ	Cost of Poor Quality
COQ	Cost of Quality
COTO	Context of the Organization
CQC	Care Quality Commission (UK)
CQI	Chartered Quality Institute—UK
CSR	Corporate Social Responsibility
DFSS	Design for Six Sigma
DOE	Design of Experiments
EBITDA	Earnings before interest, tax, depreciation, and amortization
ECO	Ecology
EFQM	European Foundation for Quality Management
ETV	Environmental Technology Verification
EU	European Union
FDA	Food and Drug Administration (USA)
FMEA	Failure Modes and Effects Analysis
GUM	Guide to Uncertainty of Measurement
HACCP	Hazard Analysis & Critical Control Point
HOQ	House of Quality
ISO	International Standards Organization
JCGM	Joint Committee for Guides in Metrology
LQ	Limiting Quality
NHS	National Health Service (UK)
OC	Operating Characteristic
OFSTED	Office for Standards in Education, Children's Services and Skills
PDCA	Plan Do Check Act

Abbreviation	Meaning
PDF	Probability Distribution Function also Portable Document Format
PMS	Project Management System
QA	Quality Assurance
QC	Quality Control
QFD	Quality Function Deployment
QHSE	Quality Health Safety Environment
QMS	Quality Management System
QOL	Quality of Life
QOL	Quality of Life
RAD	Rapid Application Development
RADAR	Results, Approach, Deployment, Assessment
SCM	Supply Chain Management
SQC	Statistical Quality Control
SWB	Subjective Well Being
TBL	Triple Bottom Line
TOWS	Threats Opportunities Weaknesses Strengths
TQC	Total Quality Control or Total Quality Costs
TQM	Total Quality Management
UNESCO	United Nations Educational, Scientific and Cultural Organization
UNFPA	United Nations Family Planning Organization
UNICEF	Was—United Nations International Children's Emergency Fund, Now—United Nations Children's Fund
VIM	International Vocabulary of Metrology
WHO	World Health Organization

APPENDIX 2

Key Addresses

ASQ - American Society for Quality, P.O. Box 3005, Milwaukee, WI 53201-3005, All other locations: +1-414-272-8575, Fax: 414-272-1734

BIPM - Pavillon de Breteuil F-92312 Sèvres Cedex Paris, FRANCE, webmaster@bipm.org, https://www.bipm.org/en/conference-centre/directions/

BSI, 389 Chiswick High Road, London, W4 4AL, United Kingdom, +44 345 086 9001

Care Quality Commission, Citygate, Gallowgate, Newcastle upon Tyne, NE1 4PA., 03000 616161, enquiries@cqc.org.uk,

CQI - The Chartered Quality Institute (CQI), 2nd Floor North, Chancery Exchange, 10 Furnival Street, London EC4A 1AB, United Kingdom. T: +44 (0) 20 7245 6722 I F: +44 (0) 20 7245 6788, www.thecqi.org

Elsevier B.V., Registered Office: Radarweg 29, 1043 NX Amsterdam, The Netherlands, Registered in The Netherlands, Registration No. 33156677, BTW No. NL 005033019B01,

Frisch, Michael B., Associate Professor, Department of Psychology and Neuroscience, Baylor University, P.O. Box 97334, Waco, TX 76798-7334 (e-mail address: michael_frisch@baylor.edu).

IEC Central Office ISO copyright office 3, rue de Varembé CH-1211 Geneva 20 Switzerland Tel.: +41 22 919 02 11 info@iec.ch www.iec.ch,

ISO - International Organization for Standardization, ISO Central Secretariat, Chemin de Blandonnet 8, CP 401, 1214 Vernier, Geneva, Switzerland. E-mail: central@iso.org. Tel.: +41 22 749 01 11

Iowa University, Mathematical Sciences, Department of Mathematics, 14 MacLean Hall, Iowa City, Iowa 52242-1419, Phone: 319-335-0714; Fax: 319-335-0627mathematics-department@uiowa.edu

International Six Sigma Institute™, c/o CreoCloud LC, Samstagernstrasse 57, 8832 Wollerau, Switzerland, Phone: +41 78 946 88 86, info@sixsigma-institute.org

National Quality Board - NQB, NHS England, PO Box 16738, Redditch, B97 9PT, 0300 311 22 33, Email: england.contactus@nhs.net

Quality-One, +1 (248) 280-4800 | information@quality-one.com

The Health Foundation 90 Long Acre London WC2E 9RA Telephone: +44 (0) 207 257 8000 Facsimile: +44 (0) 207 257 8001 www.health.org.uk, info@health.org.uk

The King's Fund 11–13 Cavendish Square London W1G 0AN Tel: 020 7307 2568 Fax: 020 7307 2801, Email: publications@kingsfund.org.uk, www.kingsfund.org.uk

The Scottish Government St Andrew's House Edinburgh EH1 3DG

UKAS, 2 Pine Trees Chertsey Lane, Staines-upon-Thames, TW18 3HR. info@ukas.com, +44 (0) 1784 429000,

UK Government Science and Technology Committee, Clerk of the Science and Technology Committee, House of Commons, London SW1A 0AA. The telephone number for general inquiries is: 020 7219 2793; the Committee's e-mail address is: scitechcom@parliament.uk.

UN/CEFACT Introduction—The United Nations Centre for Trade Facilitation and Electronic Business (UN/CEFACT) is a subsidiary, intergovernmental body of the United Nations Economic Commission for Europe (UNECE) which serves as a focal point within the United Nations Economic and Social Council for trade facilitation recommendations and electronic business standards. It has global membership and its members are experts from intergovernmental organizations, individual countries' authorities and also from the business community. UN/CEFACT Secretariat, Fax N°: +41-22-917 0629, Tel N°: +41-22-917 3254, https://www.unece.org/tradewelcome/un-centre-for-trade-facilitation-and-e-business-uncefact/contact-us.html

UNESCO Headquarters, 7, place de Fontenoy 75352 Paris 07 SP France.

APPENDIX 3

Probability Distribution Functions

Probability Distribution Functions directly relevant to Measurement Uncertainty

Table 1 *Standard uncertainty formulae for different underlying PDFs*[1]

Assumed probability distribution	Expression used to obtain the standard uncertainty	Comments or examples
Rectangular	$u(x_i) = \dfrac{a_i}{3}$	A digital thermometer has a least significant digit of 0.1°C. The numeric rounding caused by finite resolution will have semi-range limits of 0.05°C. Thus the corresponding standard uncertainty will be $u(x_i) = \dfrac{a_i}{3} = \dfrac{0.05}{1.732} = 0.029°C.$
U-shaped	$u(x_i) = \dfrac{a_i}{2}$	A mismatch uncertainty associated with the calibration of an RF power sensor has been evaluated as having semi-range limits of 1.3%. Thus the corresponding standard uncertainty will be $u(x_i) = \dfrac{a_i}{2} = \dfrac{1.3}{1.414} = 0.92\%$
Triangular	$u(x_i) = \dfrac{a_i}{6}$	A tensile testing machine is used in a testing laboratory where the air temperature can vary randomly but does not depart from the nominal value by more than 3°C. The machine has a large thermal mass and is therefore most likely to be at the mean air temperature, with no probability of being outside the 3°C limits. It is reasonable to assume a triangular distribution, therefore the standard uncertainty for its temperature is $u(x_i) = \dfrac{a_i}{6} = \dfrac{3}{2.449} = 1.2\ °C$

Normal *(from repeatability evaluation)*	$u(x_i) = s(q)$	A statistical evaluation of repeatability gives the result in terms of one standard deviation; therefore no further processing is required.
Normal *(from a calibration certificate)*	$u(x_i) = \dfrac{U}{k}$	A calibration certificate normally quotes an expanded uncertainty U at a specified, high coverage probability. A coverage factor, k, will have been used to obtain this expanded uncertainty from the combination of standard uncertainties. It is therefore necessary to divide the expanded uncertainty by the same coverage factor to obtain the standard uncertainty.
Normal *(from a manufacturer's specification)*	$u(x_i) = \dfrac{\text{Tolerance limit}}{k}$	Some manufacturers' "specifications are quoted at a given coverage probability (sometimes referred to as *confidence level*), e.g. 95% or 99%. In such cases, a normal distribution can be assumed and the tolerance limit is divided by the coverage factor k for the stated coverage probability. For a coverage probability of 95%, $k = 2$ and for a coverage probability of 99%, $k = 2.58$. If a coverage probability is not stated then a rectangular distribution should be assumed.

---

[1] See page 14 in UKAS, "M3003—Edition 3 | November 2012—The Expression of Uncertainty and Confidence in Measurement." https://www.ukas.com/download/publications/publications-relating-to-laboratory-accreditation/M3003_Ed3_final.pdf.

Examples of Opportunity and Risk Management Approaches and Their Main Uses

Table 2 Examples of opportunity and risk management approaches and their main uses[2]

Opportunity and risk approach	Main use	Summary
Cumulative risk analysis	Health, environmental protection	Cumulative risk analysis provides an approach for improving our understanding of risks and impacts in a full, real-world context. Integrated information about the range of possible effects of risk causes, events and impacts, enables a more accurate overall assessment to be made. For example, when looking at the health risks of pesticides, cumulative exposure through multiple media, such as, air, water, food, drink, soil, and dust can be taken account of.
Environmental and sustainability accounting	Sustainable development research and development	Developments in environmental and sustainability accounting are providing limited opportunities to financially account for sustainability risks. This can enable risks to be assessed on a similar basis to financial risks. Examples include putting a value on an organizations reputation and putting financial values on environmental externalities caused by the organization. Please refer to the Sustainability Accounting Guide for further information.
Hazard and operability study (HAZOP)	At design stages especially in industrial processes	A Hazard and Operability study (HAZOP) is used to identify all possible deviations from the way in which a design is expected to work and to identify all the hazards associated with these deviations. Where deviations arise that result in hazards, actions are generated which require design engineers to review and suggest solutions to either remove the hazard or reduce its risk to an acceptable level. These solutions are reviewed and accepted by the HAZOP team before implementation.
Fault tree analysis	System reliability and performance, especially in engineering	A fault tree analysis (FTA) involves specifying a key risk or top event to analyze followed by identifying all of the associated elements in the system that could cause the top event to occur. Fault trees graphically represent the interaction of failures and other events in the system. Basic events at the bottom of the fault tree are linked via logic symbols (known as gates) to one or more top events. These top events represent identified hazards or system failure modes for which predicted reliability or availability data is required.
Failure mode and effect analysis	Design of products, processes or services	Failure Mode and Effect Analysis (FMEA) examines every function and every component of the machine or system to discover the scale of the risk: What could fail or break? What is the probability of failure in operation? What are the consequences of failure? FMEA is a technique of estimating and ranking risks to guide action planning and prioritization.
Fish bone analysis (Cause-and-effect analysis, Ishikawa Diagrams)	Projects and systems	The Cause-and-Effect Diagram is a method of identifying the different factors that cause a particular problem. The fish-bone or Ishikawa diagram, as it is also known, links a problem to the inputs, methods, and processes that contribute to that problem. Parts of the system that have no bearing on the particular aspect are ignored. The problem or effect that needs influencing is placed at the head of the fish and the causes and influencing factors feed into its spine along its ribs.

Forcefield analysis	Change Management	This technique is normally used by groups to identify the key influencing forces on a situation. Driving forces help to move the situation toward a goal, whereas restraining forces prevent the situation from improving. The technique is used to identify and influence these forces helping to achieve the change sought by the group.
Risk matrices	Broad usage	Matrices are often used to bring together opportunity and risk information. This includes understanding where risks are apparent, the magnitude of the risk, risk responsibilities, management, and other information.
Suggestion schemes	Operational or product improvements	These can be employee or customer focused and generally work on the principle of rewarding good ideas for operational or product improvements.
Design for environment and sustainable design	Product and Service design	Design for Environment and Sustainable Product Design is a systematic approach to consider environmental or sustainable.
Product design		Development issues during the design process. By focusing on the actual output required and defining clear boundaries, the methods can stimulate innovation and increase competitiveness. The approaches often use indicators and assessment methods to establish sustainable development impacts of potential products or services.
Scenario planning	Strategic planning	To understand alternative visions of the future and to plan responses if these visions materialized. The aim is to stimulate innovation and test current processes and management approaches to see where enhancements can be made.
Industrial symbiosis	Manufacturing	This happens when manufacturing organizations develop partnerships to minimize waste and to develop life cycle-based solutions to waste and resource problems. Typically, this involves grouping industrial processes so that the waste of one operation can be used as the feedstock for another.
Appraisal processes	Broad usage	Providing financial and other recognition for the development of sustainable development solutions by tying results into the personal appraisal process.
Partnership and engagement based approaches	Broad usage	Using stakeholder-led approaches such as community partnerships to drive new product and service development through improved understanding of customer needs.
SWOT analysis	Broad usage	Assessment of the Strengths, Weaknesses, Opportunities, and Threats of a situation, a decision, a plan or a policy for example.

[2]See—"Sigma Opportunity and Risk Guide," The SIGMA Project—Sustainability Integrated Guidelines for Management. https://www.scribd.com/document/35665959/Sigma-Risk-Opportunity. (The SIGMA Project—Sustainability Integrated Guidelines for Management was launched in 1999 with the support of the UK Department of Trade and Industry (DTI) and is(was? Author) led by:

- British Standards Institution—the leading standards organisation
- Forum for the Future—a leading sustainability charity and think-tank
- AccountAbility—the international professional body for accountability."

Example Process Flowchart

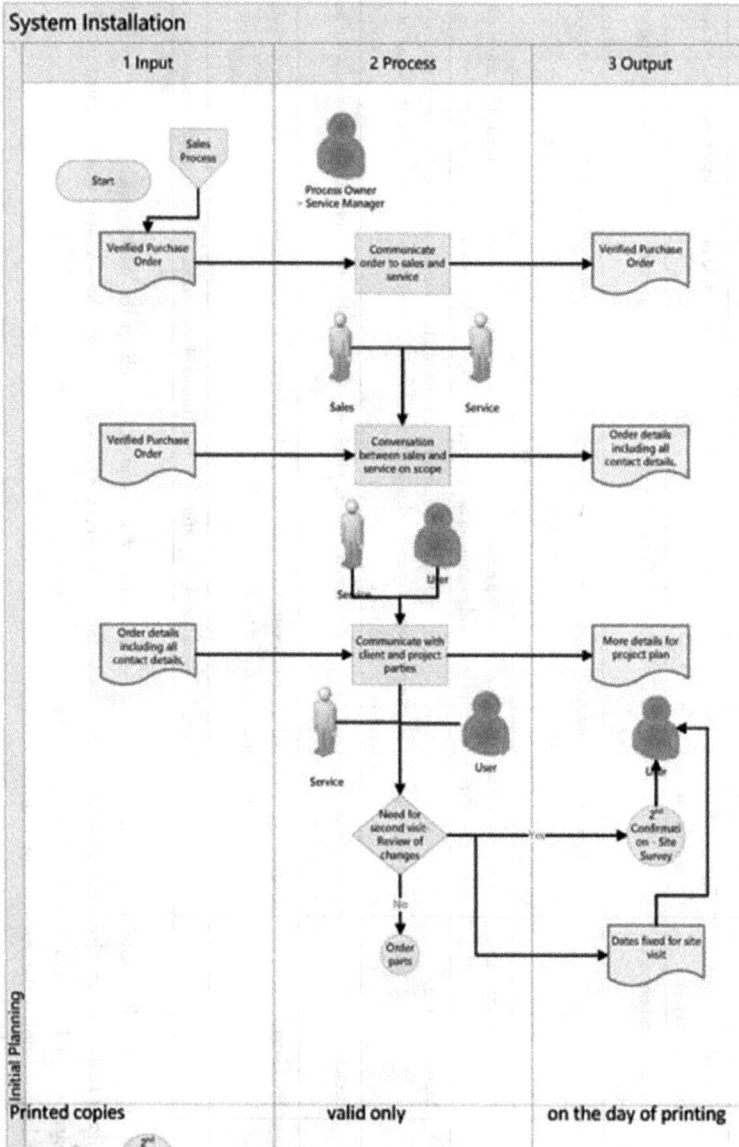

Figure 1 System installation process flowchart

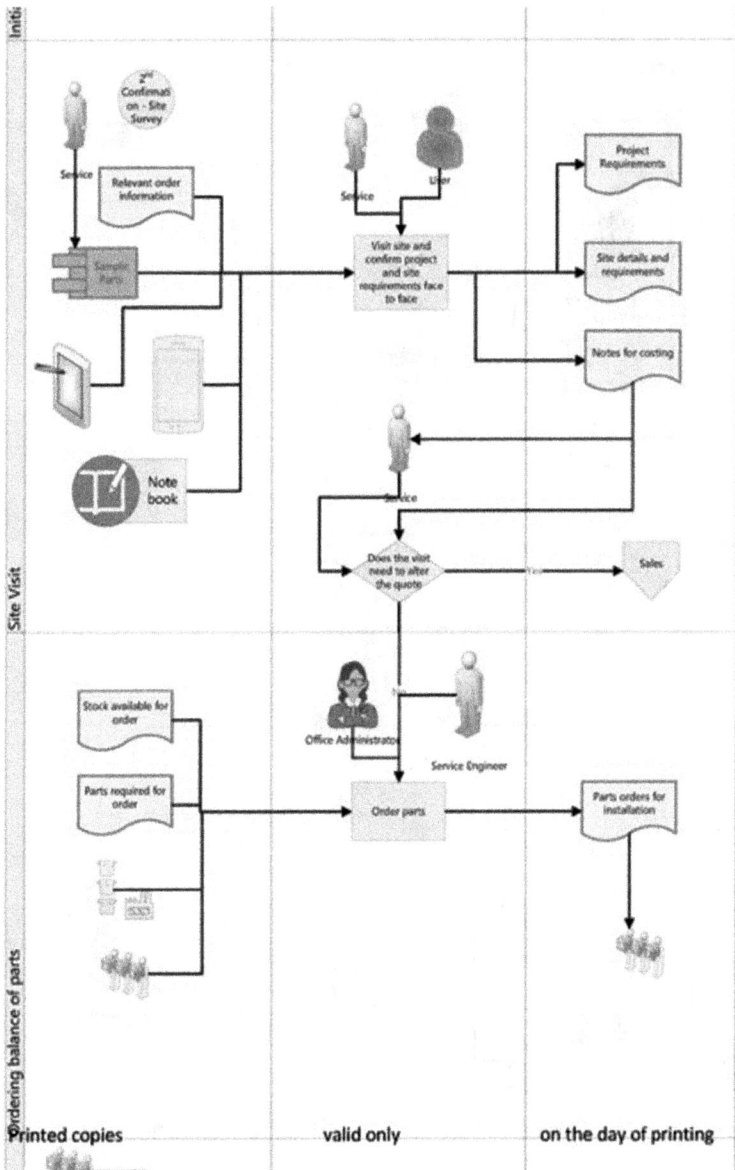

Figure 1 (Continued)

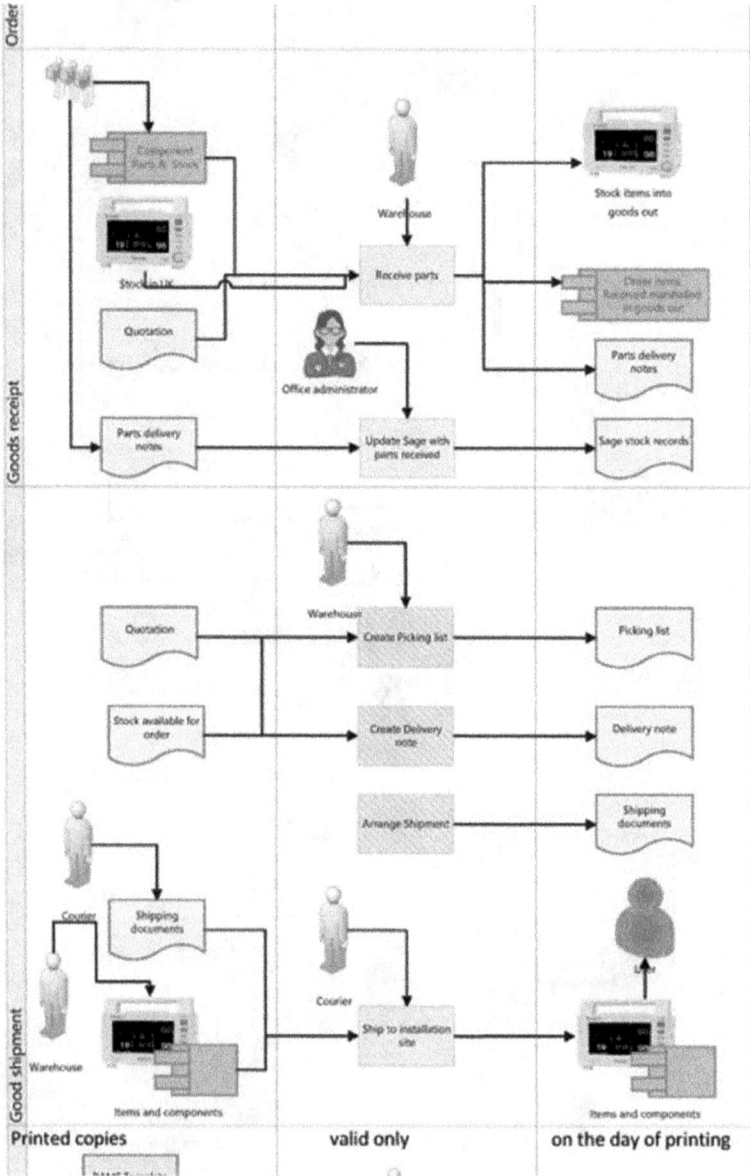

Figure 1 (Continued)

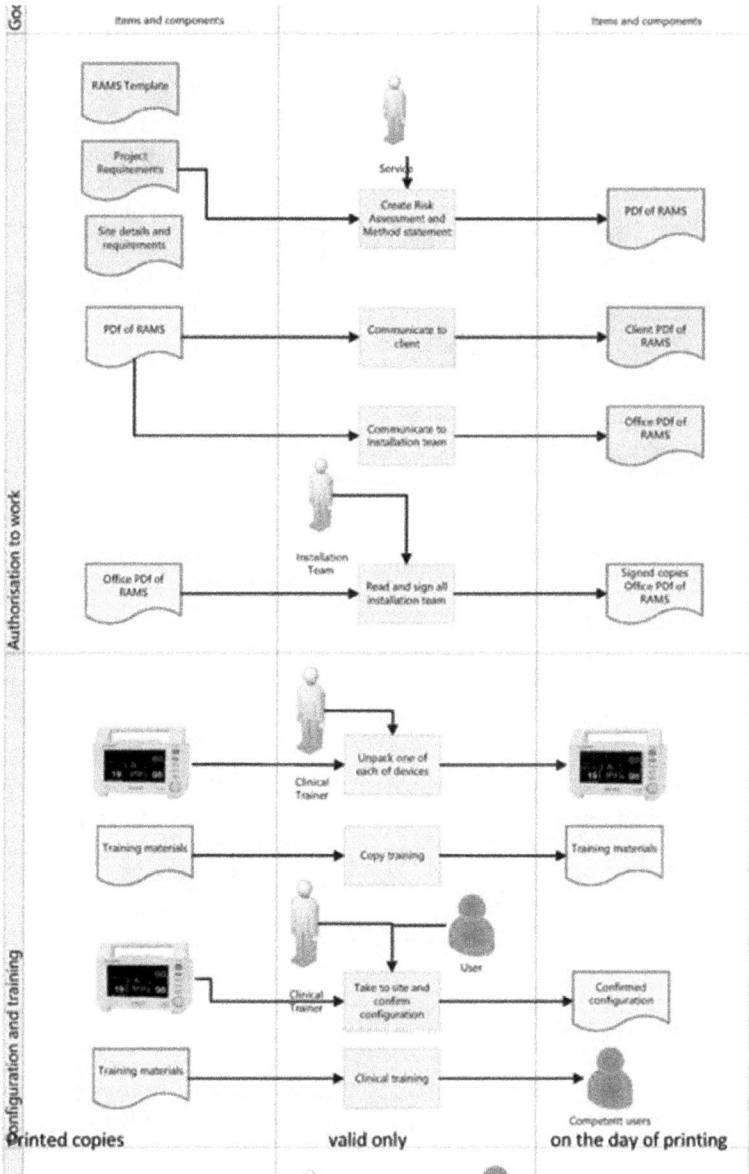

Figure 1 (Continued)

Example Section of Data Flow Diagram for PowerApps Documentation

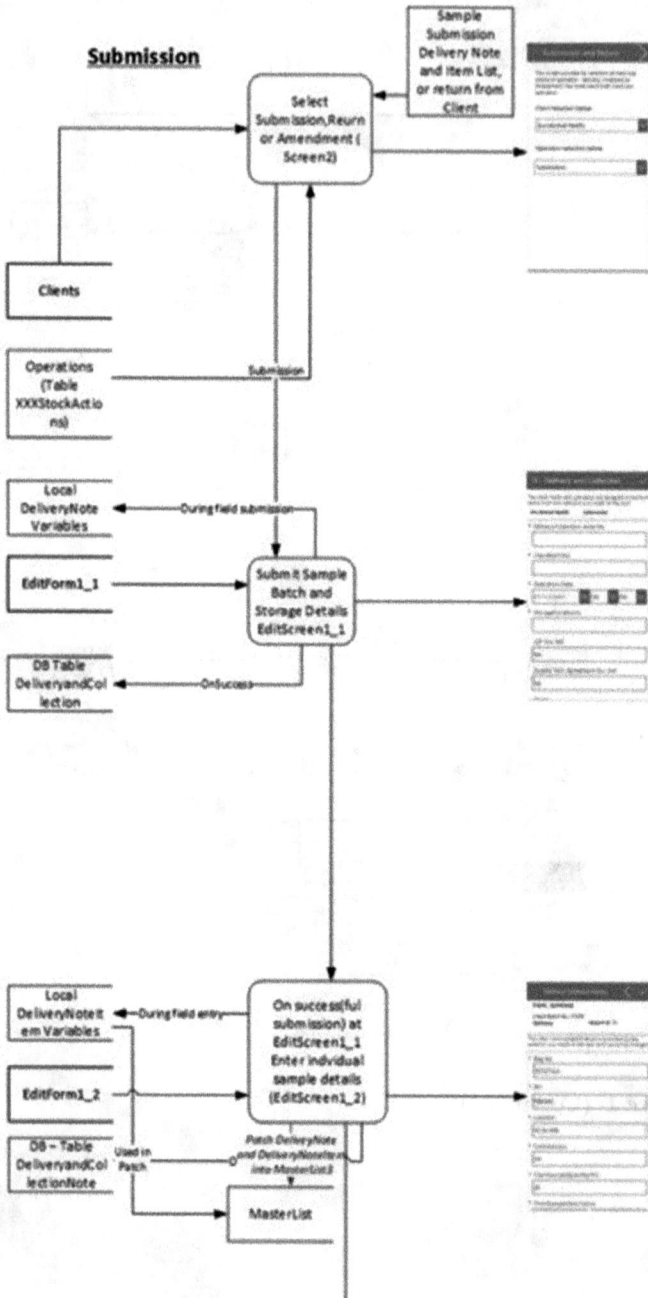

Figure 2 *Example section of data flow diagram for powerapps documentation*

Example TOWS Analysis

An example from a small business where I used the technique shows the linking to specific elements of the SWOT:

Strengths	Weaknesses
177—Modern building	180—Lack of key people
178—Financial Stability	181—Overreliance on few customers
179—Relationship with Major Suppliers	183—Poor buying power
204—Web presence general	184—No presence with some customers
175—Level of Staff Expertise	187—Lack of integrated purchasing system
176—Immediate access to Key Decision Makers	191—Small
223—Functional e-commerce site	194—Lack market client awareness
273—Established Customer Base	211—Customers are not categorized by market sector
156—Lean and Mean	174—Part Deliveries
158—Sister company shared management	278—Lack of certified management system
163—Proven Track Record	157—No on-site key staff backup
164—Location	

Opportunities	SO	WO
190—Better Sourcing	201—Customer provision of new needs—Links to SWOT—271—External Opportunity—Suppliers new products	185—Conduct Customer Survey—Links to SWOT—184—Internal Weakness—No presence with some customers—194—Internal Weakness—Lack of market client awareness—218—External Opportunity—Source specific lines for customers
199—Market Change—Certification and Regulation Emphasis	202—Keeping close to suppliers on new products	186—Marketing Plan
200—Technology—increasing sophistication and reduced and different consumables	269—Visit in-house supplier exhibitions—Links to SWOT—179—Internal Strength—Relationship with Major Suppliers—200—External Opportunity—Technology—increasing sophistication and reduced and different consumables	213—Categorize customers by sector

Opportunities	SO	WO
203—Web presence	270—Research solutions for acknowledged customer needs—Links to SWOT—179—Internal Strength—Relationship with Major Suppliers—200—External Opportunity—Technology—increasing sophistication and reduced and different consumables—271—External Opportunity—Suppliers new products	
205—Web tailoring	274—Match Technology to Potential Customer—Links to SWOT—179—Internal Strength—Relationship with Major Suppliers—212—External Opportunity—Technology sectors provide knowledge of consumables	
212—Technology sectors provide knowledge of consumables	275—Increased remote selling—Links to SWOT—203—External Opportunity—Web presence—205—External Opportunity—Web tailoring—221—External Opportunity—Remote selling and dispatch—223—Internal Strength—Functional e-commerce site	
217—Sell back on discount to supplier		
218—Source specific lines for customers		
219—Sell at a discount to customer		
221—Remote selling and dispatch		
222—Online selling		
271—Suppliers new products		
272—Targeted selling		

Table 3 *TOWS analysis for an SME lab retail business*

Threats	ST	WT
192—No USP 193—Shrinking Market 197—Better delivery from major competition 198—Middle men 209—Reduced Contact with Suppliers 210—Contact with Suppliers is Supplier Lead 215—Overpricing slow moving stock 216—Customer order flow ceases 220—Damaged packaging means a loss 277—Key contact person leaves 155—Proof of Accreditation 162—Dependence on narrow customer base	276—Maintain customer profile—Links to SWOT—179—Internal Strength—Relationship with Major Suppliers—277—External Threat—Key contact person leaves	182—Widen the customer base—Links to SWOT—181—Internal Weakness—Overreliance on few customers 189—Investigate value and means of providing integrated purchasing system 195—Increase depth and breadth of market requirements development—Links to SWOT—193—External Threat—Shrinking Market—194—Internal Weakness—Lack of market client awareness 196—Need to be more aware of potential customers—Links to SWOT—193—External Threat—Shrinking Market—216—External Threat—Customer order flow ceases 208—Membership of SciNet Group 279—ISO 9001 Management System Certification—Links to SWOT—155—External Threat—Proof of Accreditation—278—Internal Weakness—Lack of certified management system 159—Divert Phones to sister company 160—Divert e-mails and faxes to sister company 161—Call of credit controller for replacing missing key staff

Case Studies

The following case studies were kindly provided by Timothy Van Mieghem of The Proaction Group.[1]

Quality Management System Implementation—Improve Quality Performance and Customer Experience

Background	
Boat manufacturer • Informal systems relying on Tribal Knowledge • Over 12 Defects per Unit at final inspection • Defects inflated hours worked per boat to 227 • No clear quality policy or identified objectives. • High Warranty Claims • Dealer network dissatisfied	The management of a leading manufacturer of ski/wakeboard towboats was concerned with the warranty complaints from the field and poor customer experience with their product (averaged 20 warranty claims & $15K warranty cost each week). Quality and warranty issues were not being addressed on a timely basis or with effective countermeasures. Previous efforts at quality management failed to improve product quality and reduce warranty. At project start, their systems related to quality were informal, relying on personal knowledge of "how we operate". Very few systems were documented and there was a lack of a clearly defined quality policy and objectives. Manufacturing processes were mostly not documented, relying on verbal/visual training and memory. Process control techniques were not identified or documented. The quality process was highly dependent on inspection. Quality-related process data were paper-based, not easily manipulated for analysis or widespread use within the manufacturing areas. The corrective action process was undefined and activities mostly verbally communicated so it was very difficult to follow-up or track improvement. This environment led to the company having to rework units to address the 12 defects per unit they found at final inspection. This rework contributed to the 227 hours of labor required to produce each boat.

---

[1]The Proaction Group, LLC 350 N. Orleans Street, Suite 9000N, Chicago, IL 60654, +1.312.726.6111 × 313
chenson@proactiongroup.com.

Action Taken • Quality Management System Assessment and Implementation • Establish Quality Metrics • Develop Quality Management Processes, Work Instructions and Feedback Loops, and Train Workforce • Led transition from paper-based, time-consuming quality data collection to real-time electronic data collection, providing actionable, accessible data. • Incorporate Dealer and Customer Feedback into QMS • Formal Corrective Action Process for Internal and External Issues	The ProAction Group led multiple Quality Management System (QMS) assessments of their primary manufacturing facility and their design center located in the USA. We developed a comprehensive ISO-based QMS approach to address the identified deficiencies and to provide a corporate quality structure for continuous improvement. ProAction developed the implementation plan and developed the QMS elements, work instructions and other documentation, trained and coached the management team and workforce, acted as quality manager, and transitioned the quality management system to the management team. Specific implementation areas of focus included: • New Product Development (NPD)/Phase Gate process defined and utilized for new programs. • COPQ (Cost of Poor Quality) metrics developed and used to track progress and drive improvement. • AIMS data collection & analysis successfully implemented and utilized for developing metrics and supporting improvement activities. • Corrective Action process implemented and utilized to drive improvements on internal and external issues. • Process Control Plans developed for all identified processes. • Quality Manual & Quality Procedures completed. QMS Training completed for all management groups. Plant personnel introduced to QMS requirements & expectations. Electronic delivery of WIs, QMS documentation, and other plant performance information.
Measurble Results • 50% reduction in Defects per Unit. • Reduced labor hours per boat by 7% • Substantive Warranty Claim reduction • The company had the metrics and continuous improvement tools to • sustain and continue the improvements	We implemented a robust ISO-based Quality Management System at both the primary boat manufacturing facility and at the design center that resulted in the following: • Defects per unit were slashed by 50% in the first 6 months. • Labor hours per boat were reduced by 7%. • Quality data able to be accessed and analyzed in real-time. • DPU metric trend favorable since implementation. • Improved response to dealer & customer issues resulting in improved customer satisfaction. • Provided strong foundation for new Quality Director to be able to "hit the ground running" with systems already in-place within the organization.

Focused Lean Project Improved Earnings by $1.5 M

Background	A solid player in the chocolate industry had recently negotiated a long-term agreement with a major customer and was engaged in executing a diversification strategy. These distractions took focus away from the core business, and cost increases began to erode profits. Management hired an outside firm to consolidate US and Canadian operations in an effort to control costs. When the capital outlay proved to be prohibitive, the company engaged The ProAction Group to lead its Lean effort and unlock cost savings. In addition, the company had the opportunity to acquire a related business that would add important growth and diversification.
• *Chocolate Manufacturer* • Cost Reduction Effort • Space Constraint Hindered Efforts to Acquire a Business and Absorb into Current Plant	
Action Taken • Mapped Value Stream • Implemented Lean Program • Created Tracking Metrics • Consolidated Operations	Using Value Stream Mapping, the ProAction team quickly assessed the current state of operations and identified a preferred future state. Bridging the gap required the use of numerous Lean methods including Kaizen events, 5S, Quick Changeover, Visual Management, and Total Productive Maintenance. Equipment downtime was a significant drain on operations, which we targeted with a Six Sigma project. We eliminated waste by changing the line layout to improve product flow. Most importantly, we developed a series of metrics to monitor improvements and track cost reduction. The ProAction team reduced work-in-process inventory and removed obsolete equipment to free up existing floor space within the company's operations. As a result, the company's Canadian operations were absorbed into its US operations without the large capital expense previously assumed. The additional space also enabled the company to acquire and integrate a strategic player, which increased revenue by more than 50%.
Measurble Results • $1.5 M Increase in EBITDA • $2.4 M Decrease in Working Capital • Measurable Operational Improvements • Consolidated 3 Plants into 1 Existing Facility	The focused Lean initiatives had a striking impact: • Output improved by 75% • Equipment uptime (OEE) increased 50% • Labor was reduced by 20% • Scrap rates decreased by 15% • Changeovers went from 5 hours to less than 30 minutes Cost reductions added $1.5 M to EBITDA. Improved inventory management reduced working capital by $2.4 M. The increased production also allowed the company to fulfill a 60-day demand surge with a key customer, adding $0.75 M in additional margin.

References

Adair, J. 2001. "The Leadership of Jesus–and Its Legacy Today," *Canterbury Press*, p. 208.

Alexander, C.P. November 1989. "The soft technologies of quality," *Quality Progress*, pp. 24-28.

American Productivity & Quality Center. n.d. "Benchmarks on Demand." https://www.apqc.org/what-we-do/benchmarking/benchmarks-on-demand.

American Society for Quality. n.d. "Benchmarking Studies." https://asq.org/quality-resources/benchmarking-reports.

American Society for Quality. June 27, 2012. "Cost of Quality—Ask the Experts Page," *Ask the Standards Experts*. https://asqasktheexperts.com/2012/06/27/cost-of-quality-coq/?msg=fail&shared=email.

American Society for Quality. June 2017. "2017 Software Showcase & Directory," *Quality Progress*. http://asq.org/quality-progress/2017/06/software-quality/asqs-2017-software-showcase-directory.pdf.

American Society for Quality. n.d. "Cost of Quality Videos." https://videos.asq.org/cost-of-quality-appraisal-costs, https://videos.asq.org/cost-of-quality-costs-defined-part-3, https://videos.asq.org/cost-of-quality-internal-and-external-failure-costs.

American Society for Quality. n.d. "Cost of Quality (COQ) Resources," *ASQ Resources Page*. https://asq.org/quality-resources/cost-of-quality.

American Society for Quality. n.d. "Failure Mode and Effects Analysis (FMEA)," *ASQ Resources Page*. https://asq.org/quality-resources/fmea.

American Society for Quality. n.d. "The Future of Quality: Quality Throughout 2015 Future of Quality Report." https://asq.org/quality-resources/research/future-of-quality.

American Society for Quality. n.d. "What is Six Sigma?" *ASQ Resource Page*. https://asq.org/quality-resources/six-sigma.

American Society for Quality. n.d. "What is Statistical Process Control." https://asq.org/quality-resources/statistical-process-control.

American Society for Quality. n.d. "What is the Malcolm Baldrige National Quality Award (MBNQA)?" *ASQ Resources Page*. https://asq. org/quality-resources/malcolm-baldrige-national-quality-award.

American Society for Quality. n.d. "An Introduction to the PDCA Cycle Webcast, Part 1." http://asq.org/2011/07/continuous-improvement/ intro-to-pdca-1.html.

American Society for Quality. n.d. "The 7 Basic Quality Tools for Process Improvement." https://asq.org/quality-resources/seven-basic-quality-tools.

Andersen, L.H. August 1990. "Controlling Variation is Key to Manufacturing Success," *Quality Progress*, pp. 91–93.

Axelos. "What is PRINCE2?" https://www.axelos.com/best-practice-solutions/prince2/what-is-prince2.

Bafna, S. December 1997. "The Process Audit: Often Ignored but Never Insignificant," *Quality Progress*, pp. 37–40. http://asq.org/data/ subscriptions/qp/1997/1297/qp1297bafna.pdf.

Bai, Y., and W. Jin. 2016. "Risk Assessment Applied to Offshore Structures," Marine Structural Design, 2nd ed. https://www.sciencedirect. com/topics/engineering/risk-matrix.

Bainbridge, L. March 1975. "Measuring by Judgement." *Elsevier, Applied Ergonomics* 6, no. 1, pp. 9-16. doi:10.1016/0003-6870(75)90205-7.

Banerjee, A., U. B. Chitnis, S. L. Jadhav, J. S. Bhawalkar, and S. Chaudhury. July to December 2009. "Hypothesis Testing, Type I and Type II Errors." *Industrial Psychiatry Journal* 18, no. 2, pp. 127-31. https:// www.ncbi.nlm.nih.gov/pmc/articles/PMC2996198/.

Barwick, V.J and S.L.R. Ellison. January 2000. "VAM Project 3.2.1— Development and Harmonisation of Measurement Uncertainty Principles—Part (d): Protocol for Uncertainty Evaluation from Validation Data," LGC/VAM/1998/088 Version 5.1. http://blpd.dss.go.th/ training/dwdocuments/enews/VAM_uncertainty-0452.pdf.

BBC. January 14, 2020. "Italy's Invisible Cities: Venice Series 1 Episode 2 of 3." https://www.bbc.co.uk/iplayer/episode/b088nl33/italys-invisible-cities-series-1-2-venice.

BBC. June 14, 2019. "What is the Contaminated Blood Scandal?" https://www.bbc.co.uk/news/health-48596605.

BBC. n.d. "The Morecambe and Wise Show, Christmas 1971 Featuring Andre Previn." https://www.bbc.co.uk/programmes/b00gw1d0.

BBC. October 29, 2019. "Grenfell Tower: What Happened." https://www.bbc.co.uk/news/uk-40301289.

BCG. "Embracing Industry 4.0 and Rediscovering Growth." https://www.bcg.com/capabilities/operations/embracing-industry-4.0-rediscovering-growth.aspx.

Beattie, C.J., and R.D. Reader. January 1, 1971. *Quantitative Management in R&D.* 1st ed. New York, NY: Springer.

Becher, T. 1999. July 31, 1999. *Professional Practices: Commitment and Capability in a Changing Environment.* 1st ed. New York, NY: Routledge.

Becher, T. 1999. "Quality in the Professions," *Studies in Higher Education* 24, pp. 225-35. doi:10.1080/03075079912331379908.

Belbin. n.d. "The Nine Belbin Team Roles," *Belbin.* https://www.belbin.com/about/belbin-team-roles/.

Berggren, R., E. Fleming, H. Keane, and R. Moss. October 2018. "R&D in the 'Age of Agile,'" Pharmaceuticals & Medical Products, *McKinsey & Company.* https://www.mckinsey.com/industries/pharmaceuticals-and-medical-products/our-insights/r-and-d-in-the-age-of-agile.

Bergman, B., E. Cudney, P. Harding, Z. He, and P. Saraiva. January 2019. "Global Perspectives on Quality in Education." *The Journal For Quality & Participation*, pp. 33-36. http://asq.org/quality-participation/2018/07/global-quality/global-perspectives-on-quality-in-education.pdf, www.asq.org/pub/jqp.

Bemowski, K. October 1991. "America 2000—the Revolution to Change the US Education System by the Year 2000 has Begun," *Quality Progress*, pp. 45-48.

Biogen. n.d. "Aducanumab Update," *Biogen PowerPoint.* https://investors.biogen.com/static-files/5a31a1e3-4fbb-4165-921a-f0ccb1d64b65.

BIPM. March 1980. "Rapport BI PM-80/3 Report on the BIPM Enquiry on Error Statements." https://www.bipm.org/utils/common/pdf/rapportBIPM/RapportBIPM-1980-03.pdf.

Birnbaum, M.H. (ed.). 1998. *Measurement, Judgment and Decision Making—A volume in Handbook of Perception and Cognition.* 2nd ed. Amsterdam, The Netherlands: Elsevier Inc.

Bisgaard, S. and J. De Mast. January 2006. "After Six Sigma—What's Next?" *Quality Progress.* http://asq.org/data/subscriptions/qp/2006/0106/qp0106bisgaard.pdf.

Bittner, K., and I. Spence. 2006. *Use Case Modelling*. Boston, MA: Pearson Education Inc.

Blanchard, K., and P. Hodges. 2005. *Lead Like Jesus*. Nashville, TN: Thomas Nelson.

Blanchard, K., P. Hodges, and P. Hendry. 2016. *Lead Like Jesus Revisited*. Nashville, TN: Thomas Nelson.

Blas, M.J., S. Gonnet, and H. Leone. 2017. "An Ontology to Document a Quality Scheme Specification of a Software Product." *Expert Systems* 34, e12213. https://onlinelibrary.wiley.com/doi/pdf/10.1111/exsy.12213.

Boje, D.M., and R.D. Winsor. 1993. "The Resurrection of Taylorism: Total Quality Management's Hidden Agenda." *Journal of Organizational Change Manage* 6, no. 4, pp. 57-70.

Boston Consulting Group. n.d. "Embracing Industry 4.0 and Rediscovering Growth." https://www.bcg.com/capabilities/operations/embracing-industry-4.0-rediscovering-growth.aspx.

Borris, S. 2012. *Strategic Lean Mapping*. New York, NY: McGraw-Hill.

Boznak, R.G. July 1994. "When Doing It Right First Time Is Not Enough." *Quality Progress*, pp. 74-78.

Bossert, J. April 2019. "Implementing Healthcare Quality." *The Journal for Quality & Participation*. http://asq.org/quality-participation/2019/05/basic-quality/implementing-healthcare-quality.pdf.

Box, G.E.P., L.W. Joiner, S. Rohan, and F.J. Sensebrenner. May 1991. "Quality in the Community: One City's Experience," *Quality Progress*, pp. 57-63.

Boyers, P.E. May 2017. "Back to Basics—Maintaining Knowledge—How ISO 9001:2015 Is Helping Organizations Remember Their Future," *Quality Progress*, p. 64. http://asq.org/quality-progress/2017/05/back-to-basics/maintaining-knowledge.html.

Braun, R.J. February 1990. "Turning Computers into Experts." *Quality Progress*, pp. 71-75.

Brennan, C., and A. Douglas. 1999. "Striving for Continuous Improvement: The Experience of U.K. Local Government Services," *ASQ's 53rd Annual Quality Congress Proceedings*, pp. 414-22. http://asq.org/articles/aqc-proceedings/public_proceedings/53_1999/10853.pdf.

Bristol City Council. 2018. "Our Data Bristol Initiative." https://www.bristol.gov.uk/documents/20182/0/Our+Data+Bristol.pdf/6c41ae6b-5146-8c15-68cd-a3ac28277c9f.

British Quality Foundation. n.d. "BQF Awards 2020." https://www.bqf.org.uk/bqf-awards-2020/.

Brown, B. March 2012. "Listening to Shame", https://www.ted.com/talks/brene_brown_listening_to_shame

BSI. n.d. "PAS 99 Integrated Management Systems." *BSI.* https://www.bsigroup.com/en-GB/pas-99-integrated-management/.

BSI. March 2014. "BSI Unannounced Audits Frequently Asked Questions (FAQs)," *BSI.* https://www.bsigroup.com/globalassets/meddev/localfiles/en-gb/documents/bsi-md-unannounced-audits-faq-march-2014-uk-en.pdf.

Bucher, J.L. March 2010. "Measure For Measure—Out of Sync If We're Not on the Same Page, Quality Efforts Go Down the Drain," *Quality Progress*, pp. 52-53. http://asq.org/quality-progress/2010/03/measure-for-measure/out-of-sync.pdf.

Burr, J.T. March 1993. "A New Name for a Not-So-New Concept," *Quality Progress*, pp. 87-88.

Burr, J.T. April 1997. "Keys to a Successful Internal Audit," *Quality Progress*, pp. 75-77. http://asq.org/data/subscriptions/qp/1997/0497/qp-0497burr.pdf.

Business Link. February 6, 2009. "Grow Your Business Guidebook." *Business Link.*

Byrne, D.M., and S. Taguchi. December 1987. "The Taguchi Approach to Parameter Design," *Quality Progress*, pp. 19-26.

Cacciavillani, I. 1984. "Le leggi veniziane sul territorio 1471-1789. Boschi, fiumi, bonifich e irrigazioni" (Venetian laws on the territory 1471-1789: Woods, rivers, reclamations and irrigation), Limena-Padua.

Caldwell, L.J. November 1993. "To Serve a Customer Is to Touch a Life," *Quality Progress*, pp. 117-18.

Cambridge Dictionary. "Adulteration." https://dictionary.cambridge.org/dictionary/english/adulteration.

Camp, R.C. 2006. "Benchmarking: The Search for Industry Best Practices That Lead to Superior Performance," *ASQC/Quality Press.*

Campos, M, M. January 2017. "Applications of Quartering Method in Soils and Foods." *International Journal of Engineering Research and Application* 7, no. 1(Part-2), pp. 35-39. https://www.ijera.com/papers/Vol7_issue1/Part-2/F0701023539.pdf.

Care Quality Commission. 2015. "Guidance for Providers on Meeting the Regulations." https://www.cqc.org.uk/sites/default/files/20150324_guidance_providers_meeting_regulations_01.pdf.

Care Quality Commission. May 29, 2017. "The Fundamental Standards." https://www.cqc.org.uk/what-we-do/how-we-do-our-job/fundamental-standards.

Carnegie-Mellon University. "Automated Code Repair." https://www.sei.cmu.edu/research-capabilities/all-work/display.cfm?customel_datapageid_4050=4555.

Carnegie-Mellon University SEI. 2006. "CMMI® for Development, Version 1.2, CMMI-DEV, V1.2, CMU/SEI-2006-TR-008 ESC-TR-2006-008", CMMI Product Team, Pittsburgh, PA: Carnegie Mellon, Software Engineering Institute. https://resources.sei.cmu.edu/asset_files/TechnicalReport/2006_005_001_14771.pdf.

Carnegie-Mellon University SEI. "CMMI® for Acquisition, Version 1.3 CMMI-ACQ, V1.3," CMMI Product Team, Pittsburgh, PA: Carnegie Mellon, Software Engineering Institute. https://resources.sei.cmu.edu/asset_files/TechnicalReport/2010_005_001_15284.pdf.

Carnegie-Mellon University SEI. "CMMI® for Services, Version 1.3 CMMI-SVC, V1.3," CMMI Product Team, Pittsburgh, PA: Carnegie Mellon, Software Engineering Institute, 15213-3890. https://resources.sei.cmu.edu/asset_files/TechnicalReport/2010_005_001_15290.pdf.

Cartwright, M. "Medieval Guilds," *Ancient History Encyclopaedia*. https://www.ancient.eu/Medieval_Guilds/.

Castka, P., and C.J. Corbett. January 2018. "Standards—No Joking Matter—Research Analyzes Management Systems Standards and the Implications for Managers and Auditing Bodies," *Quality Progress*, pp. 32-37. http://asq.org/quality-progress/2018/01/standards/no-joking-matter.html.

Castka, P., and C.J. Corbett. May 8, 2015. "Management Systems Standards: Diffusion, Impact and Governance of ISO 9000, ISO 14000, and Other Management Systems Standards." *Foundations and Trends in Technology and Operations Management* 7, no. 3-4.

Chamberlain, J. n.d. "Unannounced Audits: A Guide to the New BRC Requirements." https://www.sgs.com/en/news/2013/11/unannounced-audits-a-guide-to-the-new-brc-requirements.

Channel 4. December 19, 2019. "The Cure." https://www.channel4.com/programmes/the-cure.

Charity Commission for England and Wales. n.d. "Tool 1: Risk management—The Risk Assessment Cycle," Charity Commission for England and Wales, in Compliance Toolkit: Protecting Charities from Harm, Chapter 2 Charities: due diligence, monitoring and verifying the end use of charitable funds. https://assets.publishing.service.gov.uk/government/uploads/system/uploads/attachment_data/file/550688/Tool_1.pdf

Charity Commission for England and Wales. n.d. "Tool 4: Risk Management—Risk Matrix," Charity Commission for England and Wales, in Compliance Toolkit: Protecting Charities from Harm, Chapter 2 Charities: due diligence, monitoring and verifying the end use of charitable funds. https://assets.publishing.service.gov.uk/government/uploads/system/uploads/attachment_data/file/550692/Tool_4.pdf in https://www.gov.uk/government/publications/charities-due-diligence-checks-and-monitoring-end-use-of-funds.

Chassin, M.R., and R.W. Galvin. 1998. "Advisory Commission on Consumer Protection and Quality in the Health Care Industry," Institute of Medicine. https://govinfo.library.unt.edu/hcquality/final/index.htm.

Chowdry, H., and P. Fitzsimons. 2016. "The Cost of Late Intervention: Eif Analysis 2016," *Early Intervention Foundation*. https://www.eif.org.uk/download.php?file=files/pdf/cost-of-late-intervention-2016.pdf.

Coaching Leaders. n.d. "What is Appreciative Enquiry," Coaching Leaders Ltd. https://coachingleaders.co.uk/what-is-appreciative-inquiry/.

Cochran, W.G., and G.M. Cox. April 20, 1992. *Experimental Designs*. 2nd ed. Hoboken, NJ: Wiley.

Cockburn, A. 2003. *Writing Effective Use Cases*. Boston MA: Pearson Education Inc.

Cohen, L. n.d. *Quality Function Deployment—How to Make QFD Work for You*. Boston, MA: Addison-Wesley.

Cohen–Rosenthal, E. March 1994. "On Arrogance and Participation." *Journal for Quality and Participation*. http://asq.org/data/subscriptions/jqp_open/1994/march/jqpv17i2cohen.pdf.

Cokins, G. September 2006. "Measuring the Cost of Quality for Management," *Quality Progress*, pp. 45-51. http://asq.org/quality-progress/2006/09/cost-of-quality/measuring-for-management.pdf

Coleman, L.B. 2015. "Advanced Quality Auditing an Auditor's Review of Risk Based Thinking, Lean Improvement and Data Analysis." http://asq.org/audit/2015/07/advanced-quality-auditing.pdf.

Community Shares. n.d. "Cooperative and Community Benefit Societies." https://communityshares.org.uk/about-cooperative-and-community-benefit-societies.

Conklin, J.D. March 2004. "DOE and Six Sigma." *Quality Progress*, pp. 66-69. http://asq.org/quality-progress/2004/03/3.4-per-million/doe-and-six-sigma.pdf.

Conti, T. December 1989. "Process Management and Quality Function Deployment." *Quality Progress*, pp. 45-48.

Cost and Management Accounting. n.d. "What is Cost and Management Accounting?" https://www.costmanagement.eu/blog-article/what-is-cost-and-management-accounting.

Counsultancy.uk. n.d. "Management Consulting." https://www.consultancy.uk/consulting-industry/management-consulting.

Covey, S.R. October 1, 1992. *Principle Centered Leadership*. 1st ed. Hoboken, NJ: John Wiley & Sons.

Cox, G. n.d. *Appreciative Enquiry*. Bristol, UK: New Directions Ltd.

Crosby, P.B. October 22, 1987. *Quality is Free*. New York, NY: Penguin.

Crow, K. n.d. "Customer-Focused Development with QFD," NPD-Solutions DRM Associates. http://www.npd-solutions.com/qfd.html.

CQI. September 2018. "ISO 19011:2018—Understanding the International Standard," The Chartered Quality Institute.

CQI. n.d. "CQI ISO 9001:2015—Understanding the International Standard." https://www.amazon.co.uk/ISO-9001-Understanding-International-Standard-ebook/dp/B07B8T9Y78/ref=sr_1_1?dchild=1&qid=1586165356&refinements=p_27%3AThe+Chartered+Quality+Institute&s=books&sr=1-1&text=The+Chartered+Quality+Institute.

Curtis, A. October 2016. "HyperNormalisation", https://www.bbc.co.uk/iplayer/episode/p04b183c/adam-curtis-hypernormalisation hypernormalisation,

Curtis, H. January 2010. "Back to Basics Customer Delight Two Key Elements to Ensure Customer Satisfaction," *Quality Progress*, p. 16.

Dalling, I. n.d. "Management System Specification and Guidance MSS 1000:2014." *CQI Integrated Management SIG*. https://www.integratedmanagement.info/mss-1000.

Darmelio, R. May 17, 2011. *The Basics of Process Mapping*. 2nd ed. New York, NY: Routledge.

Dash, G. 2017. "Occam's Egyptian Razor: The Equinox and the Alignment of the Pyramids." *The Journal of Ancient Egyptian Architecture* 2, pp. 1-8. www.egyptian-architecture.com, http://www.egyptian-architecture.com/JAEA2/article6/JAEA2_Dash.pdf.

Datta, B.N. 2004. *Numerical Methods for Linear Control Systems*. Amsterdam, Netherlands: Elsevier, pp. 640. https://www.sciencedirect.com/book/9780122035906/numerical-methods-for-linear-control-systems#book-info.

De Vera, D., A.A. Kenny, M.A.H. Khan, and M. Mayer. June 1988. "An Automotive Case Study," *Quality Progress*, pp. 35-38.

Defeo, J.A. May 2001. "The Tip of the Iceberg—When Accounting for Quality, Don't Forget the Often Hidden Costs of Poor Quality," *Quality Progress*, pp. 29-37. http://rube.asq.org/data/subscriptions/qp/2001/0501/qp0501defeo.pdf.

Dehe, B., & D. Bamford. 2017. "Quality Function Deployment and Operational Design Decisions—A Healthcare Infrastructure Development Case Study." *Production Planning & Control* 28, no. 14, pp. 1177–1192. doi:10.1080/09537287.2017.1350767.

DeCook, R. n.d. "4.2 Shapes of Distributions," Iowa University Mathematical Sciences. http://homepage.stat.uiowa.edu/~rdecook/stat1010/notes/Section_4.2_distribution_shapes.pdf.

Deming, W.E. August 11, 2000. *Out of the Crisis*. 1st ed. Boston, MA: MIT Press.

Deming, W.E. 1975. "On Probability as a Basis for Action." *The American Statistician*, 29, no. 4, pp. 146-62.

Denes, C., and M. Țîțu. 2017. "Taguchi's Quality Loss Function and Experimentation Plan Used in (author—Wire Electrical Discharge Machining)WEDM," Nonconventional Technologies Review, Romanian Association of Nonconventional Technologies Romania. http://www.revtn.ro/index.php/revtn/article/view/182/128.

Desai, M. November 1993. "Success Through Total Quality Commitment," *Quality Progress*, pp. 65-67.

Development Trusts Association Scotland (DTAS). https://dtascot.org.uk/.

Dew, J.R. April 2017. "Impacts from the First and Second World Wars on Quality Management." *The Journal for Quality & Participation*, pp. 34-38. http://asq.org/quality-participation/2017/04/quality-management/impacts-from-the-first-and-second-world-wars-on-quality-management.pdf.

Dew, J.R. July 2015. "Best Practices—Turning on the Light Bulb—Critical Reflection Needed to Get Everyone to Understand and Embrace Quality," *Quality Progress*, pp. 30-34. http://asq.org/quality-progress/2015/07/basic-quality/turning-on-the-light-bulb.pdf.

Dibley, D. n.d. "EFQM Excellence Model and the European Quality Award," *EFQM*. http://www.unece.org/fileadmin/DAM/trade/wp6/documents/2004/roundtable/efqm_uk.pdf.

Dietrich, C.F. 1991. *Uncertainty, Calibration and Probability*. Bristol, UK: Adam Hilger.

Dillon, L.S. October 1990. "Can Japanese Methods be Applied in the Western Workplace," *Quality Progress*, pp. 27-30.

Donovan, S. 2006. "Using Cost of Quality to Improve Business Results," *Making the Case for Quality*. http://www.asq.org/2006/04/cost-of-quality/using-cost-of-quality-to-improve-business-results.pdf.

Duffy, G.L., S. Peiffer, and P. Story. April 2019. "Healthcare QMS Self-Assessment Based on a Maturity Model." *The Journal For Quality & Participation*, pp. 1-22. http://asq.org/quality-participation/2019/04/best-practices/how-well-is-your-healthcare-quality-management-system-performing.pdf.

Duffy, G.L., S. Peiffer, and P. Story. April 2019. "How Well is Your Healthcare Quality Management System Performing?" *The Journal for Quality & Participation*, pp. 12-18. http://asq.org/quality-participation/2019/04/best-practices/how-well-is-your-healthcare-quality-management-system-performing.pdf.

Duncan, L., and S. Luchs. July 2017. "Down with Silos—Offering Better Value and Achieving Better Patient Care with Lean Six Sigma," *Quality Progress*, pp. 22-29. http://asq.org/quality-progress/2017/07/six-sigma/down-with-silos.pdf.

EA. n.d. "EA-4/16 G:2003—EA Guidelines on the Expression of Uncertainty in Quantitative Testing," *European Accreditation*. https://

european-accreditation.org/wp-content/uploads/2018/10/ea-4-16-g-rev00-december-2003-rev.pdf.

EFQM. n.d. "EFQM Excellence Model." Avenue des Olympiades. https://www.efqm.org/index.php/efqm-model/.

EFQM. n.d. "EFQM Recognition." https://www.efqm.org/index.php/efqm-recognition/.

Elkington, J. 2018. "25 Years Ago I Coined the Phrase 'Triple Bottom Line.' Here's Why It's Time to Rethink It." https://hbr.org/2018/06/25-years-ago-i-coined-the-phrase-triple-bottom-line-heres-why-im-giving-up-on-it.

Engels, D.E. 1978. *Alexander the Great and the Logistics of the Macedonian Army.* Berkeley, CA: University of California Press.

Epstein M.J., and K.O. Hanson. August 2005. *Praeger Perspectives—The Accountable Corporation vol 3 Corporate Social Responsibility.* Westport, CT: Praeger Publishers.

Ellison, S.L.R., and A. Williams. 2012. *EURACHEM/CITAC Guide CG 4—Quantifying Uncertainty in Analytical Measurement.* 3rd ed. https://www.eurachem.org/images/stories/Guides/pdf/QUAM2012_P1.pdf

Ericsson, A., and R. Pool. April 21, 2016. *Peak: Secrets from the New Science of Expertise.* London, UK: Bodley Head.

Erikson, H., and M. Penker. 2000. *Business Modeling with UML: Business Patterns at Work.* Hoboken, NJ: John Wiley.

EU Environment. n.d. "EU Environmental Technology Verification." https://ec.europa.eu/environment/archives/etv/, https://ec.europa.eu/environment/ecoap/etv/, https://www.youtube.com/watch?v=UOkTDwiZnyg.

EU Environment, "EU Environmental Technology Verification pilot programme General Verification Protocol Version 1.2 – July 27th, 2016", http://etv.ios.edu.pl/sites/pliki/doc/en/eu_etv_gvp_rev2.pdf

European Commission Dg Health and Consumer. n.d. "Cosmetics and Medical Devices—Medical Devices: Guidance Document—Classification of Medical Devices." European Commission Dg Health and Consumer Directorate B Unit B2 http://ec.europa.eu/DocsRoom/documents/10337/attachments/1/translations/en/renditions/native.

Fabio, A. 2018. "Margaret Hamilton takes Software Engineering to the Moon and Beyond." https://hackaday.com/2018/04/10/margaret-hamilton-takes-software-engineering-to-the-moon-and-beyond/.

Fargnoli, M., and T. Sakaob. 2017. "Uncovering Differences and Similarities Among Quality Function Deployment-based Methods in Design for X: Benchmarking in Different Domains." *Quality Engineering* 29, no. 4, pp. 690-712. doi:10.1080/08982112.2016.1253849.

Ficalora, J.P., & L. Cohen. July 17, 2009. *Quality Function Deployment and Six Sigma: A QFD Handbook*. 2nd ed. Upper Saddle River, NJ: Prentice Hall.

Fishcount.org.uk. n.d. "Quality Benefits." http://fishcount.org.uk/fish-welfare-in-commercial-fishing/quality-and-animal-welfare.

Forsha, H.I. February 1, 1992. "The Pursuit of Quality Through Personal Change Pts 1-5," *Quality Progress*, Dubuque, IA: William C. Brown.

Fortis. 2014. "Fortis' Integrated Quality, Health, Safety, and Environmental Management System Implementation." http://asq.org/mining/ming_news/2014/10/safety/fortis-integrated-quality-health-safety-and-environmental-system-implementation.pdf.

Fortuna, R.M. June 1988. "Beyond Quality: Taking SPC Upstream," *Quality Progress*, pp. 23-28.

Frank, M., M. Braginsky, V. Marchman, and D. Yurovsky. n.d. "Variability and Consistency in Early Language Learning," The Wordbank Project, Chapter 15 Variability and Consistency. https://langcog.github.io/wordbank-book/index.html.

Frankel, D.S. 2003. *Model Driven Architecture—Applying MDA to Enterprise Computing*. Hoboken, NJ: Wiley Publishing.

Frazzon, E.M., C.M.T. Rodriguez, and C.M. Pires. 2019. "Towards Supply Chain Management 4.0." *Brazilian Journal of Operations & Production Management* 16, no. 2, pp. 180-91. https://bjopm.emnuvens.com.br/bjopm/article/view/539/823.

Freeman, R., and J. Drown. October 2016. "Leading the Way Determining Leadership's Role in ISO 9001:2015," *Quality Progress*, pp. 16-20. http://asq.org/quality-progress/2016/10/auditing/leading-the-way.html.

Freiesleben, J. February 2006. "What Are Quality Reputations Worth?" *Quality Progress*, pp. 35-40. http://rube.asq.org/data/subscriptions/qp/2006/0206/qp0206freiesleben.pdf.

Friebel, R. n.d. "Measuring Quality of Health Care in the NHS—Giving a Voice to the Patients," The Health Foundation. https://www.health

.org.uk/blogs/measuring-quality-of-health-care-in-the-nhs-giving-a-voice-to-the-patients.

Frisch, M.B. November 17, 2005. *Quality of Life Therapy: Applying a Life Satisfaction Approach to Positive Psychology and Cognitive Therapy.* Hoboken, NJ: Wiley. https://epdf.pub/quality-of-life-therapy-applying-a-life-satisfaction-approach-to-positive-psycho.html.

Frisch, M.B. January 25, 2006. "Quality of Life Therapy and Assessment in Health Care," *Clinical Psychology Science and Practice.* doi:10.1111/j.1468-2850.1998.tb00132.x.

Fry, L.W., and J.W. Slocum Jr. 2008. "Maximizing the Triple Bottom Line through Spiritual Leadership." *Organizational Dynamics* 37, no. 1, pp. 86-96. https://www.researchgate.net/publication/228618000_Maximizing_the_Triple_Bottom_Line_through_Spiritual_Leadership.

Gamage, P., N.P. Jayamaha, and N.P. Grigg. 2017. "Acceptance of Taguchi's Quality Philosophy and Practice by Lean Practitioners in Apparel Manufacturing." *Total Quality Management,* 28, no. 11, pp. 1322-38. doi:10.1080/14783363.2015.1135729.

Gander, M. December 2002. "The Importance of Improved Design—How Product Design Affects Significant Factors in Manufacturing," *Quality Progress.* http://asq.org/quality-progress/2002/12/one-good-idea/the-importance-of-improved-design.html.

Gane, C., and T. Sarson. July 1977. *Structured Systems Analysis: Tools & Techniques.* St. Louis, MO: McDonnell Douglas.

Gantt, H.L. 1916. *Industrial Leadership.* New Haven, CT: Yale University Press, pp. 52-53.

Gantt, H.L. February 18, 2015. *Industrial Leadership: Scholar's Choice.* New Haven, CT: Yale University Press.

Galarnyk, M. "Explaining the 68-95-99.7 Rule for a Normal Distribution," *Towards Data Science.* https://towardsdatascience.com/understanding-the-68-95-99-7-rule-for-a-normal-distribution-b7b7cbf760c2.

Garvin, D.A. November to December 1991. "How the Baldrige Award Really Works," *Harvard Business Review.* https://hbr.org/1991/11/how-the-baldrige-award-really-works.

George, M.L., D. Rowlands, M. Price, and J. Maxey. 2005. *The Lean Six Sigma Pocket Toolbox.* New York, NY: McGraw-Hill.

Glassa, J.C., G. McCallion, D.G. McKillop, S. Rasaratnama, and K.S. Stringer. 2009. "Best-practice Benchmarking in UK Higher Education: New Nonparametric Approaches Using Financial Ratios and Profit Efficiency Methodologies." *Applied Economics* 41, 249–267. http://www.informaworld.com, doi:10.1080/00036840600994278.

Glicken, M.D., and B.C. Robinson. 2013. *Treating Worker Dissatisfaction During Economic Change*. Cambridge, MA: Academic Press.

Goodden, R. May 16, 2011. "ASQ World Conference on Quality and Improvement," Pittsburgh.

Gopalakrishnan, K.N., B.E. McIntyre, and J.C. Sprague. September 1992. "Implementing Internal Quality Improvement with the House of Quality," *Quality Progress*, pp. 57-60.

Graber, J.M., R.E. Breisch, and W.E. Breisch. June 1992. "Performance Appraisals and Deming: A Misunderstanding," *Quality Progress*, pp. 59-62.

Graessel, B., and P. Zeidler. November 1993. "Using QFD to Improve Customer Service," Quality Progress, pp. 59-63.

Gray, J. April 1995. "Quality Costs: A Report Card on Business," *Quality Progress*, pp. 51-54. http://asq.org/data/subscriptions/qp/1995/0495/qp0495gray.pdf.

Green, R. n.d. "ISO 19011:2018—The Good, the Bad and the Downright Ugly," KCS Kingsford Consultancy Services and Qualsys. https://quality.eqms.co.uk/hubfs/CQI%20presentations23_RG.pdf.

Green, R., and C. MacNee. 2015. "Implementing ISO 9001:2015-9001: 2015 Transition Training," CQI and IRCA, Implementing ISO 9001:2015 Training Course.

Gryna, F.M. April 16, 2001. *Quality Planning and Analysis: From Product Development through Use*. 4th ed. New York, NY: McGraw-Hill Education.

Gryna, F.M., and J.M. Juran. n.d. *Quality Planning and Analysis*. 3rd ed. New York, NY: McGraw Hill.

Ham, C., D. Berwick, and J. Dixon. February 2016. "Improving Quality in the English NHS—A Strategy for Action." *The Kings Fund*. https://www.kingsfund.org.uk/sites/default/files/field/field_publication_file/Improving-quality-Kings-Fund-February-2016.pdf.

Hambling, B. n.d. *Managing Software Quality—ISO 9000 3 in an Iterative World.* New York, NY: McGraw-Hill.

Hammar, M. 2015. "ISO 9001 Horizontal Audit vs. Vertical Audit," *9001 Academy—ISO 9001 Blog.* https://advisera.com/9001academy/blog/2015/03/03/iso-9001-horizontal-audit-vs-vertical-audit/.

Hammer, M., and J. Champy. August 23, 2001. *Reengineering the Corporation: A Manifesto for Business Revolution.* 3rd ed. Boston, MA: Nicholas Brealey Publishing.

Handy, C. January 15, 2009. *Gods of Management: The Changing Work of Organisations.* London, UK: Souvenir Press Ltd.

Hardin, G. 1968. "Tragedy of the Commons." *Science* 162, pp. 1243-48, The Library of Economics and Liberty. https://www.econlib.org/library/Enc/TragedyoftheCommons.html.

Hare, L. July 2003. "SPC: From Chaos to Wiping the Floor," *Quality Progress*, pp. 58-63. http://asq.org/pub/qualityprogress/past/0703/qp0703hare.pdf.

Hare, L.B. August 2001. "Chicken Soup for Processes—Understanding Process Variation is a Prerequisite to Using SPC," *Quality Progress*, pp. 76-79. http://asq.org/pub/qualityprogress/past/0801/qp0801stats.pdf.

Harrison, R. 1987. *Organization Culture and Quality of Service: A Strategy for Releasing Love in the Workplace.* London: Association for Management Education and Development.

Harrison, R. May 26, 1995. *The Collected Papers of Roger Harrison.* San Francisco, CA: Jossey-Bass Publishers.

Hashim, M., and M. Khan. June 1990. "Quality Standards—Past, Present, Future," *Quality Progress*, pp. 56-59.

Hauser, J.R., and D. Clausing. May to June 1988. "The House of Quality," *Harvard Business Review.* http://blogs.ubc.ca/nvdteamb/files/2013/10/7-The-House-of-Quality.pdf.

Havey, M. 2005. *Essential Business Process Modelling.* Sebastopol, CA: O'Reilly Media Inc.

Healey, N., & C. Sugden. n.d. "Safety Culture on the Olympic Park." Research Report RR942, Health and Safety Executive, Health and Safety Laboratory. http://www.hse.gov.uk/research/rrpdf/rr942.pdf.

Health and Safety Executive. n.d. "Industry Specific Competences," Health and Safety Executive. http://www.hse.gov.uk/competence/industry-specific-competence.htm.

Health Foundation. August 2013. *Quality Improvement Made Simple—What Everyone Should Know About Healthcare Quality Improvement.* 2nd ed. https://www.nes.scot.nhs.uk/media/3604996/qualityimprovementmadesimple.pdf.

Herper, M. n.d. "In Shocking Reversal, Biogen to Submit Experimental Alzheimer's Drug for Approval," STAT. https://www.statnews.com/2019/10/22/biogen-to-submit-aducanumab/.

Hindle, T. April 5, 2012. *Triple Bottom Line in The Economist Guide to Management Ideas and Gurus.* Main edition. Economist Books.

Hippel, P.V. n.d. "Skewness," Entry from Lovric, M., Ed. (2010). International Encyclopedia of Statistical Science. New York, NY: Springer.

Hirschmeier, J., and T. Yui. 1975. *The Development of Japanese Business: 1600-1973.* Cambridge, MA: Harvard University Press.

Hittman, J.A. October 1993. "TQM and CQI in Postsecondary Education," *Quality Progress*, pp. 77–80.

Hoel, P.G., S.C. Port, and C.J. Stone. 1971. *Introduction to Statistical Theory.* Boston, MA: Houghton Mifflin Company.

Holt, J. 2005. *A Pragmatic Guide to Business Process Modelling.* London, UK: British Computer Society.

Hopen, D.L. June 1991. "The Process of Communication," *Quality Progress*, pp. 48-50.

Horikiri, T. April 2017. The Toyota Management System. *Proceedings of the fifth Productivity Summit*, Sochi, Russia.

Horine, J.E., W.A. Haley, and L. Rubach. October 1993. "Shaping America's Future," *Quality Progress*, pp. 41-60.

Horine, J.E., W.A. Haley, and L. Rubach. October 1993. "Transforming Schools," *Quality Progress*, pp. 31-38.

Hostetter, M. n.d. "Case Study: Improving Performance at Charleston Area Medical Center," The Commonwealth Fund. https://www.commonwealthfund.org/publications/newsletter-article/case-study-improving-performance-charleston-area-medical-center.

IEC. n.d. "ISO/IEC DIR 1:2019 Edition 15.0 Consolidated with IEC SUP:2019 Edition 13.0— Procedures for the Technical

Work—Procedures Specific to IEC." https://www.iec.ch/members_experts/refdocs/iec/isoiecdir1-consolidatediecsup%7Bed15.0.RLV%7Den.pdf.

ILX Group. n.d. "PRINCE2—A Structured Project Management Methodology." https://www.prince2.com/uk/prince2-methodology.

Ingram, T. n.d. "Project Risk Management." http://www.strategic-safety-consultants.com.

Institute of Medicine. 2001. *Crossing the Quality Chasm: A New Health System for the 21st Century.* Washington, DC: The National Academies Press. https://www.nap.edu/catalog/10027/crossing-the-quality-chasm-a-new-health-system-for-the.

International Atomic Energy Authority. n.d. "The Competency Framework—A Guide for IAEA Managers and Staff," International Atomic Energy Agency. https://www.iaea.org/sites/default/files/18/03/competency-framework.pdf.

International Statistical Engineering Association. n.d. https://isea-change.org.

Isaacson, W. 2011. *Steve Jobs.* New York, NY: Simon & Schuster, p. 465.

ISACA. n.d. "Introducing COBIT." http://www.isaca.org/cobit/pages/default.aspx.

Ishikawa, K. 1991. *Guide to Quality Control.* Highlighting edition. Tokyo: Asian Productivity Organization.

ISO. 2017. "ISO and Food," *ISO.* https://www.iso.org/publication/PUB100297.html, https://www.iso.org/files/live/sites/isoorg/files/archive/pdf/en/iso_and_food_en.pdf.

ISO. n.d. "ISO 9000-3:1997—Quality Management and Quality Assurance Standards—Part 3: Guidelines for the Application of ISO 9001:1994 to the Development, Supply, Installation and Maintenance of Computer Software." https://www.iso.org/standard/26364.html.

ISO. n.d. "ISO/IEC/IEEE 90003:2018—Software Engineering—Guidelines for the Application of ISO 9001:2015 to Computer Software." https://www.iso.org/standard/74348.html.

ISO. n.d. "ISO 2859-1 Sampling Procedures for Inspection by Attributes—Part 1: Sampling Schemes Indexed by Acceptance Quality Limit (AQL) for Lot-by-lot Inspection." https://www.iso.org/search.html?q=2859.

ISO. n.d. "ISO 3951-1 Sampling Procedures for Inspection by Variables—Part 1: Specification for Single Sampling Plans Indexed by Acceptance Quality Limit (AQL) for Lot-by-lot Inspection for a Single Quality Characteristic and a Single AQL." https://www.iso.org/search.html?q=3951&hPP=10&idx=all_en&p=0.

ISO. n.d. "ISO 7439:2015 Copper-bearing Contraceptive Intrauterine Devices—Requirements and Tests." https://www.iso.org/search.html?q=7439&hPP=10&idx=all_en&p=0.

ISO. n.d. "ISO 7870-4:2011—Control Charts—Part 4: Cumulative Sum Charts." https://www.iso.org/search.html?q=7870&hPP=10&idx=all_en&p=0.

ISO. n.d. "ISO 9001:2015—Quality Management Systems—Requirements."

ISO. n.d. "ISO 9001:2008—Quality Management Systems—Requirements."

ISO. n.d. "ISO 9004: 2018—Quality Management—Quality of an Organization—Guidance to Achieve Sustained Success."

ISO. n.d. "ISO 11137:2-2006—Sterilization of Health Care Products—Radiation—Part 2: Establishing the Sterilization Dose." https://www.iso.org/standard/62442.html.

ISO. n.d. "ISO 11462-1:2001(en)—Guidelines for Implementation of Statistical Process Control (SPC)—Part 1: Elements of SPC." https://www.iso.org/obp/ui/#iso:std:33381:en.

ISO. n.d. "ISO 11737—Sterilization of Health Care Products—Radiation—Part 2: Establishing the Sterilization Dose." https://www.iso.org/search.html?q=11737&hPP=10&idx=all_en&p=0.

ISO. n.d. "ISO 13485:2016—Medical Devices—Quality Management Systems—Requirements for Regulatory Purposes." https://www.iso.org/search.html?q=13485.

ISO. n.d. "ISO 14034:2016—Environmental Management—Environmental Technology Verification (ETV)." https://www.iso.org/standard/43256.html.

ISO. n.d. "ISO 14971:2007—Medical Devices—Application of Risk Management to Medical Devices." https://www.iso.org/standard/38193.html.

ISO. n.d. "ISO 16355-1:2015—Application of Statistical and Related Methods to New Technology and Product Development Process—Part 1: General Principles and Perspectives of Quality Function Deployment (QFD)." https://www.iso.org/search.html?q=16355.

ISO. n.d. "ISO/IEC 17025, Third edition 2017-11—General Requirements for the Competence of Testing and Calibration Laboratories." https://www.iso.org/standard/66912.html.

ISO. n.d. "ISO/IEC 17043:2010—Conformity Assessment—General Requirements for Proficiency Testing." https://www.iso.org/standard/29366.html.

ISO. n.d. "ISO 19011: 2002—Guidelines for Quality and/or Environmental Management Systems Auditing." https://www.iso.org/search.html?q=19011.

ISO. n.d. "ISO 22000:2018—Food Safety Management Systems—Requirements for Any Organization in the Food Chain." https://www.iso.org/iso-22000-food-safety-management.html, https://www.iso.org/standard/65464.html.

ISO. n.d. "ISO 22514-1:2014—Statistical Methods in Process Management—Capability and Performance—Part 1: General Principles and Concepts." https://www.iso.org/search.html?q=22514.

ISO. n.d. "ISO 24333: 2009, Cereals and Cereal Products—Sampling."

ISO. n.d. "ISO/IEC 25010:2011—Systems and Software Engineering—Systems and Software Quality Requirements and Evaluation (SQuaRE)—System and Software Quality Models."

ISO. n.d. "ISO/IEC 27001:2013—Information Technology—Security Techniques—Information Security Management Systems—Requirements."

ISO. n.d. "ISO 28597:2017—Acceptance Sampling Procedures by Attributes—Specified Quality Levels in Nonconforming Items Per Million." https://www.iso.org/search.html?q=2859&hPP=10&idx=all_en&p=0.

ISO. n.d. "ISO 31000:2009—Risk Management—Principles and Guidelines."

ISO/IEC/IEEE. n.d. "ISO/IEC/IEEE 12207:2017(en)—Systems and Software Engineering—Software Life Cycle Processes." https://www.iso.org/obp/ui/#iso:std:iso-iec-ieee:12207:ed-1:v1:en.

ISO/IEC. n.d. "ISO IEC Guide 98-3—Uncertainty of Measurement—Part 3: Guide to the Expression of Uncertainty in Measurement (GUM:1995)." https://www.iso.org/standard/50461.html.

ISO/IEC. n.d. "ISO IEC Guide 99—International Vocabulary of Metrology—Basic and General Concepts and Associated Terms (VIM)." https://www.iso.org/standard/45324.html.

ISO/TC176/SC2/. n.d. "ISO 9000 Introduction and Support Package: Guidance on the Concept and Use of the Process Approach for Management Systems." https://www.iso.org/files/live/sites/isoorg/files/archive/pdf/en/04_concept_and_use_of_the_process_approach_for_management_systems.pdf.

ISO/UNIDO. n.d. "Building Trust—The Conformity Assessment Toolbox." https://www.iso.org/files/live/sites/isoorg/files/archive/pdf/en/casco_building-trust.pdf.

Jacobson, I., M. Christerson, P. Jonsson, and G. Overgaard. June 30, 1992. *Object-Oriented Software Engineering—A Use Case Driven Approach*. 1st edition. Boston, MA: Addison-Wesley Professional.

Jacobson, I., M. Ericsson, and A. Jacobson. September 28, 1994. *The Object Advantage—Business Process Reengineering with Object Technology*. Boston, MA: Addison Wesley.

Jamieson, A. July 1989. "Optimizing Quality Costs," *Quality Progress*, pp. 49-54.

Jayaram, A. 2016. Lean Six sigma Approach for Global Supply Chain Management using Industry 4.0 and IIoT. *2nd International Conference on Contemporary Computing and Informatics (IC3I)*, December 14–17, 2016, Noida, India. doi:10.1109/IC3I.2016.7917940.

JCGM. n.d. "JCGM—Joint Committee for Guides in Metrology." https://www.iso.org/sites/JCGM/JCGM-introduction.htm.

JCGM. n.d. "JCGM 100:2008 GUM 1995 with Minor Corrections—Evaluation of Measurement Data—Guide to the Expression of Uncertainty in Measurement," BIPM. https://www.bipm.org/utils/common/documents/jcgm/JCGM_100_2008_E.pdf.

JCGM. n.d. "JCGM 200:2012—International Vocabulary of Metrology—Basic and General Concepts and Associated Terms (VIM), 3rd edition—2008 Version with Minor Corrections," BIPM, https://www.bipm.org/utils/common/documents/jcgm/JCGM_200_2012.pdf.

Jing, G.G. May 2019. "A Fundamental FMEA Flaw—How to Increase the Efficiency and Effectiveness of Failure Mode and Effects Analysis," *Quality Progres*, pp. 26–33. http://asq.org/quality-progress/2019/05/auditing/a-fundamental-fmea-flaw.html.

Jones-Farmer, L.A., and R.W. Hoerl. May 2019. "A Unified Approach," *Quality Progress*, pp. 48-51. http://asq.org/quality-progress/2019/05/statistics-spotlight/a-unified-approach.html.

Jozwiak, G. January 15, 2019. "Ofsted Inspections to Focus on 'Quality of Education' Over Performance Data," *Children and Young People Now*. https://www.cypnow.co.uk/cyp/news/2006260/ofsted-inspections-to-focus-on-quality-of-education'-over-performance-data.

Juran, J.M. 1964. *Managerial Breakthrough: A New Concept of the Manager's Job*. New York, Toronto, and London: McGraw-Hill.

Juran, J.M., and F.M. Gryna. 1970. *Quality Planning and Analysis*. New York, NY: McGraw Hill.

Juran, J.M., F.M. Gryna, and R.S. Bingham Jr. 1951. *Quality Control Handbook*. 3rd ed. McGraw Hill.

Juran, J.M. "The Juran Trilogy: Quality Planning." https://www.juran.com/blog/the-juran-trilogy-quality-planning/.

Juran, J.M. July 1990. "China's Ancient History of Managing for Quality—Pt. 1." *Quality Progress*, 23, no. 7, pp. 31-35.

Juran, J.M. December 1991. "World War II and the Quality Movement," *Quality Progress*, pp. 19-24.

Juran, J.M. 1995. *A History of Managing for Quality—The Evolution, Trends and Future Directions of Managing for Quality*. Milwaukee, WI: ASQC Quality Press.

Juran, J.M. August 1995. "A History of Managing for Quality," *Quality Progress*, pp. 125-9. http://asq.org/data/subscriptions/qp/1995/0895/qp0895juran.pdf.

Juran, J.M. January 1, 1995. *Managerial Breakthrough*. Revised edition. New York, NY: McGraw Hill.

Kaçmaz, E. "Acceptance Sampling," *PowerPoint*. https://slideplayer.com/slide/13594292/, https://slideplayer.com/slide/download/, http://ceng.eskisehir.edu.tr/emrekacmaz/%C4%B0ST252/icerik/25.6-Acceptance-Sampling.pptx.

Kachoui, D. April 2018. "Personal Improvement—Becoming A Master—Do You have What It Takes to Achieve Mastery?" *Quality Progress*, pp. 38-43. http://asq.org/quality-progress/2018/04/career-development/becoming-a-master.pdf.

Kahler, D. September 15, 2008. Management of Design Quality. Presented at the American Society for Quality Energy & Environmental

/Design & Construction Conference Sheraton Imperial Convention Center Raleigh, North Carolina Session M21, Monday. http://asq. org/ee/2008/06/management-of-design-quality.pdf.

Karabatsos, N. June 1988. "Listening to the Voice of the Customer," *Quality Progress*, p. 5.

Keller, P., and T. Pyzdek. 2013. *Goal of Quality Cost System: The Handbook for Quality Management.* McGraw-Hill.

Kelly, T. October 1991. "Elementary Quality," *Quality Progress*, pp. 51-56.

Kenny, A.A. June 1988. "A New Paradigm for Quality Assurance," *Quality Progress*, pp. 30-32.

Kimothi, S.K. 2002. *The Uncertainty of Measurement—Physical and Chemical Metrology Impact and Analysis.* Milwaukee, WI: ASQ Quality Press.

Kingsfund. n.d. "Lessons from Stafford." https://www.kingsfund.org.uk/ sites/default/files/field/field_document/robert-francis-lessons-from-stafford.pdf.

Kingsfund. n.d. "Robert Francis QC in Conversation with Catherine Foot." https://vimeo.com/112280675.

Kingsfund. n.d. "The Francis Inquiry Report." https://www.kingsfund.org.uk/projects/francis-inquiry-report?gclid=CjwKCAiAw ZTuBRAYEiwAcr67OcnSD55hH2k52yWLZbQczQd6WN5U QCngHK7b2UgkAEpSNyrt664bDxoCLwEQAvD_BwE.

Kingsfund. n.d. "The Francis Inquiry Report." https://www.kingsfund. org.uk/projects/francis-inquiry-report.

Kirkpatrick, I., and M.M. Lucio. 1995. *The Politics of Quality in the Public Sector.* New York, NY: Routledge.

Kirkup, L., and B. Frenkel. 2006. *An introduction to Uncertainty in Measurement using the GUM.* Cambridge, UK: Cambridge University Press.

Kluse, C. n.d. "TQM and the Government—The Importance of Leadership and Personal Transformation," pp. 27-31. http://asq.org/ quality-participation/2009/10/total-quality-management/case-study-tqm-and-the-government-the-importance-of-leadership-and-personal-transformation.pdf.

Koltko-Rivera, M.E. 2006. "Rediscovering the Later Version of Maslow's Hierarchy of Needs: Self-Transcendence and Opportunities for

Theory, Research, and Unification." *Review of General Psychology* 10, no. 4, pp. 302-17. https://www.simplypsychology.org/maslow(2).pdf.

Kovach, J.V. April 2018. "The Path to Personal Quality," *Quality Progress*, p. 16. http://asq.org/quality-progress/2018/04/career-coach/the-path-to-personal-productivity.html.

Kramer, B.S. September 1990. "The Consumer's Risk in Clinical Trials." *Molecular Biotheraphy* 2, no. 3, pp. 132-6. https://www.ncbi.nlm.nih.gov/pubmed/2222896.

Kremer, W., and C. Hammond. n.d. "Abraham Maslow and the Pyramid that Beguiled Business." https://www.bbc.co.uk/news/magazine-23902918.

Kulier, R., P. O'Brien, F.M. Helmerhorst, M. Usher-Patel, and C. d'Arcangues. 2007. "Copper Containing, Framed Intra-uterine Devices for Contraception." *Cochrane Database of Systematic Reviews* no. 4. Art. No.: CD005347. https://www.cochranelibrary.com/cdsr/doi/10.1002/14651858.CD005347.pub3/epdf/full.

Kurzweil, R. March 9, 2006. *The Singularity is Near*. London, UK: Duckworth.

Lane, F.C. 1978. "Storia di Venezia," Turin, p. 421.

Law Society. n.d. *Lexcel—the Legal Practice Quality Mark*. London, UK: The Law Society's Hall. https://www.lawsociety.org.uk/for-the-public/quality-marks/legal-practice/.

Learn about Quality. n.d. "Continuous Improvement," *ASQ*. https://asq.org/quality-resources/continuous-improvement.

Legal Services Panel. September 2010. *Quality in Legal Services*. London, UK: Legal Services Panel. https://www.legalservicesconsumerpanel.org.uk/publications/research_and_reports/documents/VanillaResearch_ConsumerResearch_QualityinLegalServices.pdf.

Lendrich, P. Winter 2014. "QHSE Programs Ensuring Quality for Australian Businesses," *gastoday.com.au*. https://web.a.ebscohost.com/ehost/pdfviewer/pdfviewer?vid=2&sid=8c542d5a-9433-42ab-ba17-32ef529cbc13%40sdc-v-sessmgr03.

Lewis, C.J. 1995. "Implementing Total Quality Management in The Public Sector." *Theses Digitization Project*. https://scholarworks.lib.csusb.edu/etd-project/1106, https://pdfs.semanticscholar.org/8612/9 50e65ad75155508bc9ea2dbb5e3ec0bdf9a.pdf.

S. Lewis, 1922, "Babbit"

Limpert, E. and W.A. Stahel, 14 Jul 2011, "Problems with Using the Normal Distribution – and Ways to Improve Quality and Efficiency of Data Analysis", Plos One, https://journals.plos.org/plosone/article?id=10.1371/journal.pone.0021403 and https://www.ncbi.nlm.nih.gov/pmc/articles/PMC3136454/

LMS. n.d. "Farm Quality Assurance," Livestock & Meat Commission for Northern Ireland. https://www.lmcni.com/farm-quality-assurance/.

Lockheed Martin. n.d. "Risk and Opportunity Management Overview." https://www.lockheedmartin.com/content/dam/lockheed-martin/eo/documents/suppliers/training-2017-risk-opportunity-mgmt.pdf.

Low Incomes Tax Reform Group. n.d. "Digital Exclusion," Low Incomes Tax Reform Group of The Chartered Institute of Taxation. https://www.litrg.org.uk/sites/default/files/digital_exclusion_-_litrg_report.pdf.

Lowe, C.W. November 1969. *Critical Path Analysis by Bar Chart: The New Role of Job Progress Charts (A Business Management Book)*. Revised edition. London: Business Books.

Lowe, T.A., and G.M. McBean. November 1989. "Honesty Without Fear," *Quality Progress*, pp. 30-34.

Lowenthal, J.N. January 1994. "Reengineering the Organization: A Step-by-Step Approach to Corporate Revitalization—Part 1," *Quality Progress*, pp. 93-95.

Lowenthal, J.N. February 1994. "Reengineering the Organization: A Step-by-Step Approach to Corporate Revitalization—Part 2." *Quality Progress*, pp. 61-63.

Lowenthal, J.N. March 1994. "Reengineering the Organization: A Step-by-Step Approach to Corporate Revitalization—Part 3," *Quality Progress*, pp.131-33.

Lira, I. 2002. *Evaluating the Measurement Uncertainty: Fundamentals and Practical Guidance*. Bristol, UK: Institute of Physics Publishing.

Liu, S. February 2018. "Six Sigma—The Crown Jewels of Design—Overcoming Vulnerabilities with Axiomatic and Taguchi Robust Parameter Design," *Quality Progress*, pp. 22-29. http://asq.org/quality-progress/2018/02/engineering/the-crown-jewels-of-design.pdf.

Luko, S. 2019. "Risk and Uncertainty." *ASQ Statistics Digest* 38, no. 3, pp. 35-47.

Machiba, T. n.d. "OECD Project on Sustainable Manufacturing and Eco-innovation," OECD Directorate for Science, Technology and Industry. www.oecd.org/sti/innovation/sustainablemanufacturing.

Mader, D.P. January 2008. "Lean Six Sigma's Evolution—Integrated Method uses Different Deployment Models," *Quality Progress*, pp. 40-48. http://asq.org/quality-progress/2008/01/economic-case-for-quality/lean-six-sigmas-evolution.pdf.

Mader, D.P. July 2004. "Selecting Design for Six Sigma Projects," *Quality Progress*, pp. 65-70. http://asq.org/data/subscriptions/qp/2004/0704/qp07043.4permillion.pdf.

Madison, J. n.d. "Federalist No. 51 (1788)." https://billofrightsinstitute.org/founding-documents/primary-source-documents/the-federalist-papers/federalist-papers-no-51/.

Mahbod, R., and D.H. Captain. Winter 2019. "Blockchain: The Future of the Auditing and Assurance Profession." *Armed Forces Comptroller* 64, no. 1, pp. 23-27. https://www.rmafed.com/blockchain-the-future-of-the-auditing-and-assurance-profession/, https://cdn.flipsnack.com/widget/v2/widget.html?hash=fc3eoiflu&bgcolor=EEEEEE&t=1548875669.

Manchanda, A. June 2019. "Constructing Quality," *Quality Progress*, pp. 26-35. http://asq.org/quality-progress/2019/06/cost-of-quality/constructing-quality.html.

Martin, J., and C. McLure. n.d. "Structured Techniques for Computing," 2 Vols, Savant Research Institute.

Maslow, A.H. 1987. Motivation and Personality, Pearson, 3 ed, 7 Jan. 1997, In ed. R. Frager, J. Fadiman, C. McReynolds, & R. Cox. Addison Wesley.

Maslow, A.H. January 7, 1997. *Motivation and Personality*. 3rd ed. London: Pearson.

Massachusetts Institute of Technology. April 23, 20. "Explainer: What is a Blockchain?" *MIT Technology Review*, p. 18. www.technologyreview.com/s/610833/explainer-what-is-a-blockchain/.

Mathsisfun. n.d. "Normal Distribution." https://www.mathsisfun.com/data/standard-normal-distribution.html.

McArthur, E. n.d. "Our Mission is to Accelerate the Transition to a Circular Economy." https://www.ellenmacarthurfoundation.org/our-story/mission.

McClelland, D.C. June 12, 2015. *The Achievement Motive*. Eastford, CT: Martino Fine Books.

McFadden, F.R. June 1993. "Six-Sigma Quality Programs," *Quality Progress*, pp. 37-42.

McIver, K.D. February 2017. "Good Shepherds—Applying Tragedy of the Commons Theory for More Effective Resource Management," *Quality Progress*, pp. 30-34. http://asq.org/quality-progress/2017/02/project-management/good-shepherds.html.

McLeod, S.A. May 21, 2018. "Maslow's Hierarchy of Needs." Retrieved from https://www.simplypsychology.org/maslow.html.

McMaster, B. n.d. "Supporting Excellence in the Arts—From Measurement to Judgement," Department for Culture, Media and Sport. https://webarchive.nationalarchives.gov.uk/+/http:/www.culture.gov.uk/images/publications/supportingexcellenceinthearts.pdf.

McNamee, M. November 1, 2016. "Taking Risk Management by StORM—How Strategic Objective-based Risk Management Changes Everything," *LinkedIN*. https://www.linkedin.com/pulse/taking-risk-management-storm-mark-mcnamee/.

Mead, M. (Ed.) 1954. *Cultural Patterns and Technical Change*. Paris: United Nations Educational, Scientific and Cultural Organisation.

Mellat-Parast, M., E.C. Jones, and S.G. Adam. September 2007. "Six Sigma and Baldrige: A Quality Alliance," *Quality Progress*, pp. 45-51. http://asq.org/quality-progress/2007/09/baldrige-national-quality-program/six-sigma-and-baldrige-a-quality-alliance.pdf.

Merrill, P. May 2015. "A Brief History of Quality—Recognizing the Past while Anticipating Future Customers' Needs," *Quality Progress*, pp. 42-44. http://asq.org/quality-progress/2015/05/innovation/a-brief-history-of-quality.pdf.

Merrill, P. March 2012. "Seize the Opportunity Who will Improve Food Safety?" *Quality Progress*, pp. 44-45. http://asq.org/quality-progress/2013/03/innovation/seize-the-opportunity.pdf.

Merry, M.D., and M.G. Crago. September to October 2001. "The Past, Present and Future of Health Care Quality—Urgent Need/or Innovative) External Review Processes to Protect Patients," The Physician

Executive. https://pdfs.semanticscholar.org/eefd/b183d2c81eb90df1
1899716339aee3ae9228.pdf.

McGill, B.K. November 1990. "Return to Chaos," *Quality Progress*,
pp. 55-57.

Miura, A. September 2004. "MIL-Q-9858A, the Origin of ISO 9001,"
ASQ CSD Partnership News. http://asq.org/fdc/2012/06/mil-
q-9858a-the-origin-of-iso-9001.pdf.

Moen, R., and N. Clifford. "Evolution of the PDCA Cycle." http://www
.idemployee.id.tue.nl/g.w.m.rauterberg/lecturenotes/DG000%20
DRP-R/references/Moen-Norman-2009.pdf.

Moen, R.D. November 1989. "The Performance Appraisal System:
Deming's Deadly Disease," *Quality Progress*, pp. 62-66.

Moen, R.D., and C.L. Norman. June 2016. "Quality History—Always
Applicable Deming's System of Profound Knowledge Remains Relevant for Management and Quality Professionals Today," *Quality
Progress*, pp. 46-53. http://asq.org/quality-progress/2016/06/basic-
quality/always-applicable.pdf.

Montano, C.B., and G.H. Utter. August 1999. "Total Quality Management in Higher Education—An Application of Quality Improvement
in a University," *Quality Progress*, pp. 52-59. http://asq.org/data/sub-
scriptions/qp/1999/0899/qp0899montano.pdf.

Montgomery, D.C. August 7, 2012. *Statistical Quality Control: A Modern
Introduction*. 7th Edition International Student Version. Hoboken,
NY: John Wiley & Sons.

Morgan, J.D. 2019. It's No Longer Enough to Simply Be Agile. Presented
at the 6th Annual University of Maryland Project Management Symposium, College Park, Maryland, May 2019. https://pmworldjournal.
com/article/its-no-longer-enough-to-simply-be-agile.

Motschman, T., C. Bales, and L. Timmerman. April 2016. "Improving Healthcare Monograph Series, A Hospital-Based Healthcare
Quality Management System Model," Healthcare Technical Committee. http://asq.org/2016/04/quality-management/a-hospital-based-
healthcare-quality-management-system-model.pdf.

MSC. n.d. *The MSC Fisheries Standard*. London: Marine Stewardship
Council. https://www.msc.org/standards-and-certification/fisheries
-standard.

Muelaner, J. October 31, 2019. "An Introduction to Statistical Process Control (SPC)—Keeping an Eye on the Big Picture." *Quality Digest.* https://www.qualitydigest.com/print/32965, https://www.qualitydigest.com/inside/management-article/introduction-statistical-process-control-spc-102419.html.

Murthy, J. n.d. "What is the Difference between Accreditation and Certification?" *Planning and Building Control Today.* https://www.pbctoday.co.uk/news/planning-construction-news/accreditation-and-certification-difference/32133/, https://www.ukas.com/download/case-studies/pr/Plannin-and-Building-Control-Today-April-issue-2017.pdf.

National Quality Board. April 2013. "Quality in the New Health System—Maintaining and Improving Quality." https://assets.publishing.service.gov.uk/government/uploads/system/uploads/attachment_data/file/213304/Final-NQB-report-v4-160113.pdf.

National Quality Board. 2016. "Shared Commitment to Quality," National Quality Board, NHS England Publications Gateway. https://www.england.nhs.uk/wp-content/uploads/2016/12/nqb-shared-commitment-frmwrk.pdf.

Naur, P., and B. Randell. October 11, 1968. "Software Engineering—Report," Garmisch, Germany: Nato Science Committee. http://homepages.cs.ncl.ac.uk/brian.randell/NATO/nato1968.PDF.

NHS Improvement. n.d. "Statistical Process Control." https://improvement.nhs.uk/documents/2171/statistical-process-control.pdf.

NHS Improvement. October 2011. "An Overview of Statistical Process Control (SPC)." https://www.england.nhs.uk/improvement-hub/wp-content/uploads/sites/44/2017/11/An-Overview-of-Statistical-Process-Control-SPC.pdf.

NHS National Patient Safety Agency. January 2008. "A Risk Matrix for Risk Managers." https://www.neas.nhs.uk/media/118673/foi.16.170_-_risk_matrix_for_risk_managers_v91.pdf.

Nichols, A. 2018. "How Football Can Help with Auditing a Process-Based QMS," Michigan Manufacturing Technology Center. https://www.the-center.org/Blog/June-2018/How-Football-Can-Help-with-Auditing-a-Process-Base.

Nicholson, S.D. January to April 2013. "Quality in the New Health System—Maintaining and Improving Quality." https://assets.

publishing.service.gov.uk/government/uploads/system/uploads/attachment_data/file/213304/Final-NQB-report-v4-160113.pdf.

Niemann, C. November 2015. "Measure for Measure, Lab Without a Mask—Getting Value from Inspections," *Quality Progress*. http://asq.org/quality-progress/2015/11/measure-for-measure/lab-without-a-mask.html.

NIST. n.d. "Baldrige Performance Excellence Program—Baldrige Excellence Framework." https://www.nist.gov/baldrige, https://www.nist.gov/baldrige/publications/baldrige-excellence-framework.

NIST. September 2012. "NIST Special Publication 800-30 Revision 1 Guide for Conducting Risk Assessments," Computer Security Division Information Technology Laboratory National Institute of Standards and Technology Gaithersburg. https://nvlpubs.nist.gov/nistpubs/Legacy/SP/nistspecialpublication800-30r1.pdf.

NIST/SEMATECH. n.d. "6.1.6. What is Process Capability?" e-Handbook of Statistical Methods. http://www.itl.nist.gov/div898/handbook/, https://www.itl.nist.gov/div898/handbook/toolaids/pff/pmc.pdf,https://www.itl.nist.gov/div898/handbook/pmc/section1/pmc16.htm.NIST/SEMATECH. n.d. "6.1.6. What is Process Capability?" e-Handbook of Statistical Methods. http://www.itl.nist.gov/div898/handbook/, https://www.itl.nist.gov/div898/handbook/toolaids/pff/pmc.pdf,https://www.itl.nist.gov/div898/handbook/pmc/section1/pmc16.htm.NIST/SEMATECH. n.d. "6.1.6. What is Process Capability?" e-Handbook of Statistical Methods. http://www.itl.nist.gov/div898/handbook/, https://www.itl.nist.gov/div898/handbook/toolaids/pff/pmc.pdf, https://www.itl.nist.gov/div898/handbook/pmc/section1/pmc16.htm.

Nolan, T.W., and L.P. Provost. May 1990. "Understanding Variation," *Quality Progress*, pp. 70-78.

Nova, "Einstein's Quantum Riddle", https://www.pbs.org/wgbh/nova/video/einsteins-quantum-riddle/ and https://www.youtube.com/watch?v=Mn4AwineA5o

Nolan, T.W., R.J. Perla, and L.P. Provost. November 2016. "Understanding Variation—26 Years Later—Correctly Assessing Variation is Fundamental to Sound Decisions," *Quality Progress*, pp. 28-37. http://asq.org/quality-progress/2016/11/best-practices/understanding-variation26-years-later.pdf.

Nonaka, I. September 1993. "The History of the Quality Circle," *Quality Progress*, pp. 81-83.

NPD Solutions. n.d. "Failure Modes and Effects Analysis (FMEA)," DRM Associates. http://www.npd-solutions.com/firm-overview.html.

NPL. n.d. "Traceability and Uncertainty," NPL. http://resource.npl.co.uk/docs/publications/newsletters/metromnia/issue14_traceability_poster.pdf.

Oakland, J., and R.J. Oakland. October 22, 2018. *Statistical Process Control*. 7th ed. New York, NY: Routledge.

Organisation for Economic Co-Operation and Development. n.d. "Sustainable Manufacturing And Eco-Innovation Framework, Practices and Measurement Synthesis Report." https://www.oecd.org/innovation/inno/43423689.pdf.

Office of Financial Management. n.d. "Competency Examples with Performance Statements," Washington State Office of Financial Management. https://www.google.co.uk/url?sa=t&rct=j&q=&esrc=s&source=web&cd=19&cad=rja&uact=8&ved=2ahUKEwiOwaugwnkAhUUTBUIHb4iDnQQFjASegQICRAC&url=https%3A%2F%2Fofm.wa.gov%2Fsites%2Fdefault%2Ffiles%2Fpublic%2Fshr%2FStrategic%2520HR%2FWorkforce%2520Planning%2FCompetencyExamples.doc&usg=AOvVaw1JVptqUz1WrStj52zFWkfJ.

Operational Excellence. n.d. "EFQM Excellence Model—A Model for Business Excellence." https://www.slideshare.net/oeconsulting/e-25124937.

Øvretveit, J. 2009. "Does Improving Quality Save Money? A Review of Evidence of Which Improvements to Quality Reduce Costs to Health Service Providers," *The Health Foundation*. https://www.health.org.uk/sites/default/files/DoesImprovingQualitySaveMoney_Evidence.pdf.

Pai, W.C. Summer 2002. "A Quality-Enhancing Software Function Deployment Model," Information Systems Management..

Pang, V.K. February 1992. "Scientifically Selecting Suppliers," *Quality Progress*, pp. 43-45.

Pant, S. n.d. "Dive into PowerApps: Building Apps That Mean Business Without Writing Code," Channel 9. https://channel9.msdn.com/Events/Ignite/2016/BRK3326-TS.

Paris, C. April 12, 2019. *Surviving ISO 9001: 2015*. 2nd ed. Tampa, FL: Oxebridge Quality Resources International.

Pascale, R. 1990. *Managing on the Edge*. New York: Simon & Schuster.

Paul, D., J. Cadle, and D. Yeates (eds.). 2014. *Business Analysis*. Swindon: BCS Learning and Development.

Paulk, M.C. 2009. "A History of the Capability Maturity Model for Software," *SQP* 12, no. 1. http://citeseerx.ist.psu.edu/viewdoc/download ?rep=rep1&type=pdf&doi=10.1.1.216.199.

Pearson. n.d. "Acceptance Sampling Plans," Pearson MyLab Operations Management. https://www.pearsonmylabandmastering.com/global/myomlab/, https://wps.prenhall.com/wps/media/objects /7117/7288732/65767_28_SuppG.pdf.

Pena-Rodriguez, M.E. April 2018. "Serious About Samples," *Quality Progress*, p. 19. http://asq.org/quality-progress/2018/04/process-management/serious-about-samples.html.

Peters, T.J., and R. H. Waterman, Jr. 1982. *In Search of Excellence*. New York, NY: Harper & Row.

Peiffer, S.E., P.B. Story, and G.L. Du. October 2016. "The Impact of Human Factors on a Hospital-Based Quality Management System," *The Journal for Quality & Participation*, pp. 19-23. http://asq.org/quality-participation/2016/10/quality-management/the-impact-of-human-factors-on-a-hospital-based-quality-management-system.pdf.

Peiffer, S., G. Kollm, C. Graham-Clark, R. Denis, G.L. Duffy, V. Araujo, and P. Story. January 2018. "Finding Solutions to Quality Issues That Affect the Healthcare Industry." *The Journal for Quality & Participation*, pp. 1-11. http://asq.org/quality-participation/2018/01/best-practices/finding-solutions-to-quality-issues-that-affect-all-aspects-of-healthcare-across-the-globe.pdf.

Pollo, M.V. n.d. "The Ten Books on Architecture—Book IX Introduction." https://www.math.nyu.edu/~crorres/Archimedes/Crown/Vitruvius.html.

Population Council. 1984. "NDA 18–680 Application to FDA for CuT380A IUD," Population Council.

Powell, T. July 11, 2019. "Early Intervention." House of Commons Library, Briefing Paper Number 7647. https://researchbriefings.files.parliament.uk/documents/CBP-7647/CBP-7647.pdf.

Powers, J. July 1993. "TQM in Software Development Organizations," *Quality Progress*, pp. 79-80.

PWC. n.d. "Student Careers." https://www.pwc.co.uk/careers/student-jobs/work-for-us/graduateopportunities/consulting/management-consulting.html.

Pursuit of Happiness. n.d. "Abraham Maslow and the Hierarchy of Happiness." http://www.pursuit-of-happiness.org/history-of-happiness/abraham-maslow/.

Pyzdek, T. April 1993. "Process Control for Short and Small Runs," *Quality Progress*, pp. 51-60.

QMS. n.d. "Whole Chain Assurance," Quality Meat Scotland.

Quality-One. n.d. "Gage Repeatability & Reproducibility (Gage R&R)." https://quality-one.com/grr/.

Quality-One. n.d. "Introduction to Failure Mode and Effects Analysis (FMEA)." https://quality-one.com/fmea/.

Quality Magazine. May 16, 2003. "Motorola: A Tradition of Quality." https://www.qualitymag.com/articles/84187-motorola-a-tradition-of-quality?

Quality World. September 2019. "Nestlé to Pilot Blockchain Technology," *Quality World*, p. 2. https://members.quality.org/SelfService/My_Professional_Development/Quality_World_Magazine.aspx https://www.flipsnack.com/5F6FB67EFB5/qw-september-2019/download-pdf.html.

Radziwill, N. October 2018. "Let's Get Digital," *Quality Progress*, pp. 24-29. http://asq.org/quality-progress/2018/10/basic-quality/lets-get-digital.html.

Raistrick, C., P. Francis, J. Wright, C. Carter, and I. Wilkie. 2004. *Model Driven Architecture with Executable UML*. Cambridge, UK: Cambridge University Press.

Rallings, J., and L. Payne. 2016. "The Case for Early Support." https://b.barnardos.org.uk/case-for-early-support-2016.pdf.

Ramsey, M.H., and S.L.R. Ellison (eds.). "Measurement Uncertainty Arising from Sampling: A Guide to Methods and Approaches," Eurachem, EUROLAB, CITAC, Nordtest and the RSC Analytical Methods Committee. https://www.eurachem.org/index.php/publications/guides/musamp, https://www.eurachem.org/images/stories/Guides/pdf/UfS_2007.pdf.

Rao, N. October 2018. "The Time Is Now," *Quality Progress*, pp. 19-23. http://asq.org/quality-progress/2018/10/global-quality/the-time-is-now.html.

Ravanavar, G.M., and P.M. Charantimath. "Strategic Formulation Using Tows Matrix–A Case Study." *International Journal of Research and Development* 1, no. 1. http://ijrdonline.com/journal/1344316744strategic.pdf, http://blog.oxfordcollegeofmarketing.com/2016/06/07/tows-analysis-guide/.

Reber, M.F. May 2019. "In No Uncertain Terms," *Quality Progress*, pp. 18-24. http://asq.org/quality-progress/2019/05/continuous-improvement/in-no-uncertain-terms.html.

Red Tractor. n.d. "Red Tractor Assurance," *Red Tractor*. https://assurance.redtractor.org.uk/.

Reichman, W. August 30, 1973. *Use and Abuse of Statistics*. New Impression edition. New York, NY: Penguin.

Reid, R.D. July 2015. "Standards—Open to Change—How Expected Revisions to ISO 9001:2015 May Affect Sector-specific Standards," *Quality Progress*, pp. 18-23. http://asq.org/quality-progress/2015/07/standards/open-to-change.pdf.

Reid, R.D. November 2017. "Standard Issues—IATF 16949—Navigating Difficult Requirements—An In-depth Look at Process Control, One of the Most-cited IATF 16949 Requirements," *Quality Progress*, pp. 63-65. http://asq.org/quality-progress/2017/11/standards-issues/navigating-difficult-requirements.html.

Renault Institute of Quality Management. n.d. *Renault Quality Dealership Programme Step 9—How to Improve Teamwork*. Hertfordshire, WD: The Rivers Office Park.

Resnick, B. November 16, 2018. "The World Just Redefined the Kilogram—It Involves Complex Science and Beautifully Simple Philosophy." *EST*. https://www.vox.com/science-and-health/2018/11/14/18072368/kilogram-kibble-redefine-weight-science.

ReVelle, J.B. November 2017. "Forward Progress—Looking Back at Quality's Evolution Over the Past 50 Years and Seeing Where the Movement Is Headed," *Quality Progress*, pp. 16-32. http://asq.org/quality-progress/2017/11/basic-quality/forward-progress.pdf.

Roberts, M. October 22, 2019. "First Drug That Can Slow Alzheimer's Dementia," Health Editor, *BBC News*. https://www.bbc.co.uk/news/health-50137041.

Robitaille, D. July 2019. "Cost of Quality—The Language of Value—A New American National Standard Aligns Cost of Quality with Management Systems," *Quality Progress*, pp. 47-50. http://asq.org/quality-progress/2019/07/standards-issues/the-value-of-change.pdf.

Rodríguez, M., M. Piattini, and C.M. Fernβndez. September 2015. "Software Quality—A Hard Look at Software Quality—Pilot Program Uses ISO/IEC 25000 Family," *Quality Progress*, pp. 30-36. http://asq.org/quality-progress/2015/09/software-quality/a-hard-look-at-software-quality.pdf.

Rollefson, M.M. November 1991. "The Total Quality Appraisal Survey: Where Do You Stand?" *Quality Progress*, pp. 54-57.

Ross, J.E. n.d. "Total Quality Management—Quality Costs." https://totalqualitymanagement.wordpress.com/2008/09/12/cost-of-quality/.

Ross, P.J. June 1988. "The Role of Taguchi Methods and Design of Experiments in QFD," *Quality Progress*, pp. 41-47.

Ross, R. April 26, 2017. "Eureka! The Archimedes Principle," *LiveScience/Pure Science*. https://www.livescience.com/58839-archimedes-principle.html.

Roy, R.K. 2010. *A Primer on the Taguchi Method*, 2nd ed. Dearborn, MI: SME.

Russell, J.P. February 2007. "Know and Follow ISO 19011's Auditing Principles," *Quality Progress*, pp. 29-34. http://asq.org/quality-progress/2007/02/auditing/iso-19011-principles.pdf.

Ryan, S.M.J. June 3, 2016. "The Heart and Science of Health Care Quality," IAQ General Meeting in Helsinki, Finland. https://img1.wsimg.com/blobby/go/f9efea8c-f34b-41d8-a64d-aac8dd7f72ca/downloads/1cpkoibv1_179495.pdf?ver=1572443644267.

Salmon, V.R. n.d. "Quality in American Schools," *Quality Progress*, pp. 73-75.

Samohyl, R.W. June 2018. "Acceptance Sampling for Attributes via Hypothesis Testing and the Hypergeometric Distribution." *Journal of Industrial Engineering International* 14, no. 2, pp. 395-414. https://link.springer.com/article/10.1007/s40092-017-0231-9.

Sarin, S. May 1997. "Teaching Taguchi's Approach to Parameter Design," *Quality Progress*, pp. 102-106. http://asq.org/data/subscriptions/ qp/1997/0597/qp0597sarin.pdf.

SAS. n.d. "Big Data—What It Is and Why It Matters." https://www.sas .com/en_gb/insights/big-data/what-is-big-data.html.

Sayers, D.L. 2013. "Why Work." http://malyonworkplace.org.au/wp- content/uploads/2013/12/Why-Work-Dorothy-Sayers-Essay.pdf.

Sayle, A.J. 1988. *Management Audits—The Assessment of Quality Manage- ment Systems*. 2nd ed.

Schmidt, S.R., and R.G. Launsby. 1989. *Understanding Industrial De- signed Experiments*. 4th ed. Colorado Springs, CO: Air Academy Press.

Schniederman, A.M. November 1986. "Optimum Quality Costs and Zero Defects: Are They Contradictory Concepts?" *Quality Progress*, pp. 28-31. http://asq.org/quality-progress/1986/11/cost-of-quality/ optimum-quality-costs-zero-defects.pdf.

Schnoll, L. April 1993. "One World, One Standard," *Quality Progress*, pp. 35-29.

Schuhmacher, A., O. Gassmann, & M. Hinder. 2016. "Changing R&D Models in Research-based Pharmaceutical Companies." *Journal of Translational Medicine* 14, 105. https://translational-medicine. biomedcentral.com/articles/10.1186/s12967-016-0838-4.

ScienceDirect. n.d. "Design Specification," Elsevier. https://www .sciencedirect.com/topics/engineering/design-specification.

ScienceDirect. n.d. "Reliability Engineering," Elsevier. https://www .sciencedirect.com/topics/engineering/reliability-engineering.

ScienceDirect. n.d. "Quality of Life," Elsevier. https://www.sciencedirect. com/topics/social-sciences/quality-of-life.

ScienceDirect. n.d. "Quality of Life Measure," Elsevier. https://www.scien- cedirect.com/topics/medicine-and-dentistry/quality-of-life-measure.

Schaefer, C. n.d. "How the Latest Baldrige Award Winners Manage for Innovation," *NIST Blogrige The Official Baldrige Blog*. https:// www.nist.gov/blogs/blogrige/how-latest-baldrige-award-winners- manage-innovation.

Schargel, F.P. October 1993. "Total Quality in Education," *Quality Prog- ress*, pp. 67-70.

Schmidt, S.R., and R.G. Launsby. *Understanding Industrial Designed Experiments*. Cambridge, MA: Air Academy Press.

Scottish Government. 2008. "Curriculum for Excellence: Building the Curriculum 3: A Framework for Learning and Teaching: Key Ideas and Priorities." https://www2.gov.scot/resource/doc/226155/0061245. pdf, https://www2.gov.scot/Publications/2010/06/02152520/1.

Scottish Government. 2010. "The Healthcare Quality Strategy for NHSScotland," The Scottish Government St Andrew's House Edinburgh EH1 3DG, https://www2.gov.scot/resource/doc/311667/0098354. pdf.

Scottish Government. 2008. "Early Years and Early Intervention—A Joint Scottish Government and COSLA Policy Statement." https:// www.gov.scot/publications/early-years-early-intervention-joint-scottish-government-cosla-policy-statement/pages/4/.

Scottish Social Services Council. n.d. "Appreciative Inquiry Resource Pack." Scottish Social Services Council Compass House. http://learn. sssc.uk.com/course/view2770.html?id=67.

Scribed. n.d. "Sigma Opportunity and Risk Guide," The SIGMA Project—Sustainability Integrated Guidelines for Management. https:// www.scribd.com/document/356655959/Sigma-Risk-Opportunity.

Seddon, J. September 15, 2000. *The Case Against ISO 9000*. 2nd ed. Dublin, Ireland: Oak Tree Press.

Seddon, J. October 1, 2003. *Freedom from Command & Control: A Better Way to Make the Work Work*. Buckingham, UK: Vanguard Consulting Ltd.

Select Business Solutions, Inc. n.d. "What is the Capability Maturity Model? (CMM)." http://www.selectbs.com/process-maturity/ what-is-the-capability-maturity-model.

Select Business Solutions, Inc. n.d. "What is Capability Maturity Model Integration? (CMMI)." http://www.selectbs.com/process-maturity/ what-is-capability-maturity-model-integration.

SGS. n.d. "QHSE Management." https://www.sgs.com/-/media/global/ documents/flyers-and-leaflets/sgs-ind-wind-qhse-a4-en-10.pdf.

Shah, D. July 2015. "Measure for Measure—Estimating Uncertainty— Metrological Traceability to Non-SI Units," *Quality Progress*. http://

asq.org/quality-progress/2015/07/measure-for-measure/estimating-uncertainty.html.

Shah, D. May 2015. "Measure for Measure—Measuring Confidence Determining a Measuring Device's Accuracy," *Quality Progress*, pp. 46-48. http://asq.org/quality-progress/2015/05/measure-for-measure/measuring-confidence.pdf.

Shah, D. March 2015. "Measure for Measure—Measuring Device Revolution Who Monitors Precision in a New World of Consumer Electronics?" *Quality Progress*, pp. 46-47.

Shah, D. September 2014. "Measure for Measure–Measuring Proficiency Evaluating Laboratory Measurement Performance," *Quality Progress*, pp. 46-47. http://asq.org/quality-progress/2014/09/measure-for-measure/measuring-proficiency.pdf.

Sharples, K.A., M. Slusher, and M. Swaim. May 1996. "How TQM Can Work in Education," Quality Progress, pp. 75-78. http://asq.org/data/subscriptions/qp/1996/0596/qp0596sharples.pdf.

Shewhart, W.A. April 2015. "The Economic Control of Quality of Manufactured Product", ASQ Quality Press.

Shiplee, H., L. Waterman, K. Furniss, R. Seal, and J. Jones. May 2011. "Delivering London 2012: Health and Safety." *Proceedings of the Institution of Civil Engineers—Civil Engineering* 164, no. 5, pp. 46-54. https://www.icevirtuallibrary.com/doi/10.1680/cien.2011.164.5.46.

Siemens. n.d. "How to Conduct a Failure Modes and Effects Analysis (FMEA)," Siemens PLM Software. https://polarion.plm.automation.siemens.com/hubfs/Docs/Guides_and_Manuals/Siemens-PLM-Polarion-How-to-conduct-a-failure-modes-and-effects-analysis-FMEA-wp-60071-A3.pdf.

Simon, K. n.d. "SIPOC Diagram," *ISixSigma*. https://www.isixsigma.com/tools-templates/sipoc-copis/sipoc-diagram/.

Singman, J.L. November 22, 2013. *The Middle Ages (Everyday Life)*. Sterling.

Sixsigma, I. n.d. "What is Six Sigma," International Six Sigma Institute. https://www.sixsigma-institute.org/What_Is_Six_Sigma.php.

Skrabec, Q.R. Jr. November 1990. "Ancient Process Control and Its Modern Implications," *Quality Progress*, pp. 49-52.

Smartsheet. n.d. "Six Sigma for Beginners," Smartsheet. https://www
.smartsheet.com/all-about-six-sigma#the-six-sigma-methodologies.

Smolenyak, M. July/August 1995. "Improving Quality in a Long Term
Care Facility." *Journal for Quality and Participation*. http://asq.org/
data/subscriptions/jqp_open/1995/july_august/jqpv18i4smolenyak.
pdf.

Soares, N.F. September 2017. "Unannounced, and Unexpected—Challenges Surround Unannounced Audits of Food Safety Standards,"
Quality Progress, pp. 16-19. http://asq.org/quality-progress/2017/09/
food-safety/field-notes-unannounced-and-more-unexpected.pdf.

Spears, J.L., and H. Barki. September 2010. "User Participation in
Information Systems Security Risk Management," *MIS Quarterly* 34, no. 3, pp. 503-522. https://web.a.ebscohost.com/ehost/
pdfviewer/pdfviewer?vid=0&sid=2934acb0-f300-4c03-8e47-
634443ec4407%40sdc-v-sessmgr03.

Spinellis, D. April 3, 2006. *Code Quality—The Open Source Perspective*.
Boston, MA: Pearson Education Inc.

Standards Australia. 2013. "Risk Management Guidelines—Companion
to AS/NZ ISO 31000:2009," SA/SNZ HB 436:3013. https://www
.standards.org.au/standards-catalogue/sa-snz/publicsafety/ob-007/
sa--snz--hb--436-2013.

Standards Store. n.d. "What Is an Integrated Management System?"
https://integrated-standards.com/articles/what-is-integrated-management-
system/.

Starcher, R. December 1992. "Mismatched Management Techniques,"
Quality Progress, pp. 49-52.

Statistics How To. n.d. "Correlation in Statistics: Correlation Analysis
Explained." https://www.statisticshowto.datasciencecentral.com/
probability-and-statistics/correlation-analysis/.

Stein, B. July 1991. "Management by Quality Objectives," *Quality Progress*, pp. 78-80.

Stoneburner, G., A. Goguen, and A. Feringa. July 2002. "Risk Management Guide for Information Technology Systems—Recommendations of the National Institute of Standards and Technology," NIST
Special Publication 800-30, Computer Security Division Information Technology Laboratory National Institute of Standards and

Technology. https://www.ucop.edu/information-technology-services/initiatives/resources-and-tools/sp800-30.pdf.

Sullivan, L.P. June 1988. "Policy Management Through Quality Function Deployment," *Quality Progress*, pp. 18-20.

Surak, J.G. March 2013. "Apples to Oranges? Clearing up the Differences between ISO 22000 and ISO 9001 Standards," *Quality Progress*. http://asq.org/quality-progress/2013/03/food-safety/apples-to-oranges.html.

Swanson, R. December 1993. "Quality Benchmark Deployment," *Quality Progress*, pp. 81-84.

Taormina, T. November 2019. "Risk Avoidance—Clearing a Safe Path—A Breakthrough Approach to Avoid and Evade Risk," *Quality Progress*, pp. 16-25. http://asq.org/quality-progress/2019/11/risk-management/clearing-a-safe-path.html.

Tay, L., & E. Diener. 2011. "Needs and Subjective Well-being Around the World." *Journal of Personality and Social Psychology* 101, no. 2, pp. 354-56. doi:10.1037/a00. http://academic.udayton.edu/jackbauer/Readings%20595/Tay%20Diener%2011%20needs%20WB%20world%20copy.pdf.

Taylor, F.W. June14, 2014. *The Principles of Scientific Management*. Scotts Valley, CA: CreateSpace Independent Publishing Platform.

Taylor, J.R.A., S. Reid, and A. Tweed. 2017. "Quality, Service Improvement and Redesign (QSIR) Tools," NHS Improvement. https://improvement.nhs.uk/resources/quality-service-improvement-and-redesign-qsir-tools/.

Thickpenny, R. September 2019. "Protecting Society," *Quality World*, pp. 14-19.

Treichler, D., R. Carmichael, A. Kusmanoff, J. Lewis, and G. Berthiez. January 2002. "Design for Six Sigma: 15 Lessons Learned," *Quality Progress*, pp. 33-42. http://asq.org/data/subscriptions/qp/2002/0102/qp0102rreichler.pdf.

Troy, B. n.d. "Is Every Quality Professional a Leader?" Quality in Mind for the Global Quality Community. *ASQ Blog*, http://asq.org/blog/2014/11/every-quality-professional-a-leader/.

Truity. n.d. "Myers & Briggs' 16 Personality Type Profiles," Truity Psychometrics LLC. https://www.truity.com/page/16-personality-types-myers-briggs.

Tsuda, Y., and M. Tribus. April 1991. "Planning the Quality Visit," *Quality Progress*, pp. 30-34.

UK Gov. October 30, 2018. "Evidence-based Early Years Intervention— Eleventh Report of Session 2017–2019," House of Commons Science and Technology Committee. https://researchbriefings.files.parliament.uk/documents/CBP-7647/CBP-7647.pdf.

UK Gov DTI. May 2004. "Corporate Social Responsibility—A Government Update," Department of Trade and Industry. www.dti.gov.uk/DTI/Pub 7201/1k/05/04/NP.

UK Gov Department of Health. n.d. "Transforming Care: A National Response to Winterbourne View Hospital," Department of Health Review: Final Report, Mental Health, Disability and Equality Department of Health. https://assets.publishing.service.gov.uk/government/uploads/system/uploads/attachment_data/file/213215/final-report.pdf.

UK Gov NHS Transforming Care and Commissioning Steering Group. n.d. "Winterbourne View—Time for Change—Transforming the Commissioning of Services for People with Learning Disabilities and/or Autism." https://www.england.nhs.uk/wp-content/uploads/2014/11/transforming-commissioning-services.pdf.

UK Gov Ofsted. n.d. "Ofsted Is Changing How It Inspects Schools." https://www.gov.uk/government/news/ofsted-is-changing-how-it-inspects-schools.

UK Gov Publications. n.d. "Report of the Mid Staffordshire NHS Foundation Trust Public Inquiry." https://www.gov.uk/government/publications/report-of-the-mid-staffordshire-nhs-foundation-trust-public-inquiry.

UKAS. n.d. "M3003—Edition 3|November 2012—The Expression of Uncertainty and Confidence in Measurement." https://www.ukas.com/download/publications/publications-relating-to-laboratory-accreditation/M3003_Ed3_final.pdf.

UKAS. n.d. "ISO 17025 Remote Assessment Webinar." https://www.ukas.com/news/iso-17025-remote-assessment-webinar/.

UKAS. n.d. "What is the Difference between Accreditation and Certification?" https://www.ukas.com/news/what-is-the-difference-between-accreditation-and-certification/.

UNESCO. n.d. "Education for All: The Quality Imperative; EFA Global Monitoring Report, 2005." https://unesdoc.unesco.org/ark:/48223/pf0000137333, http://www.unesco.org/education/gmr_download/chapter1.pdf.

UNICEF. 2000. "Defining Quality in Education," United Nations Children's Fund 3 United Nations Plaza. http://www.oosci-mena.org/uploads/1/wysiwyg/Quality_Education_UNICEF_2000.pdf.

USFDA. n.d. "Approaches to GMP Inspection." https://www.fda.gov/media/89231/download.

U.S. Department of Transportation Federal Aviation Administration Flight Standards Service. 2009. "Risk Management Handbook." https://www.faa.gov/regulations_policies/handbooks_manuals/aviation/media/faa-h-8083-2.pdf.

Van Mieghem, T. January 1998. "Lessons Learned from Alexander the Great," *Quality Progress*, pp. 41-46. http://asq.org/data/subscriptions/qp/1998/0198/qp0198vanmieghem.pdf.

Vandenbrande, W. April 2006. "Design of Experiments for Dummies," *Quality Progress*, pp. 59-65. http://asq.org/data/subscriptions/qp/2005/0405/qp0405vandenbrande.pdf.

Voehl, F. n.d. "Recovering Prosperity Through Quality: Community Quality Councils Operating System Guidebook," https://www.comminit.com/africa/content/recovering-prosperity-through-quality-community-quality-councils-operating-system-guideb.

Waters, L., and M. White. 2015. "Case Study of a School Wellbeing Initiative: Using Appreciative Inquiry to Support Positive Change." *International Journal of Wellbeing* 5, no. 1, pp. 19-32. doi:10.5502/ijw.v5i1.2.

Watson, G.H. March 2019. "The Ascent of Quality," *Quality Progress*, pp. 24-30. http://asq.org/quality-progress/2019/03/career-development/the-ascent-of-quality-40.html.

Watson, G.H., and E.A. Spiridonova. August 2019. "Quality Tools—Fish(bone) Stories—Reimagining the Fishbone Diagram for the Digital World." *Quality Progress*, pp. 14-23. http://asq.org/quality-progress/2019/08/basic-quality/fishbone-stories.pdf.

Weaver, J.B. 2007. "A Standards-based Approach to Information Security and Risk Management," *ASQ*. http://asq.org/software/2007/10/

introduction-to-iso-27001-information-security-management-systems-webinar-speaker-slides.pdf.

Weeks, J.B. October 2011. "Is Six Sigma Dead?—If It Is, How Can We Revive It?" *Quality Progress*, pp. 22-28. http://asq.org/quality-progress/2011/10/six-sigma/is-six-sigma-dead.pdf.

Weetman, C. December 3, 2016. *The Circular Economy Handbook for Business and Supply Chains: Repair, Remake, Redesign, Rethink*. 1st ed. Kogan Page.

Weiler, G. May 2004. "What Do CEOs Think About Quality?" *Quality Progress*, pp. 52-56. http://rube.asq.org/data/subscriptions/qp/2004/0504/qp0504weiler.pdf.

Weihrich, H. "The TOWS Matrix—A Tool for Situational Analysis." https://www.academia.edu/34211017/The_TOWS_Matrix_A_Tool_for_Situational_Analysis.

West, J.E.J., and C.A. Cianfrani. April 2017. "Standard Issues—Beyond the Requirements—ISO 9001 Compliance Alone Isn't Sufficient to Sustain an Organization," *Quality Progress*. http://asq.org/quality-progress/2017/04/standard-issues/beyond-the-requirements.html.

Wheatley, M.J. January 16, 2001. *Leadership and the New Science*. 2nd ed. New York, NY: McGraw-Hill Education.

WHO. 1997. "WHOQOL—Measuring Quality of Life," Division of Mental Health and Prevention of Substance Abuse—World Health Organization, WHO/MSA/MNH/PSF/97.4. https://www.who.int/mental_health/media/68.pdf.

WHO. February 1995. "WHOQOL-100—The 100 Questions with Response Scales." https://www.who.int/healthinfo/survey/WHOQOL-100.pdf?ua=1

WHO/UNFPA. 2016. "TCu380A Intrauterine Contraceptive Device (IUD), WHO/UNFPA Technical Specification and Prequalification Guidance," UNFPA. https://www.unfpa.org/sites/default/files/resource-pdf/TCu380A_IUD_WHO_UNFPATechnicalSpec_Guidance_updated2017.pdf.

Wilkins, J.O. Jr. May 2000. "Putting Taguchi Methods to Work to Solve Design Flaws," *Quality Progress*, pp. 55-59. http://asq.org/data/subscriptions/qp/2000/0500/qp0500wilkins.pdf.

Wilkinson, A., T. Redman, and E. Snape. Winter 1995. "New Patterns of Quality Management in the United Kingdom." *Quality Management Journal.* http://asq.org/data/subscriptions/qmj_open/1995/february/qmjv2i2wilkinson.pdf.

Wikipedia. n.d. "SGS S.A." https://en.wikipedia.org/wiki/SGS_S.A.

Willink, R. 2013. *Measurement Uncertainty and Probability.* Cambridge, UK: Cambridge University Press.

Wood, D.C. July 2008. "Blurred Vision," *Quality Progress*, pp. 29-33. http://rube.asq.org/quality-progress/2008/07/economic-case-for-quality/blurred-vision.pdf.

Woodhall, W.H. October 2000. "Controversies and Contradictions in Statistical Process Control." *Journal of Quality Technology* 32, no. 4, pp. 341-50. http://asq.org/pub/jqt/past/vol32_issue4/qtec-341.pdf.

Yang, T., C. Ku, and M. Liu. 2016. "An Integrated System for Information Security Management with the Unified Framework." *Journal of Risk Research* 19, no. 1, pp. 21-41. doi:10.1080/13669877.2014.940593.

YouTube. n.d. "Deep Water Horizon." https://www.youtube.com/watch?v=9NQ8LehUWSE.

YouTube. n.d. "Piper Alpha." https://www.youtube.com/watch?v=Nwbw5PHZnqk.

Yumpu. n.d. "The Small Business Standard—Chartered Quality Institute." https://www.yumpu.com/en/document/view/4363996/the-small-business-standard-chartered-quality-institute.

Zillow. n.d. "52246 Home Prices and Home Values." https://www.zillow.com.

About the Author

Paul Hayes is a quality practitioner, professional, and manager with 47 years' experience in a range of industry sectors and virtually all quality disciplines and tools together with a burning passion to see the holistic, integrated application of principles at the root of quality practice applied to the whole of life and society. He is a mathematics and chemistry graduate with experience in chemicals and paper manufacture followed by quality roles in paper converting, dental chemicals, medical devices, computer hardware and software, DNA testing, and marine renewable energy complemented by medical device and diagnostics prequalification work and publication of international specifications and guidelines. In addition, audit training with live practice and uncertainty of estimate work within environmental technology verification mark his long and varied career. Paul can be contacted at WhyQuality@kmsltd.com

Index

OTHER TITLES IN OUR SUPPLY AND OPERATIONS MANAGEMENT COLLECTION

Joy M. Field, Boston College, *Editor*

- *The Barn Door Is Open: Frameworks and Tools for Success and Fulfillment in the Workplace* by Serge Alfonse
- *Operations Management in China* by Craig Seidelson
- *Logistics Management: An Analytics-Based Approach* by Tan Miller and Matthew J. Liberatore
- *The Practical Guide to Transforming Your Company* by Daniel Plung and Connie Krull
- *Leading and Managing Strategic Suppliers* by Richard Moxham
- *Moving the Chains: An Operational Solution for Embracing Complexity in the Digital Age* by Domenico LePore
- *The New Age Urban Transportation Systems, Volume I: Cases from Asian Economies* by Sundaravalli Narayanaswami
- *The New Age Urban Transportation Systems, Volume II: Cases from Asian Economies* by Sundaravalli Narayanaswami
- *Optimizing the Supply Chain* by Jay E. Fortenberry
- *Sustain: Extending Improvement in the Modern Enterprise* by W. Scott Culberson
- *Managing Using the Diamond Principle: Innovating to Effect Organizational Process Improvement* by Mark W. Johnson
- *Insightful Quality, Second Edition: Beyond Continuous Improvement* by Victor E. Sower and Frank K. Fair
- *The Global Supply Chain and Risk Management* by Stuart Rosenberg
- *Moving into the Express Lane: How to Rapidly Increase the Value of Your Business* by Rick Pay
- *The Effect of Supply Chain Management on Business Performance* by Milan Frankl

Concise and Applied Business Books

The Collection listed above is one of 30 business subject collections that Business Expert Press has grown to make BEP a premiere publisher of print and digital books. Our concise and applied books are for...

- Professionals and Practitioners
- Faculty who adopt our books for courses
- Librarians who know that BEP's Digital Libraries are a unique way to offer students ebooks to download, not restricted with any digital rights management
- Executive Training Course Leaders
- Business Seminar Organizers

Business Expert Press books are for anyone who needs to dig deeper on business ideas, goals, and solutions to everyday problems. Whether one print book, one ebook, or buying a digital library of 110 ebooks, we remain the affordable and smart way to be business smart. For more information, please visit **www.businessexpertpress.com**, or contact **sales@businessexpertpress.com**.

www.ingramcontent.com/pod-product-compliance
Lightning Source LLC
Chambersburg PA
CBHW061146220326
41599CB00025B/4372